SHAKING THE FAITH

Mary Marshall.

"Elizabeth De Wolfe's account of Dyer's circumstances, motives, and activities as a prominent Shaker apostate sheds new light on a lifelong quest to fulfill her role as wife and mother and on the larger world of career apostates that she entered. Drawing on scholarly resources dealing with gender and family as well as with religious history and print culture, De Wolfe integrates her narrative of this remarkable woman into the larger story of nineteenth-century American religion, society, and culture."

—Stephen J. Stein, Chancellors' Professor of Religious Studies, and Adjunct Professor of History, Indiana University, Bloomington

"In this skillfully researched and deftly written study, Elizabeth De Wolf suggests new perspectives for understanding the Shakers, the role of women in new religious and communal movements, and the problems that a capable woman had as she tried to develop an independent life and have a public impact in a society where women's roles were severely circumscribed."

—Lawrence Foster, author of *Religion and Sexuality: The Shakers, the Mormons, and the Oneida Community*

"Shaking the Faith tells the compelling story of a woman and a religious sect locked in a dangerous duel on the margins of American culture. Elizabeth De Wolfe vividly exposes the historical roots of questions that continue to perplex contemporary society: What happens when a marriage falls apart? How should a mother behave? What constitutes a proper family? *Shaking the Faith* offers a fascinating look at the very public fracturing of the Dyer marriage, and explores what the couple's tempestuous divorce revealed about gender, family and faith in the early American republic."

—Nancy Lusignan Schultz, author of *Fire & Roses: The Burning of the Charlestown Convent, 1834*

"Carefully researched and thoughtfully argued, Shaking the Faith is a valuable case study of one woman's struggle to live up to society's and her own expectations. Elizabeth De Wolfe is particularly adept at connecting Dyer's campaign to larger tensions in antebellum America: the debate over the proper roles for husbands and wives, the relationship between government and the family, and the limits of religious toleration."

—Priscilla Brewer, Associate Professor of American Studies, University of South Florida, and author of *Shaker Communities, Shaker Lives*

SHAKING THE FAITH

WOMEN, FAMILY, AND MARY MARSHALL DYER'S
ANTI-SHAKER CAMPAIGN, 1815–1867

ELIZABETH A. DE WOLFE

To SCOTT

SHAKING THE FAITH
© Elizabeth De Wolfe, 2004

All rights reserved. No part of this book may be used or reproduced in any manner whatsoever without written permission except in the case of brief quotations embodied in critical articles or reviews.

First published 2002 by PALGRAVE™

First paperback published 2004
by PALGRAVE MACMILLAN™
175 Fifth Avenue, New York, N.Y. 10010 and
Houndmills, Basingstoke, Hampshire, England RG21 6XS
Companies and representatives throughout the world

PALGRAVE MACMILLAN is the global academic imprint of the Palgrave Macmillan division of St. Martin's Press, LLC and of Palgrave Macmillan Ltd. Macmillan® is a registered trademark in the United States, United Kingdom and other countries. Palgrave is a registered trademark in the European Union and other countries.

ISBN 1–4039–6612–5

The Library of Congress has catalogued the hardcover edition as follows:

Library of Congress Cataloging-in-Publication Data
De Wolfe, Elizabeth A., 1961–
    Shaking the faith : women, family, and Mary Marshall Dyer's anti-Shaker campaign, 1815–1867 / by Elizabeth A. De Wolfe
        p. cm.
    Includes bibliographical references and index
    ISBN 0-312-29503-0 (hc)
    1. Dyer, Mary M., b 1780. 2. Shakers—Biography. 3. Shaker women—Biography. I. Title.

BX9793.D45 D4 2002
289′.8′092—dc21   2002025174

A catalogue record for this book is available from the British Library.

Design by autobookcomp.

First edition: June 2002
10 9 8 7 6 5 4 3 2 1

Printed in the United States of America.

Contents

PERMISSIONS

The author and publisher gratefully acknowledge permission for use of the following material:

Excerpts from original Shaker manuscripts. Used with the permission of the Western Reserve Historical Society, Cleveland, Ohio.

Excerpts from the Francis Jackson Papers and from the correspondence of William Barrett Shedd. Used with the permission of the Massachusetts Historical Society.

The discussion of the mob at Enfield in chapter three is adapted from Elizabeth A. De Wolfe, "The Mob at Enfield: Community, Gender and Violence Against the Shakers." Reprinted by permission from *Intentional Community: An Anthropological Perspective* by Susan Love Brown, ed., the State University of New York Press. ©2001 State University of New York. All rights reserved.

Chapter four is adapted from Elizabeth A. De Wolfe, "Mary Marshall Dyer, Gender, and *A Portraiture of Shakerism*," ©1998 by the Center for the Study of Religion and American Culture. Reprinted from *Religion and American Culture*, Volume 8, Number 2, by permission of the University of California Press.

Excerpts from original Shaker Manuscripts are used courtesy of The Winterthur Library: The Edward Deming Andrews Memorial Shaker Collection.

Excerpts from the Papers of the History of Enfield, New Hampshire, and from the correspondence of Mills Olcott are used with the permission of the Dartmouth College Library.

Excerpts from the papers of the Yandell and Waller families are used courtesy of The Filson Historical Society, Louisville, Kentucky.

Excerpts from the Journal of Miner Kilbourne Kellogg are used with the permission of the Cincinnati Historical Society Library, Cincinnati Museum Center.

Illustration of Joseph Dyer's advertisement is used with the permission of the New Hampshire Department of State, Division of Records Management and Archives.

Illustration of Mary Dyer's handbill, "Free Lecture to the Ladies," is used courtesy of the American Antiquarian Society.

ILLUSTRATIONS

ACKNOWLEDGMENTS

This book began as a dissertation for the American and New England Studies program at Boston University. I remain grateful for the financial support provided by the program, and by the Boston University Women's Guild. Additional generous funding came in the form of research fellowships from the Winterthur Museum and Library, the Pew Program in Religion and American Culture, and the National Endowment for the Humanities. The University of New England has provided ongoing support in the form of faculty research grants.

Mary Dyer's story was quilted together from bits and pieces found in libraries, historical societies, and research centers spread across New England and beyond. Some are well endowed, well staffed, and well known, others are lightly staffed, lightly funded, and little known. All provided invaluable assistance with letters, newspapers, town records, apostate accounts, and soot-covered court documents, and to each I owe my sincere thanks. They include: Ann Gilbert and Gay Marks at the Sabbathday Lake (Maine) Shaker Library; Renée Fox, Canterbury (N.H.) Shaker Village; Jerry Grant, Emma B. King Library (Old Chatham, N.Y.); Richard McKinstry and Iris Snyder, Winterthur Library; Ralph Stenstrom, Hamilton College; Marjorie Carr at the Enfield Public Library; and the staff at the New Hampshire Department of State, Division of Records Management and Archives. Staff, archivists, and librarians at numerous institutions offered welcome assistance in this research project. They include: the New Hampshire Historical Society; New Hampshire State Library; Warren County (Ohio) Historical Society; Cincinnati Public Library; Cincinnati Historical Society; Boston Public Library; Boston Atheneum; Massachusetts Historical Society; New York State Library; Connecticut State Library; American Antiquarian Society; Holy Cross College; Worcester PolyTech; the Filson Historical Society; Enfield Shaker Museum; the Fruitlands Museums;

Rauner Special Collections Library at Dartmouth College; the Orford (N.H.) Public Library; and the Orford Social Library. One letter here, an old map there—all were important pieces in the big picture and I'm grateful for the knowledgeable and enthusiastic assistance received in my travels.

Parts of the puzzle fell into place with the generous sharing of resources, scarce imprints, and ideas. I'm grateful for the generosity of David Newell, Jerry Grant, the Milton Sherman Collection, the late Wendell Hess, Frank P. Wood, Scott De Wolfe, Barbara Roberts, Richard Candee, Daniel Cohen, and the late John Shea. As the end-notes will attest, Mary Ann Haagen's copious knowledge, meticulous research, and generosity of spirit (and references) filled in gaps in my own research, suggested new avenues to follow, and enhanced my own understanding of life among the Enfield Shakers. At the Sabbathday Lake Shaker community I found food for thought in the archives, and food for the body at noontime meals. I am grateful for the sustenance both provided.

Lawrence Foster was an early and steadfast supporter for my work, from first glimmer of idea, to critiquing the present tome. My dissertation committee, Nina Silber, Dana L. Robert, Stephen Marini, Richard Candee, and Richard W. Fox provided helpful suggestions that initiated the transition from dissertation to book. Colleagues and friends were pressed into service to look at copies of Mary Dyer's *A Portraiture of Shakerism* in far-flung libraries as they completed their own research, and others read multiple versions of various chapters and offered their insightful critiques. Thank you Joan Sullivan, Cheryl Boots, Candace Kanes, Rebecca Noel, Magda Hotchkiss, David Richards, and David Shawn. Mark DeFazio lent his honest eyes and read the entire manuscript, as did Shirley Theresa Wajda, whose careful reading and astute comments helped sharpen my argument. At Palgrave, Jennifer Stais provided gentle reminders and helpful answers. Editor Deborah Gershenowitz understood the project from our first meeting; her skillful guidance and perceptive questions strengthened the manuscript in its journey from draft to monograph. A special thanks to Allie Lee, who was there when the work commenced, and Pearl Lynn, who was there when it was completed.

Before this book was a dissertation, it was an idea for a term paper and for that idea, I thank Scott De Wolfe, best friend, best critic, and best supporter. With Scott, I have found myself in the place just right.

Introduction: Shakers and Anti-Shakers

In 1853, Mary Marshall Dyer set her earthly affairs in order. Two of her three surviving children, by then grown adults, lived in the Enfield, New Hampshire, Shaker community where they had resided with their siblings and father since 1813. To these "beloved children," her first born Caleb and her second son Orville, Mary left each one dollar. But to Jerrub Dyer, her youngest surviving child, Mary bequeathed two houses, railroad stock, and all her personal property. Why the difference in her gifts? Mary, in her will, explained that Caleb and Orville "while Shakers" would receive only a minimal bequest. But after she reviewed what she had written, Mary returned to her will and, with a caret mark, added one word, changing her explanation, and providing the small bequest to her sons "while *with* Shakers."[1] Mary Dyer's distinction between her sons *being* Shakers and her sons simply living *with* the Shakers revealed her continued antipathy towards the Shaker community she had once called home. Mary Dyer had seceded from the Enfield Shakers and left behind her husband and five children in 1815, and had battled the sect ever since. Her revision also divulged her fervent hope that, even after four decades, her sons Caleb and Orville would leave the Shakers as their brother Jerrub had, just months before Mary penned her will. In Mary's view, her children lived *with* the Shakers, but even after four decades, were not Shakers themselves.

During the first half of the nineteenth century an aggressive and well-organized anti-Shaker campaign sought to destroy what is today considered a model of virtuous and simple living. Of the many players in this highly visible drama, Mary Marshall Dyer (1780–1867) was the best known. A linchpin of anti-Shaker activity, Dyer fought tenaciously to retrieve her children from the Shakers. In the 1820s, Mary Dyer was a household name in many parts of the country, recognized for her tragic story of family loss, or for her vindictive nature, depending on one's point of view. What made Dyer notorious was her gender, her association with Shakerism, and her astounding skill at public presentation. What made Dyer successful was her unparalleled use of print culture to wage her public campaign.

Shakerism has been often cited as one of America's most successful communal experiments by virtue of its longevity, nineteenth-century membership, and infiltration into American culture. While the mid-nineteenth-century peak of some 4,000 members in nineteen communities has today given way to one small Shaker enclave in Sabbathday Lake, Maine, the classic furniture, architecture, and craft products remain well-recognized features of American material culture. Documentaries, trade and scholarly texts, and even Shaker-themed murder mysteries keep the beliefs and practices (to varying degrees of authenticity) of Shakerism alive.

Shakerism is a Protestant faith whose members subscribe to three principle beliefs. Shakers believe that the Second Coming of Christ occurred within individuals open to His spirit. Founder Ann Lee was the first to realize that Christ's return would take the form of His spirit dwelling within each individual. To work towards this state, Shakers attempt to live a Christ-like life. Shakers practice confession of sins and live a celibate life, believing that the original sin was lustful sexual intercourse between Adam and Eve.[2] Shakers believe that God incorporates both masculine and feminine characteristics. From this belief arises the Shaker ideal of gender equality and the Shaker practice of parallel male and female leadership positions. Despite this ideal, work roles within Shaker communities were divided along traditional gender lines, and not all male Shakers were supportive of what was described as the "petticoat government" of female leaders.[3]

Shaker roots extend to eighteenth-century England where membership was drawn from burgeoning industrial communities such as Manchester. There the predecessors to Shakerism practiced an ecstatic style of worship that led to the derogatory name of Shaking Quakers. One young member, Ann Lee, became an active participant and an influential leader. According to Shaker history, while jailed for profaning the Sabbath, Lee had a vision to lead her sect to the American colonies. In August 1774, Ann Lee arrived in New York City with seven followers. For the first few years, Lee and her followers lived separately and worked in various occupations to save money to purchase land.

By 1776 this band had reunited in upstate New York and set to clearing the land they had purchased eight miles northwest of Albany in an area known as Niskeyuna. In a period of social upheaval brought by the Revolution, individuals wearied by war, tired of doctrinal debates, and confused by changing norms and uncertain times saw in Shakerism a chance to recreate the world. With its promising and straightforward message, Shakerism spread with the winds of religious revivals throughout New England, to Kentucky, Ohio, and Indiana, and later, briefly, to Georgia and Florida.[4]

By the end of the eighteenth century, Shakers were living in communal villages apart from the surrounding populace that Shakers referred to as the "world." All property was shared and biological kinship relations were abandoned in favor of the communitywide family of brothers and sisters. Many Shaker villages grew quite large with hundreds of members, and to maintain organization and structure, the villages were subdivided into what were called "families." Each family was a self-sufficient unit with their own buildings, agriculture, industries, and leadership. The most committed Shakers lived in the Church Family (also called the Center Family). One (or more) family in each community served as the novitiate order and housed newcomers to Shakerism. Additional families were added as necessary when membership in Shaker villages increased.

Two elders and two eldresses served as the leaders of each Shaker family. Pairs of trustees governed temporal concerns that included the sales and purchases of goods, legal disputes, and other interactions with the world. Within each Shaker community deacons and deaconesses oversaw specific tasks and industries such as the kitchen, apple orchard, or medicinal products. These latter positions rotated among the membership. The ministry, two men and two women, provided spiritual guidance as they traveled between geographically close villages under their care. The ministry leaders were under the direction of the Central, or Parent, Ministry of all of Shakerism at New Lebanon, New York. Shaker communities kept in touch with one another through a steady stream of correspondence and frequent intercommunity visits.

Potential Shakers, like Mary Dyer and her family, would have lived in the novitiate order for a trial period of varying length. The Shakers separated biological families to lessen kin ties and redirect individual loyalty towards the Shaker group. Any property brought into the village was distributed, as all items were owned communally. Novitiates signed a probationary agreement in which they consented to their voluntary participation in Shakerism and agreed that, should they defect, they would not hold the Shakers responsible for back wages or a reimbursement of property donated, a frequent demand of seceders. Once firmly established in the faith, a member would be reassigned to another family within the Shaker community and would sign the community covenant, a spiritual and legal document that recapitulated the communal aspirations of the community.

The Shakers did not expect everyone to take up the difficult challenge of a life of purity, but they fervently hoped that those who joined the sect would remain among the faithful. Yet over the long course of Shaker history, more individuals tried and left the faith than those who tried it and remained. Some individuals came to the Shakers during the cold winter months, only to leave again in the spring. These so-called "winter Shakers," more interested in a warm bed and a hot meal than spiritual enlightenment, had little intention of adopting a religious life. A good number of potential converts came to and went from Shaker villages several times before deciding between a life within, or without, the community of Believers, as Shakers called themselves. Some on-again, off-again Shakers even traveled from one Shaker community to another, at each stop asking the elders for one more "privilege" or chance at a Shaker life. Promising individuals, and sometimes entire families, would stay for a novitiate year, only to have a change of heart and secede at the moment they might have formally joined. Some seceders found celibacy too great a challenge, some chafed at the strictly governed life, and others found in the communal society no respite from hard work. Despite the turmoil and uncertainty of these constant comings and goings, with their celibate lifestyle the Shakers relied on conversion for new members, enduring the frustration of so many losses in the hopes of gaining one new member.[5]

When their attraction to Shakerism—genuine or feigned—faded, most seceders simply left the Shaker community and went on with their worldly lives. A disgruntled seceder might have spoken against the Shakers in private conversations, but these conversations left scant marks in the historical record, leaving us to wonder at what might have been said.[6] However, a small but vocal group of seceders engaged in more public behavior, leaving traces of anti-Shaker activity we can examine. These more public seceders, known as apostates, spoke out on what they saw as the Shakers' unjust or immoral behavior. Apostates are a special category of religious seceders who make a break from their faith and then turn around to attack what they had once espoused.[7] Shaker apostates related how they had been tricked into joining, had suffered under Shaker religious practice, or had seen their families separated. In several states, particularly New York, New Hampshire, and Kentucky, apostates brought local and legislative action against Shaker communities. In Kentucky apostates attempted to force the Shakers to pay back wages for their communal labor. Other apostates disregarded the law and took matters into their own hands, whipping the public into a fury of anti-Shaker sentiment with allegations that children were held in bondage among the Shakers and then storming a Shaker community with a frenzied mob. In 1810 500 angry villagers attacked the Union Village, Ohio, community, terrorizing the Shakers and destroying their property. In Kentucky, Sally Bryant attempted to retrieve her daughter Lucy who had been indentured to the Shakers by her father. Shakers recorded how Bryant dressed entirely in black and looked like a "fury from the lower regions" when she led 200 to 300 local residents against the Pleasant Hill Shakers in 1825. Bryant successfully retrieved her daughter despite the fact that Lucy did not wish to leave her new communal home. Not all mobs were successful. In 1818 Mary Dyer and Eunice Chapman, whose three children were abducted by Eunice's husband-turned-Shaker, rallied support from 100 residents of Enfield, New Hampshire, in an ill-conceived attempt to steal their own children away from the Shakers.[8]

Although mobs led to injury and destruction of Shaker property, and legal actions discriminated against and restricted Shaker communal life, the most threatening form of apostate activity was the publication and distribution of anti-Shaker books and pamphlets. As literacy rates rose and the cost of production of books and pamphlets fell, apostate authors in the years between the Revolution and the Civil War found an anxious and willing audience for their carefully crafted diatribes that offered an insider's account of a suspicious sect. In a period of rapid economic growth, technological change, and increasing diversity, printed materials offered a convenient and inviting means to debate and define the coalescing national culture. Apostate authors did what literary scholar Jane Tompkins termed "cultural work," that is, their texts helped define American identity by illustrating, in their attacks on the Shakers, what Americans should disdain.[9] Lasting longer than a momentary mob, and with the potential to stretch far beyond a particular court's jurisdiction to all areas of the country, anti-Shaker books furthered the message that the Shakers were not welcome—and indeed were potentially dangerous—participants in the new American nation.

Mary Dyer excelled at the use of print culture to advance her cause and make her claims. Dyer explained and defined herself in the published books, pamphlets, and newspaper essays she crafted. And while crafting texts, she crafted a community of supporters connected by her literary activity as well as by a larger identity—those who disliked the Shakers. As literary critic Richard Brodhead explored in his study of authorship in America, an author's literary activity was not unidirectional: the communities Dyer's writing fostered in turn shaped the writing created within them.[10] In addition, Dyer was written about as Shakers, newspaper editors, supporters, and detractors published their views on Dyer and her claims. Her gender—the public understanding of the role, obligations, and duties of females—framed the ensuing discussions all these writing and reading communities prompted.

Mary Dyer lived a Shaker life for two years, willingly joining the sect that offered her a chance to preach and an opportunity to move away from the relentless work and isolation of Stewartstown, New Hampshire, on the northern New England frontier. With her husband Joseph, their five children, a stepson, and several neighbors, Mary Dyer joined the Enfield, New Hampshire, Shakers in January of 1813. For the first year or so, both Mary and Joseph found satisfaction with their new communal life. Yet while Joseph grew evermore attached to Shakerism, Mary's interest waned, frustrated with her lack of advancement to a leadership position. In January 1815 she announced her decision to leave. Since she had been a troublesome convert—frequently suggesting improvements for the faith—the Shaker leaders were likely glad to see her go. But when Mary requested the return of her children, legally indentured to the Shakers the year before, the elders and Joseph refused to yield. Distraught, angry, and very much alone, on a cold January day Mary Dyer fled the Shakers.

Shakerism had split apart many families, but Mary Dyer, unlike most women in her situation, turned her lonely anguish into action and began a campaign against the Shakers that would last five decades. Dyer placed petitions before the New Hampshire legislature, wrote books and pamphlets, distributed broadsides, penned articles in newspapers, and led a mob against the Enfield Shakers. Assisted by a network of family, friends, and sympathizers, Dyer sold her own books, gave public lectures, and solicited support from both men and women throughout New England as she traveled alone from town to town and maintained her quest to thwart the Shaker experiment. Yet despite Dyer's public recognition, Mary struggled to manage the day-to-day tasks of survival—food, shelter, and the necessities of life. Tied to her Shaker husband through unbreakable marriage bonds, yet alone in the world, Mary Dyer existed in a cultural limbo for fifteen years after she left the Shakers. When she and Joseph ultimately divorced, made possible through an amendment to New Hampshire divorce law prompted by the Dyers' unusual marital situation, Mary finally became free to govern her own life. She remained active in the anti-Shaker cause throughout her remaining years, arguing first for the return of her own children, and later, for legislation to prevent what had happened to her from happening to other women. Shakerism defined Mary's life even in her apostasy. Dyer replaced her hopes of preaching Shakerism with her message of anti-Shakerism. And having lost her biological family, Dyer cared for the apostate family, a surrogate family of sorts to replace the one she had left at the Shakers. But although Mary Dyer clung tenaciously to her claims of Shaker crimes and abuse, the public perception of Shakerism during the first half of the nineteenth century shifted from fear of the sect to admiration of Shaker material and economic successes, upright character, and self-supporting communities. By 1860, the anti-Shaker movement was dead, and a few years later, so was Mary Marshall Dyer.

The story of Mary Dyer's fight against the Shakers provides a new window into understanding antebellum Shakerism by examining closely the workings, and especially the writings, of one of its most tenacious detractors. Although today the Shakers are considered a respected and admired part of American history, in the last decades of the eighteenth and first decades of the nineteenth centuries, Shakers were seen as a strange new people and the faith as something to be feared. Like those who fight so-called cults today, two centuries ago concerned citizens organized to prevent Shakerism from spreading. These "anti-Shaker" activists worried that the Shakers used deceptive means to lure new members into a faith that was dangerous to one's physical and spiritual well-being. Anti-Shakers used violent confrontation, legal wrangling in the courts and state legislatures, and harassment to achieve their goals of destroying the Shakers. Anti-Shaker activists included local people who did not want a Shaker community in their neighborhood, ministers who opposed Shakerism on theological grounds, family and friends of Believers who feared for their friends' safety, and most importantly, the Shaker apostates who had turned away from the faith and turned around to spurn publicly what they had once embraced. The key in this public battle was print culture—the books, pamphlets, newspaper articles, and broadsides that were printed and distributed by both the apostates and the Shakers.

As historian Ann Fabian argues in her recent work on personal narratives in early-nineteenth-century America, individuals beset by tragedy, personal loss, or odd circumstance could "turn misfortunes into assets, [and] experiences into published books."[11] Dyer and other seceders from the Shaker faith did just that and used the power of the pen to invite the public into their personal lives and their private experiences as one-time Shakers. Such texts offered readers an opportunity to experience Shakerism vicariously and from the safety of their homes. Shaker apostate authors offered a window into the lived experience of Shakerism through the eyes of those who found it unsatisfying. Their texts offered readers information and a warning about the dangers of religious difference. Further, the specific concerns about Shaker tenets, beliefs, and practices that apostate authors placed at the center of their tracts—part biography, part exposé—provide insight into areas of tension in a rapidly growing and changing American society.

Apostate narratives are a subset of a larger corpus of writing about the Shakers. Beginning in the late eighteenth century and growing in the antebellum nineteenth century, numerous authors took pen in hand to describe the curious communal Shakers. Some writers were hostile and composed anti-Shaker tracts, including a good number of ministers who watched with alarm as members of local (including their own) congregations flocked to the Shakers.[12] Other authors took it upon themselves to refute Shaker publications, such as the theological treatise *The Testimony of Christ's Second Appearing*.[13] By the first quarter of the nineteenth century, spending a day at a Shaker village became a not uncommon tourist experience. Accounts of visiting the Shakers, published in periodicals, newspapers, or in travelogues, became increasingly popular in the late 1820s and following decades. Many authors pointed out "peculiarities" of the Shakers, often focused on the physical form of Shaker women who were seen to be pale and ghostly in the absence of romantic love. Nonetheless, most visitors praised the neatly organized villages and productive agricultural endeavors. Some noted visitors included well-known authors of the day whose experiences found their way into short stories and novels. Fiction with Shaker themes, notably stories of love within the celibate community, formed an important source of Shaker imagery for public consumption.[14] But the apostate narratives, fourteen authors publishing two dozen texts from 1780 to 1860, offered something the writers of fiction, theological tracts, or visitor's accounts could not: a unique insider's perspective on Shaker life. As eighteenth-century apostate author Valentine Rathbun promised his readers, his text was based not on "mere speculation but [on] sorrowful experience."[15] But the apostate author walked a fine line. Because the Shakers were a suspect sect (especially before 1830), apostate authors had to contend with the question of why they had joined such a subversive organization in the first place. Their credibility in telling their tale was a combination of their insider status, plus the distance they had achieved from their former communal home.[16] To gain the reader's trust, the apostate author built the tale around the twin processes of religious conversion and deconversion in a narrative supported by personal biography and contextual history.[17]

Passing on information via the printed media was analogous to an earlier, oral tradition of information distribution. Mary Dyer first worked out her apostate tale in oral form, telling her story to several diverse audiences before it was committed to print. Once printed, the story found new audiences, and as information was passed along in books, so too were the books themselves as reader shared with reader. Print proved a powerful force to persuade, to educate, and to document events. For apostate authors, print provided an arena in which to wage their public dispute with Shakerism. Former Shaker Absolem Blackburn, writing his apostate tract in Kentucky in 1824, styled himself a "modern pamphleteer," reflecting the growing ease with which those with modest means could place their selves in print. Information in print could travel beyond the geographic space and the time of the author, thus adding a previously unknown, and potentially powerful, longevity to the claims made. As the availability of printed material exploded in the early republic, reading became a fundamental part of American life. The Shakers were well aware of the power and complained that " . . . no sooner does a family set out to obey the gospel, then the writings of the Rathbuns, Tho' Brown, Mary Dyer, Eunice Chapman, &c are brought up and thrown in their way as a stumbling block. . . ."[18] The Shakers were forced to respond in kind, defending their faith in print against the printed accusations of the apostate authors.

Shaker apostates wrote their narratives for a wide variety of reasons: to air grievances (including the loss of property and wages while engaged in communal life), to make money, to promote their own ideas, or to seek support for changes in custody and divorce laws in order to retrieve Shaker-held children or break marital bonds with a still-believing spouse. Writing an apostate narrative was also a way to defend oneself, to distance themselves publicly from their dalliance with the Shakers, and to reintegrate into mainstream society; as sociologists would phrase it, to "manage" a "spoiled identity."[19] Most authors claimed they wrote not for personal glory or gain, but as a "duty" to the public who needed to know—for their own safety and well-being—the information that the apostates possessed.

The Shaker apostate narrative has its literary base in the captivity narrative.[20] In the apostate version of the captivity archetype, the individual innocently joins the Shakers, seduced by the compelling words of elders. Valentine Rathbun complained in his 1780s works that Shaker leaders, in order to prompt conversion, " . . . sometimes use great severity, and sometimes great flattery, to frighten on the one hand and allure on the other."[21] Once a member, the novice is subjected to subversive techniques and suffers tribulation and humiliation: Daniel Rathbun saw his family torn apart, Thomas Brown was ordered to give up reading, apostates in the 1840s claimed the elders used mesmerism, a hypnotic force, to control members. Finally, by pluck, luck, fate, chance, or God, the individual escapes, or is rescued, from Shakerism, and then, despite danger to self, renounces the group and publishes as a duty to warn others.[22]

The titles of apostate works reveal the unexpected nature of what lurked below Shakerism's pleasant facade: through apostates' pens Shakerism was "unmasked," "revealed," "unveiled," "exposed," "discovered," and "detected." Apostate Aquila Bolton featured a title page verse declaring his text would "expose [the Shakers] to the world and ask, that world's assistance to tear off the mask."[23] Apostate accounts launched a barrage of charges towards the Shaker faith and its leaders designed to portray the Shakers as outsiders and a threat to American society. And while this Shaker threat shifted over time from a threat to the stability of the nation, to a threat to the integrity of the family, and, finally, to a threat to individual body and spirit, the unifying theme of anti-Shaker writings was that Shakerism represented a dangerous variation on the patriarchal nation, proper American family, and traditional Protestant faith.[24] The resulting apostate narrative participated in the social construction of the Shaker evil and provided a means by which individuals could justify participation—by claiming they were tricked into joining—as well as justify the anti-Shaker movement.[25]

Like the former slaves, escaped prisoners, and cross-dressing sailors who produced pamphlets of their unique experiences, Mary Dyer found herself in unusual circumstances. In her lifetime, Dyer would publish five major works, several newspaper articles, and two broadsides.[26] After leaving the Shakers and finding herself without property or money and with limited power to govern her own life, Dyer turned to the public and entered print culture with her own hard tale of deception, abuse, and hardship. Dyer herself was the subject of numerous articles and rebuttals, including four books, several remonstrances, and a series of articles published by the Shakers who engaged in a counterattack no previous, or later, apostate would endure. As both the Shakers and Mary Dyer vied for public support, their battle became the subject of intense public debate. The public eagerly followed the conflict but did so not just because Dyer's texts offered a peak behind the Shakers' closed doors, but because her heart-wrenching experience reflected all too vividly changes in the family and gender roles that blurred and confused the structure of American society. And when the Shakers defended themselves, their texts in conjunction with those of their detractors participated in a larger public debate about the definition of a proper home, family, and religious practice.

Mary and Joseph Dyer had joined the Shakers in a period of intense change in American family structure. The strictly hierarchical structure where wives and children obeyed husbands was giving way to a more shared, or companionate, structure of marriage where husband and wife had distinct but complimentary roles. While fathers still ruled the family, mothers gained increasing cultural importance in the post-Revolutionary era. Mothers were responsible for raising the next generation of Americans, and their inherent nature made them the ideal, and only, choice for this critical role. As historians of women have described the "cult of true womanhood," women were understood to be naturally pious and virtuous. Kept safe from the corrupting influence of the public world of commerce, women in their private domestic sphere created a haven against corruption that protected her family. Within this haven, mores and culture were transmitted to the next generation.[27]

But this change did not happen overnight, nor equally within any one family. The seeds of the Dyers' marital discord are found in this cultural shift: Joseph expected a strictly hierarchical structure to his family, while Mary expected a greater role in decisions affecting the welfare of her children. The Dyers' marriage was troubled before their encounter with the Shakers, and certainly life at a celibate village did little to rekindle any flames of passion. Joseph liked the strict order and discipline of Shaker life as it mirrored his societal expectations. But at the Shakers Mary saw her marital woes writ large: little input into her community, lack of autonomous decision making, and a forced dependence on others. Believing she would have more freedom outside the Shakers, Dyer left, only to find that her marital status kept her bound, with or without the presence of her husband. While in a cultural sense, the structure of family was shifting, in the legal arena, little had changed. Wives were united with their husbands under the doctrine of coverture, effectively turning two individuals into one. That one was the husband. Wives were expected to obey their husbands, husbands were expected to provide bed and board and reasonable supplies for living, "necessities" that might include cloth and thread for making clothing. Joseph and Mary were one legal entity, and regardless of whether the Dyers shared bed and board, Mary could not sue or be sued, sell property, enter a contract, or keep wages from work she had done. Although Dyer had left the Shakers and Joseph, these legal and cultural expectations were still in force plunging Mary into a social limbo were she had no social, and importantly, legal identity apart from that of Joseph Dyer's wife.

Dyer's gender constrained her ability to pursue legal action against Joseph. Her gender also presented challenges as an apostate writer. In telling her tale Dyer had to defend her initial activities with the Shakers, as all apostate authors did. But she also had to defend her actions as a woman. Literary scholar Susan M. Griffin has argued in her study of tales of escaped Catholic nuns that the female subject was both author of *and* evidence for the tale she told. As such, she was subject to intense examination on her motives, experiences, and culpability.[28] Likewise, Dyer came under investigation. No one questioned apostate author Daniel Rathbun's actions as a father, yet Mary Dyer's skill and history as a mother received intense scrutiny. No one questioned Thomas Brown's travels to sell his Shaker apostate text, yet Dyer's similar travels were commented upon in newspapers throughout New England. Where Absolem Blackburn's presentation as a "modern pamphleteer" was seen as evidence of the best of democracy and literacy, Dyer's foray into print stimulated aggressive response against her and a suspicion about her "true" motives for appearing in public. Dyer's use of print culture in her anti-Shaker campaign shared thematic characteristics with her male predecessors, yet her gender added a layer of complexity that threw into sharp relief gender issues of the day.

The first apostate authors, publishing in the last two decades of the eighteenth century, supported their experiences with scriptural argument. Writing nearly forty years later, Mary Dyer crafted a narrative supported by sentiment. Sentimentality—the affections of the heart—became increasingly important in the late eighteenth and into the nineteenth centuries. Growing out of philosophical ideas from John Locke, and others, it was believed that morality was developed through the senses.[29] When reading a sentimental novel (which emerged as a popular literary form at this time), the reader, if a moral person, should be moved to tears by the pain or suffering of others. A lack of response indicated a flawed morality. Dyer invoked sentiment in several of her works. In her first work, *A Brief Statement* (1818), Dyer asked "Who can have sensations with me?" inviting the reader into her moral universe, and in several places Dyer related to the reader that she must put down her pen, so overcome with tears was she.[30] When Dyer used these scenes of tears she illustrated how moral individuals viscerally reacted to Shaker life. Further, because the Shakers remained unmoved by Dyer's tears, readers "read" the Shakers as immoral and thus unfit to raise children, Dyer's included. Physical responses were not only statements reflecting moral standards, they also demanded action.[31] Historian Thomas Laqueur has described nineteenth-century "humanitarian narratives" in which the pain of ordinary people detailed in texts connected subject and reader in a bond of "those who suffer and those who would help."[32] Dyer asks who can share her sensations, then answers her own question: "I think some mothers can, but they can not relieve me. I call for the tender feelings of fathers to have pity on the feminine sex."[33] She calls on her readers to take their tears and "tender feelings" and pass laws to prevent this moral outrage of families torn apart by Shaker belief. While the male apostate authors did not rely as heavily as Dyer on sentiment, they, too, used physical responses to indicate moral difference. Absolem Blackburn, for example, noted how the Shakers' prayers caused his hair "almost to stand on end." And when the Shakers compared Ann Lee to Christ, the memory caused him to shudder.[34]

Mary Dyer used the female captivity story to portray the Shakers as savage. A familiar and acceptable format for women authors, the captivity narrative, tales of abduction by Indians and rescue by the power of God, offered Mary Dyer a mental framework for interpreting her experiences, a literary guidepost for writing about them, and a familiar dramatic tableau for her readers. Eunice Chapman, struggling in New York to regain her Shaker-held children, described the loss of her two daughters and young son as "similar . . . to those mothers who have had their children forced from their arms by the savages."[35] The use of this format was not limited to women fighting the Shakers. In the early nineteenth century Abigail Abbot Bailey, suffering in an abusive marriage, adapted the captivity format to describe her marital difficulties, her fears of her husband's incest with a daughter, and Abigail's struggle to return home to New Hampshire after her husband abandoned her in upstate New York.[36] Dyer, Chapman, and Bailey told tales that intrigued readers, but also instructed. As literary scholar Gary Ebersole has argued, captivity narratives provided "vehicles for reflection on larger social, religious, and ideological issues."[37] In these tales, Dyer, Chapman, and Bailey provided images of a society that captured women in marital bonds difficult to break even when husbands abandoned their wives, stole children away, or engaged in incest.

Dyer drew on the works of several previous anti-Shaker authors, using their male voices to voice her complaints. For example, Dyer reprinted selections from Daniel Rathbun's 1785 work. When Rathbun, within Dyer's text, wrote how as a deluded Shaker convert he felt that his "wife and children were all dead to me," his authoritative voice (male, and eyewitness to Shakerism) reinforced Dyer's claim that Shakerism destroyed families.[38] Further, his account indicated how Mary's husband (as a male Shaker) would have been taught to feel towards her. In *A Portraiture of Shakerism* (1822), Mary Dyer's most

complex work, she reprinted long sections of male-authored theological debate and legal proceedings, topics about which women did not
routinely write. With this strategy of co-opting male voices, Dyer could
present arguments normally outside of a woman author's domain.

Dyer also presented pages and pages of affidavits in her publications. At first used as part of her legal strategy during hearings in front
of the New Hampshire legislature, Dyer's affidavits later became a significant portion of her published texts. Dyer's authorial voice receded
as affiant after affiant described how the Shakers had destroyed their
families, abused their children, and ignored the desperate pleas of mothers. The affidavits exposed Dyer to intensive public scrutiny as the
Shakers challenged her claims with affidavits of their own, which testified that Mary Dyer herself had neglected her children, ignored her
husband, and destroyed the Dyer family. The exchange initiated a heated
dispute on the nature of authenticity and veracity that newspaper editors and readers debated across New England.

Although the Dyer drama is set in a sectarian religious community,
religious beliefs formed a relatively minor aspect of this debate. While
the mainstream Protestant clergy issued scriptural rebuttals to Shaker
belief, the general public focused their concern on Shaker practices, especially in regards to the foundation unit of American society—the family. In the conjugal American family religious and social values were
passed to the next generation. The very stability of the social order relied
on the proper workings of family that imparted authority and discipline within its own internal bounds. The Shakers' communal lifestyle
challenged the widely held notion that the family unit was a unique
entity isolated from the surrounding community. Instead, the Shaker
family and the Shaker community were coexistent. Celibacy presented
an even greater challenge to Protestant society. New England ministers
had long condemned celibacy as unscriptural, unnatural, and a state
that would lead one to other, more perverse, sexual sins. The earliest
anti-Shaker writers drew on this tradition in their critiques of Shakerism
denouncing the Shakers for their refusal to "go forth and multiply," as
the Bible commanded, and help populate the American wilderness that
stretched before them.[39] By subverting the patriarchal reproductive family, and especially in a faith led by women, Shakers threatened to break
up all of society. Apostate Benjamin West described the consequences
of celibacy and female leadership in his 1783 apostate account: husbands would disown wives, and wives disown natural affection for their
husbands and children, "Thus women become monsters, and men worse
than infidels in this new and strange religion."[40] To its opponents, this
"strange" religion turned the social order upside down.

The Shakers considered the natural attraction of men and women, and the emotional bonds between spouses for each other, and parents, especially mothers, for children, as evidence of carnal lusts to be driven out through physical separation, hard work, and worship. Nonetheless, the Shakers recognized the obligations of husbands for wives, and in situations where a wife refused to join a believing husband, the Shakers insisted that the husband provide for his wife before he could be admitted as a full member. The Shakers thus challenged the cultural definition of family while simultaneously upholding the prevalent role definitions of husband, wife, and children.

Shakerism thus embodied a conflict between conservatism and progress. The Shakers did not reject the notion of family, but rather redefined its structure and purpose. The faith offered the opportunity for a woman's advancement in religious or business leadership roles but the community relied on the traditional division of labor to survive. It stood opposed to the traditional reproductive family, yet relied on the reproduction of others for new members. Shakerism offered an alternative for women without the protection of husbands and fathers, yet reinforced the necessity of males to provide for females both in their own trustees and in their formerly married members. Both within and without Shakerism, the world of men and women was changing in the first decades of the nineteenth century. It was in this period of change, conflict, and confusion that the lives of Mary and Joseph Dyer intersected with Shakerism.

Mary Marshall Dyer stood at the heart of the nineteenth-century attack on the Shakers. But this quintessential apostate has been overlooked in most studies of the Shakers. Dismissed by early-twentieth-century writers as an emotion-driven fury or, worse, as so crazed as to have lost all reason, Dyer and apostates like her have received little serious scholarly attention. Legal historian Carol Weisbrod studied litigation between apostates and four utopian groups, including the Shakers. Although financially, physically, and emotionally draining, apostate-initiated court battles ultimately helped reaffirm state support for the Shakers in decisions that upheld Shaker indentures and covenants as binding legal documents.[41] Historian Lawrence Foster considered Mary Dyer's difficulty subordinating her independent will to that of the authoritarian Shaker leaders. Recognizing in Dyer's written attacks shades of earlier apostate accusations, Foster coined the phrase "career apostate" to describe Dyer's lengthy attack that grew in part from her failure to obtain a leadership position. Instead of seeing Dyer as the solitary fury, Foster brought Dyer into the broader context of apostate activity over time. Similarly, historian Jean M. Humez described Dyer

as thwarted in her desires for a preaching career. She saw Dyer as rein-
venting herself as a "heroic avenger of the female victims of the religion that had once seemed to offer opportunities for women like her."[42]
Foster and Humez suggest Mary Dyer replaced her desire for leadership and preaching within the Shakers with a life-long career of leadership and preaching against the Shakers.

Building on Foster and Humez's work, I examine Mary Dyer's activities as part of a wider anti-Shaker campaign. I view Dyer's apostasy
as a public, cultural performance where the apostate (performer) and
readers (audience) share a set of beliefs, ideas, and symbols that were
called upon to communicate a specific message. In Dyer's books, public lectures, and court appearances, Dyer drew on religious ideas, gender roles, and concepts of the family to make her argument that the
Shakers were a danger to American society, the family, and to individual well-being. This performance occurred in what I call the public theater of apostasy. The "public theater" is a metaphor, or way of
interpreting the world, in use by the Shakers and their detractors. The
Shakers saw themselves as actors, or participants, in a cosmological
battle between good (the forces of Zion) and evil (the devil and his
apostate minions). Observers from the world used theater metaphor-
ically as well. Newspaper editor Isaac Hill, for example, wrote about
Dyer's "performance" in front of the New Hampshire legislature. To
explore Mary Dyer's life in the public theater of apostasy, diverse sources
are used. The public Dyer is revealed in her books, legislative appearances, and public lectures, all of which were further discussed in newspaper accounts, letters, and memoirs. The private Dyer remains more
elusive. No journals, diaries, or lengthy letter in Dyer's hand survives.
Yet through court records, eyewitness accounts, Shaker correspondence,
town histories, and additional sources, Mary Dyer emerges.

In the chapters that follow I examine the structure and strategies of
Dyer's anti-Shaker campaign. This is a challenging story to tell—a microhistory where in looking at one woman's life we learn about larger cultural issues.[43] But we know little of Mary's private thoughts and
motivations beyond what Mary tells us in each of her written works.
We know quite a bit about her public thoughts and desires. Dyer crafted
her texts to attract paying customers for her books, an audience of
readers who could potentially assist Dyer achieve her goals. As we read
her works we read, and read around, her personal agenda. With each
new work published, Dyer provided additional details on events discussed in her prior publications. Even more interesting, albeit challenging, in her later publications, like a palimpsest, one written version
of Dyer's life replaced a previous version. For each event in this pro-

tracted battle we have multiple versions and multiple vantage points for analysis: the event as revealed by Mary Dyer in her publications, the same event as described by Joseph Dyer and the Shakers, and the event portrayed by other observers in letters, memoirs, newspapers, or court records.

In a roughly chronological fashion, Dyer's story unfolds. Chapter one examines Dyer's conversion to and subsequent deconversion from Shakerism and how Dyer began to perform the role of a Shaker apostate. In chapter two, Dyer enlarged her apostasy, pleading her case to the New Hampshire legislature and publishing the first of her anti-Shaker works. In chapter three, Dyer rallied community support: a mob attack on the Shakers, a town petition to the legislature, and a lawsuit against Joseph Dyer. Although Dyer was buoyed by the support received from the leading men of the town, these men had their own agendas quite distinct from that of Mary Dyer. Chapter four examines Dyer's campaign in the 1820s when she published her largest work, *A Portraiture of Shakerism,* and embarked on a remarkable, multi-year bookselling campaign. At the end of the decade, Dyer divorced Joseph and, finally, regained her independent status and her social and legal identity. Following her divorce, Dyer disappeared from public anti-Shaker activities. Chapter five examines Dyer's reemergence to the forefront of anti-Shakerism, motivated by the sad and mysterious death of her youngest son. In chapter six, Dyer's legacy—one of communities and commodities—is assessed.

A close study of Mary Marshall Dyer's remarkable apostate career expands our understanding of the vital role anti-Shaker activities played in the evolution of the faith. Anti-Shakerism played an active role in the evolution of Shaker religion and, while destructive, ultimately, anti-Shakerism strengthened the Shaker faith by weeding out malcontents, by leading the Shakers to print culture, and by forcing the Shakers to articulate their beliefs and practices simply, clearly, and honestly in multiple public venues. Sociologist Rosabeth Moss Kanter has argued that aggressive actions towards utopian groups act as a "social vaccination" preparing the group in small doses for the next, potentially larger, assault.[44] Ironically, then, these diverse anti-Shaker acts served in part to strengthen the faith that apostasy and aggressive opponents weakened.

Mary Dyer's activities are part of a broader context of social protest in the antebellum period, illustrating that Shakerism and anti-Shakerism are coexistent with the changing social world, not isolated from it. As historian David B. Davis has argued, anti-Catholic, anti-Mason, and anti-Mormon movements shared a fear of conspiracy and subversion and directed that fear in acts designed to repress difference. Recent works on anti-Mormonism, anti-Catholicism, and contemporary anti-cult campaigns illustrate the shared concerns that undergird opposition campaigns in the nineteenth century and today.[45] The current work of national and international anti-cult organizations and frequent media attention to alternative groups often reflects the same agenda and actions of anti-Shakers two centuries ago. Thus the Shaker experience with anti-Shakers can be seen as part of a broader and pervasive American experience of fear, mistrust, and suspicion of difference.[46] Two centuries ago, Shaker/anti-Shaker conflict engaged the public because these debates provided a means of figuring out what America should be, by giving clear examples of what it should not. Understanding the conflicts around Shakerism provides insight into the ever-present conflicts in contemporary life, conflicts that suggest Americans still ask, and attempt to answer, the same questions of identity.

While Dyer was not unique in her anti-Shaker quest, her nearly fifty-year campaign to eradicate the group she feared was "subversive of Christian morality" and "detrimental to the well-being of society" was the lengthiest and the most complex.[47] This is a story set in a sectarian religious community—but it is also a story about women and family, and the roles and rules society enacted and enforced to maintain social stability. When Dyer wrote her last will and testament, she put forth her ideal vision of family. Her son Jerrub would inherit the fruits of her labor, as long as he upheld expected filial duties including providing for Mary "in sickness and in health," paying her debts and funeral costs, finding a "safe burying place," and erecting a "proper gravestone." When the Shakers offered new members a novitiate covenant, they defined their family as one of shared goods and communitywide bonds. Members who gave freely to the community would share equally in its bounty. The Shakers and Mary Marshall Dyer in their own distinctive ways challenged family structure and gender roles and used the power of print to gain adherents to their visions. Although neither Mary Dyer nor the Shakers would concede the point, Mary, a mother without children and a wife without a husband, and the Shakers, a celibate, communal sect that disavowed the marriage bond, shared similar positions on the margins of society. In this tension-filled and conflicted area, we find a determined woman, a struggling faith, and an American public anxious to understand themselves as they read to understand others.

1

Conversion, Deconversion, and Apostasy

Mary Dyer's mind had been under "serious contemplation" some time before smallpox made its way to Stratford, New Hampshire, in April 1803.[1] When Mary, three-year-old Caleb, and one-year-old Betsey became infected, Mary took her children to a pesthouse, an isolated cabin thirteen miles into the woods where the sick were sent to prevent them from infecting others. Alone and fevered, Mary begged God to spare her children and promised to serve Him if their lives were prolonged. With "a promise in [her] mind," Mary gave herself up and "God ... appeared [her] friend."[2] Her mind and body were then at ease, and a week later Mary and her children went home.

Mary's pesthouse conversion represented one of many religious peaks in her life, moments when Mary turned to God for assistance with the trials she endured. Subservient to God's will, yet nonetheless taking direct action in offering her service in exchange for her children's lives, Mary sought a personal relationship with God. Her experiences in the first years of the nineteenth century mirror those of many religious seekers and tell us about the process of converting and deconverting from religious belief. Far from reflecting an instantaneous decision, the twin processes are marked by shifting levels of commitment and satisfaction. For Mary Dyer, her continued quest for religious satisfaction, and the ideas carried in the Shakers' theological treatise, the 1810 *Testimony of Christ's Second Appearing*, would lead her first into, then out of, Shakerism.

Conversions

Born in newly settled Northumberland, New Hampshire, on August 7, 1780, Mary would later describe with pride that her parents Caleb Marshall (1750–1800) and Zeruiah Harriman (1753–1842) raised twelve children, ten of whom, including Mary, became schoolteachers.[3] Her parents were both of Scottish ancestry; Caleb a fourth generation colonist from coastal New Hampshire, and Zeruiah the daughter of a Scottish father from Rowley, Massachusetts. Caleb and Zeruiah married in Hampstead, New Hampshire in 1773 and, as part of a contingent of family and friends, they moved from the settled seacoast to Northumberland on the Connecticut River in northwestern New Hampshire. This was the New England frontier, where Caleb built his house "without hammer or nails" and where Indian attacks forced early settlers, including the Marshalls, to return temporarily to more settled areas.[4] Of the Marshalls' twelve children, eleven lived to adulthood and most remained in northern New England, settling in New Hampshire or neighboring Vermont.[5]

During Mary's youth, Northumberland was a small, close-knit community with a 1790 population of 117. Primarily a farming community, Northumberland shared goods and resources with Guildhall, Vermont, directly across the Connecticut River. As roads were little more than paths through the dark forests, religious services were held only two or three months a year. Itinerant Methodist and Baptist ministers occasionally preached. The aptly named Reverend Selden Church took residence in Northumberland but a meetinghouse was not built until 1799, and no formal church was organized until well into the nineteenth century.[6] In the decade following the Revolution, Northumberland experienced rapid migratory growth. As the younger generation matured and the population grew in "the Coös," as the region was known, family groups moved northward, settling new towns and extending the population of New Hampshire towards the Canadian border.

Mary described her childhood as filled with sickness; around the age of ten illness prompted her to fear for her life. By age sixteen her unspecified illness had not abated and she went to live on her paternal grandfather Marshall's farm in Hampstead, in an attempt to regain her health in the coastal setting.[7] Mary enjoyed her two years on the coast, describing her life at that time as filled with "vain amusements." Her health restored in Hampstead, Mary found energy for socializing and she became attached to a young man who owned a "handsome situation" in the center of town. But missing her family, Mary returned to Northumberland in February 1798. Her young man planned to visit the following fall but in the intervening months, Mary found a new romantic interest, the widower Joseph Dyer.

Joseph Dyer was eight years Mary's senior, born June 19, 1772 in Canterbury, Connecticut. The youngest of eight children of Captain Elijah Dyer (1716–1793) and Elizabeth Williams (1733–1817), Joseph was baptized in the Congregational church. His father died in 1793, and the estate was settled two years later. Joseph received one-sixth of the real estate (a total of approximately fifty acres divided into two lots) and one-sixth of his father's personal estate including a half share in a sorrel mare and a share in a grindstone. In early 1796, Joseph sold the larger of his two lots (just over thirty-seven acres) to his brothers Ebenezer and Elijah for seventy pounds "lawful money"[8] and used the money to settle in Stratford, New Hampshire, a participant in one of the last great migrations north before settlers would head west.[9] In Stratford, Joseph married Elizabeth Peverly, the daughter of one of the town's leading men and a former schoolmate of Mary's. Elizabeth died in early 1798 at their Stratford home, possibly due to complications from the birth of their only child, a son named Mancer, born February 5, 1798.[10]

In 1798 eighteen-year-old Mary Marshall met twenty-six-year-old Joseph Dyer. Reverend Church married them the following year. The Dyers settled in Stratford where Joseph had previously established his home near the Connecticut River. Stratford was a long and narrow town, following the Connecticut River for ten miles with settlers and their farms extending inward up to one mile away from the river. The soil, long shaded by thick forests, was rich and fertile. The Dyers were among the first settlers to push north into Stratford. In 1800, the population of the town was 281, nearly double what it had been a decade prior.[11] Here the Dyers farmed and began their family. Their first son, Caleb Marshall Dyer, born August 25, 1800, was named in honor of Mary's father who had died just two days before his namesake's birth. Two more children followed: Betsey on January 6, 1802 and on June 15, 1804, Orville.[12]

Joseph was active in the small village. He had been a member of the North Star Lodge of Masons since the lodge organized in Northumberland in 1798. Lodge records indicate a number of achievements. On September 26, 1798, Joseph received his "First Degree" and two months later became a Master Mason. At the January 21, 1800 meeting, the last gathering before the lodge relocated to Lancaster, Joseph was elected junior deacon. In 1803, he held the office of Steward. One of his fellow Masons was Benjamin Marshall, Mary's brother.[13] In Stratford, Joseph also served as a militia captain and attended "trooping, training, and other public days" and later admitted that at those events he sometimes "spent more time and money than wisdom."[14] Property-owning men rotated responsibility for a number of town jobs. Joseph held a number of positions in Stratford including selectman (briefly, in 1800), constable (1800), and highway surveyor (1804).[15] In the winter of 1805, the Dyers exchanged their farm in Stratford for one in Stewartstown, about thirty miles north, where some of Joseph's Connecticut relatives lived.[16] In Stewartstown the Dyers completed their family with Jerrub, born March 27, 1806, and Joseph, Junior, born February 9, 1809.

Stewartstown rests at the junction of Vermont, New Hampshire, and Canada. A range of hills two miles east from the river set the initial boundary for the town. The river area was settled first, and like the settlements to the south, Stewartstown had deep, fertile soil lying under wild forests and scenery described as "rich and sublime."[17] When the area was first settled, neighbors would come together to "roll up a log cabin," a community bee to set up housing quickly.[18] The area experienced rapid migratory growth in the first decade of the nineteenth century with the population rising from ninety-nine in 1800 to 186 in 1810 and doubling again to 363 by 1820. Attracted by the rich soil, settlers quickly developed Stewartstown and by the 1820s the community supported saw mills, a grist mill, and a clothing mill as well as post offices, schools, and stores.

The Dyers, like most of their neighbors, were farmers and kept cows, oxen, and horses. Joseph marked his cattle with "both ears cropt square."[19] They grew a variety of vegetables for their own use, grains including wheat, oats, barley, and rye for bread, and flax for cloth. Many of the settlers raised grass seed and carried it to sell in markets in Dover and Concord, New Hampshire, and Portland, Maine. The land was among the best farming and grazing land in the state, and pure spring water was easily accessible. Trout filled the streams and plentiful game included moose, bear, partridges, grouse, hares, and rabbits. Wolves, bobcats, foxes, and pigeons were also abundant and were problematic to the farming community. The first saw mill was erected in 1803, followed by a gristmill the next year. The season dictated local activities, and tasks undertaken included hunting, lumbering, ice cutting, farming, and the production of maple sugar.

The Dyers' hard work paid off. They were among the largest landowners in Stewartstown, owning both cleared land and wild land, including 200 acres intended for future farms for their four sons. They traveled by horse and by sleigh. Joseph occasionally took long journeys, sometimes as far away as Portsmouth, New Hampshire, to sell crops, or back to Connecticut to visit family. Joseph was a Stewartstown selectman in 1806–1807 and again in 1809–1810. As Town Clerk (1809–1810), Joseph signed many documents regarding land transactions or other town business.[20] Mary occasionally provided her signature as witness to these exchanges, leaving a record that her nickname was Polly. At their farm, the Dyers sold "spirituous liquor," finding a good number of Canadian customers who would slip over the border for Sunday purchases. Mary had talent with a needle and made garments for both men and women. This income allowed the Dyers to keep a succession of hired men to help Joseph in the fields and hired girls to help Mary with work in the house, including child rearing, nursing, washing, cooking, and cleaning. While Joseph tended to the fields, Mary undertook a variety of tasks, some she had done before as a young girl in the relatively more settled Northumberland, and some new tasks as demanded by the frontier life of Stewartstown. Mary's domestic labor, in conjunction with the more visible labor of her husband, was crucial to the economic development of the agricultural community.[21]

Farming kept the Dyers busy, but their life was not solitary. With their neighbors, friends, and family, the Dyers attended social gatherings. One party featured apples and cider "brought from the lower towns." Another gathering featured rum and a fiddler.[22] These social events fostered community bonds and interdependence. Both by building structures and by building community, the residents of Stewartstown saw their frontier life as a temporary step on the way to a settled, prosperous life. Like many American communities, Stratford and Stewartstown looked to the future, and when the Dyers lived in the Coös, plans were underway for the construction of roads, schools, and a meetinghouse.[23]

Yet despite this busy community life, in the first decades of the nineteenth century there were few established churches in the Coös. In their later writings, both Mary and Joseph emphasized how the revival spirit marked their religious experiences in the middle of the first decade of the nineteenth century. The revivals sweeping through the area brought excitement and a new religious focus and intensity to both Dyers' lives, as they had to many Americans anxious to make the nation a Godly nation. But the Dyers' books also revealed that the while revivals and new attention to matters of religion were personally invigorating, this same excitement brought confusion to their household. Mary and Joseph were frequently out-of-step in their conversions and religious beliefs. As both sought to define their lives within new religious bounds, their marriage became increasingly strained. And when an itinerant preacher arrived in town with tales of a new and curious religion, both Mary and Joseph were intrigued by the possibility of altering their life, setting the stage for their eventual, and fateful, conversion to Shakerism.

Religion made the Dyer household a stage for a battle of self-discipline and will. The smallpox crisis had prompted Mary's 1803 pesthouse conversion and she emerged with a new focus in her life. She longed to attend Methodist meetings, the only religious service in the area, but Joseph objected. He was more interested in "parties and balls" and lived an undisciplined, intemperate life.[24] Liquor and differing levels of religious commitment stressed the Dyers' marriage. In her later testimony Mary would blame the Shakers for her marital discord, but the Dyer marriage was strained long before they learned of Shakerism. Mary objected to Joseph's drinking habits, evidence of his lack of self-discipline and self-control. Activities in the Dyer household presented a constant test of Mary's spiritual strength. Visitors frequented the farm and played card games, despite a new law that attempted to curtail the growing problem of gambling. This rowdy, frivolous behavior angered her even more than Joseph's drinking. Mary took two forms of action to deal with these troubles. During one card game, Mary grabbed the deck and threw the cards into the fire, effectively stopping that day's gambling. Mary later portrayed her aggressive, physical response as illustrating the strength of her convictions, destroying the cards as surely as God would smote sinners. Mary Dyer enacted the promise she had made in the pesthouse to serve God, challenging her husband's lack of self-discipline to resist sin with a strong will of her own. In addition to her physical outbursts, Mary also took a more spiritual approach to her troubles and prayed for a resolution to her unhappy life.

The resolution to the Dyers' troubles came in Joseph's "remarkable" and terrifying dream that convinced him he would soon die a sinner.[25] Mary offered her own interpretation. Reflecting her desire for family stability, Mary told Joseph the dream was a warning to forsake sin. Shortly after this, Elder Quimby, a Baptist missionary, preached nearby. The Freewill Baptist revival that had blazed across Maine and southern New Hampshire had reached the Coös.

The Freewill Baptist movement was part of an evangelical sectarian impulse whose roots were found in the dynamic preaching of Methodist preacher George Whitefield in the 1740s. Eschewing contemplative scriptural study for intense oral development, Whitefield broke with traditional Calvinist doctrine and urged reflection on a history of Redemption, key events that shaped human destiny. Many sectarian groups, the Shakers and the Freewill Baptists among them, built on these "scriptural narratives" and by the early nineteenth century had solidified their own unique philosophies.

The Freewill Baptists, like other sectarians, denied the doctrine of predestination where humans were damned at God's will. Likewise, the sectarians reduced the efficacy of original sin in removing its heritable quality that had long cursed humans. The sectarians, and particularly Freewill Baptists, placed a greater emphasis on volitional sin and the individual's ability to select or reject temptation. This formed the backbone of the Freewill Baptist beliefs. Each person at one point in his or her life would be presented "with a clear and conscious choice between true faith and fatal error."[26] Another crucial doctrine was the appearance of Christ in the human person of Jesus. At the time of Christ, humans had been saved from original sin but still committed volitional sin in their fallen state. Christ's atonement would reunite humans and God. The emphasis of the act of atonement was on the personal volition of the event. Christ's atonement offered humans another chance for salvation by believing in Him as a Savior. It was the individual's free choice to accept Jesus and receive salvation, or to reject Him and suffer damnation.[27]

The Freewill Baptist message appealed to northern New England. The Congregationalism of southern, settled New England had not established much of a hold in the new towns of northern New England, evident in the few settled churches on the frontier. The lack of churches and other institutions, and a community organized in isolated farms rather than a central village, placed greater reliance on the family as the primary social unit. The family was a collection of individuals with distinct roles and duties. As self-reliant and independent individuals on the frontier, the doctrine of free choice appealed. One was not directed to forgo sin, but had the choice and the power to do so.

Joseph attended Elder Quimby's meeting and left "much alarmed with his state of mind."[28] For several days he was agitated and cried to God for forgiveness for his sins. "At length," wrote Mary, he "appeared to find peace and his mind filled with extacy [sic] of joy."[29] For Joseph, conversion came unaware. Mary had initiated her "deal" with God during the pesthouse crisis, but Joseph was a more passive recipient, first of Mary's interpretation of his dream and then of Elder Quimby's preaching.

The Dyers' farm became a center for religious activity, and a life of frivolity became one of stability. Elder Quimby preached twice at the Dyers' house, and Mary reported that by October 1806 "our house changed from drunkards and swearing to Christians, reading and praying."[30] The revival and the charismatic preachers who traveled in the area brought the Dyers' unhappy period to an end. They sold their farm in Stewartstown for $1,600 and moved to a new one of 200 acres.

With the profit from the sale, they paid off their debts. Reinvigorated by religion, the Dyers lived a settled life, although without an organized church, they stood alone.[31]

In August 1809, Joseph encouraged Mary to meet Elder Benjamin Putnam, a dark-eyed twenty-one-year-old Freewill Baptist minister who had been preaching since age fourteen.[32] When Mary heard the dynamic young preacher, the spirit filled her. Putnam baptized Mary, Joseph, and several of their neighbors. Community support kept the spirit alive. Following a meeting held at a nearby Canaan (Vermont) home, Putnam united the Dyers and eleven others in a pledge to watch over one another, a pledge many of the group would keep in their support of Mary's later quest against the Shakers.

Religion had brought some peace to the Dyer household, but now that same religious spirit reintroduced marital tension. Inspired by Putnam's Freewill Baptist message, the Dyers traveled to various area religious meetings and hosted religious services at their home. The Dyers were not simply acted upon by forces of conversion, they acted as agents of conversion as well. Joseph served as a teacher and led area-Freewill Baptist community members in worship. He housed itinerant preachers and traveled into nearby Canada to do some preaching himself, at least once accompanied by Mary. The oldest Dyer children were affected as well. Caleb and Betsey "became serious," and one "was hopefully converted."[33] Although Joseph had given up drinking and both he and Mary had found religion, a new stress divided the Dyers. Mary saw herself as called to preach and had become quite attached to the young Elder Putnam with whom she shared intense conversations. Mary described her relationship with Elder Putnam as spiritual, yet Joseph thought otherwise, particularly when Mary made her marriage celibate, declaring that "living in the works of natural generation . . . would destroy both body and soul." Joseph reluctantly acquiesced "tho not all together agreeable to [his] feelings."[34] Here is one form of power that Mary utilized, namely access to sex. Whether motivated by a desire to avoid another pregnancy, to reach a higher spiritual plain, or simply by a desire to avoid Joseph, Mary denied her husband sexual access for three years prior to their joining the Shakers. Caleb Dyer, in later testimony about his family's pre-Shaker life, recalled those days as a time of tension and stated that the Shakers had cared for him and his siblings better than his parents had or would have been able.

Like Mary, Joseph longed to preach, but the responsibilities of farm and family prevented him. When Lemuel Crooker, a self-professed itinerant preacher, came into Stewartstown in 1811, Joseph found they shared similar religious ideas, especially concerning joint interest of property. Crooker intrigued Mary as well, and while he boarded with the Dyers, she made him clothing, and she and Lemuel spent long hours in private conversation, to the further detriment of her marriage. As with her attachment to Elder Putnam, Mary was spiritually excited by the itinerant preacher who perhaps provided a strength and religious fulfillment her husband and isolated community did not provide. Crooker had also impressed several members of the Stewartstown community where he fasted often and preached two or three times a week.[35] Desirous of a permanent preacher, the community sent Crooker to New York state to retrieve his family and return to settle permanently in New Hampshire. During his trip, Crooker visited the New Lebanon, New York, Shaker community. And when he returned to New Hampshire, Crooker arrived not with his family but with *The Testimony of Christ's Second Appearing*, the Shakers' first extensive treatise on their theology. This unexpected occurrence brought confusion to the community, and to the Dyer household.

Speaking for the Shakers and covering more ground than missionary leaders could, *Testimony* brought Shakerism a new and powerful visibility as print brought Shaker theology to widespread public attention. The first edition of *Testimony*, published in Ohio in 1808, launched the Shakers into print culture. But distribution of the book from the distant western Shaker communities was problematic, and also, on reviewing the first edition, the Parent Ministry at New Lebanon, New York, had discovered numerous typographical mistakes, binding errors, omitted sheets, and confused doctrinal points. In addition to correcting the errors, the Ministry wanted the second edition to be less costly and more intellectually accessible to "afford the poorer class of people with the privilege of participating equally with the rich in the benefit of this publication."[36] This second edition of the work, published in Albany in 1810, presented Shaker beliefs and defended the faith against persistent rumors that founder Ann Lee was nothing more than a drunken, old woman. "Corrected and improved," the second edition very quickly became known popularly as the Shaker Bible.[37] Crooker carrying *Testimony* to Stewartstown demonstrated how the printed volume could travel in place of Shaker leaders and spread the faith in their stead.

Several Stewartstown neighbors met at the Dyers' home to discuss this new material, attracted to, but also repelled by, the Shaker beliefs. The assembled neighbors listened carefully to Crooker, who spoke approvingly of the Shakers whom he had visited at New Lebanon. But several of the Dyers' Canaan friends had previously lived near the Canterbury, New Hampshire, Shaker community, and they voiced

strong warnings about how Shaker life disrupted the biological family. Others who had read the *Testimony* shared the Canaan friends'
misgivings about celibacy, Ann Lee's connection to Christ, and the
necessity to confess sins to elders. William Plumer, who would be governor when Mary Dyer first appeared before the New Hampshire legislature, read the *Testimony* and recorded his mixed impressions in
his private diary. "The work," wrote Plumer, "bears strong marks of
genius, talents, and information & is wrote in a bold . . . style. On
most occasions it is clear & definite but on some questions, like the
subject, it is obscure & mystical."[38] Four diary pages later, Plumer
concluded his summary of *Testimony*. Although he asserted that the
Shakers were "remarkable for their industry; & are peaceable good
members of society," the *Testimony* was "proof of the fallacy of the
argument that a doctrine is right because men of learning, extensive
knowledge, great talents & fair moral characters embrace it."[39] Plumer's
comments reflected public sentiment of the day. Shaker material
works—attractive buildings and productive farms—were admirable,
but Shaker words—their sometimes clear and sometimes obscure theological writings—were questionable.

Despite the cautions expressed about Shaker practice and belief, the
Dyers, Crooker, and Mary's sister Susanna Marshall traveled to the
nearest Shaker village in Enfield, New Hampshire, to see the Shakers
firsthand. Their actions repeated a familiar pattern. Knowledge of the
Shakers brought curiosity, which then prompted a visit and was often
followed by conversion. The Dyers were already in a highly awakened
religious state when Crooker brought the Shaker message to
Stewartstown. In the Dyers' introduction to the faith, books first carried the Shaker message, confirmation of the Shaker leaders' correct
perception that publications could bring new members to the faith.
Unlike their neighbors, the Dyers were more curious about than repelled
by Shakerism and, wanting to add a new dimension to their lives, traveled to Enfield to learn more.

The party of potential converts arrived in Enfield on a Friday night
after a 130-mile journey. Mary and her sister shared a room while Joseph
and Crooker stayed elsewhere. During the weekend, the visitors observed
Shaker life and work in the bustling Enfield community. A visitor's
account published in 1808, just a few years prior to the Dyers' visit,
described the Enfield Shaker village where "everything wore the mark
of industry, neatness and prudence." Joseph would have been
impressed by Shaker agricultural endeavors: "the fields were in the highest cultivation, their barns large and convenient, and their cattle numerous and goodly."[40] Following the norm of gender separation at the

Shaker community, Mary saw little of her husband until Sunday meeting where she saw him participate in Shaker worship, an indication that Joseph had joined the sect. Mary, although encouraged to join the patterned marches that formed the heart of a Shaker service, declined to participate and watched her husband's enthusiasm with a worried eye. As an earlier visitor had described, in Shaker public worship, "the principal ceremony was dancing, but in the dancing there was nothing of the grace or majesty of motion. It was the stiff movements of a clown in the frenzy of a Pythia. . . . The males and females on this day mingle in this wild devotion."[41] Their short visit completed, the Dyers, Susannah, and Crooker started their journey north, stopping in Northumberland to share their experience with family and friends. Joseph found the Shaker principles "agreeable to his own conviction," seeing firsthand the productive benefits of joint property and communal work.[42] But Mary, for reasons that aren't entirely clear, didn't share in Joseph's positive report. Having observed Joseph participate so enthusiastically in Shaker worship, Mary may have worried at the potential loss of her husband. Mary and Crooker continued their close relationship. Joseph, excluded from the intense religious conversations he had once enjoyed with Crooker, complained that Crooker and Mary's relationship was one he thought closer than proper. But Crooker's sentiments for Mary and for Shakerism evidently changed, and shortly after their return from Enfield, Crooker left New Hampshire.

Although books and the visit to Enfield had captivated Joseph's interest, isolation from practicing Shakers and a lack of community support challenged his ability to practice the faith in Stewartstown. Joseph tried to practice Shaker worship in his home, including "ceremonies and dance."[43] Still filled with his preaching desires, Joseph planned to set up a Stewartstown Shaker community. He carried with him and read repeatedly *The Testimony of Christ's Second Appearing* and discussed it with all who would listen. But there was little local interest in Shakerism. Joseph's only success seemed to be Mary who, although hesitant about the faith during her visit to Enfield, became increasingly attracted to Shaker ideas. As Joseph preached to his wife the new ideas he gleaned from *Testimony,* Mary learned more of the faith, particularly intrigued by women's spiritually equal standing with men, the possibility of preaching, and the opportunity to share in the communal ownership of property.[44] Joseph and Mary had replaced Crooker as their religious sounding board with each other. But, curiously, as Mary grew more interested in Shakerism, Joseph's enthusiasm waned. The Dyers seemed trapped in a subtle battle for religious dominance—either Mary or Joseph took the lead, but rarely both. When Joseph left

Stewarstown and preached, Mary felt religiously isolated and trapped in her domestic role; when Mary preached, Joseph bemoaned the lack of a wife to maintain the household. By August of 1811, out-of-step again in their religious preferences, the Dyers mutually abandoned the idea of becoming Shakers.

Although his enthusiasm had faded, Joseph had not given up entirely the idea of becoming a Shaker. On a trip to Portsmouth, New Hampshire, Joseph detoured north and stayed overnight at the Alfred, Maine, Shaker village. The personal visit recharged Joseph, and he returned to Stewartstown invigorated.[45] In the fall of 1812, Enfield Shakers Moses Jewett and John Lyon, alerted by a letter from the Dyers to the potential for Stewartstown converts, made the long journey north and preached at the Dyers' home. The Dyers invited family and friends to the meeting, including Sarah Curtis, their hired girl and a member of the Canaan group who had pledged to watch over one another. Mary wore a Shaker dress that she had no doubt sewn for herself. Affidavits from both Joseph and Mary's later books indicated that Shakerism had taken hold of the Dyers but to varying and changing degrees. Some witnesses claimed Mary was the more zealous; others said Joseph took the lead. Regardless of who was more enthusiastic, the Dyers had again become very interested in Shakerism. Spirituality—the influence of Shakers in their home—and practicality—the Dyers' growing economic difficulties and the threat of war—motivated Mary and Joseph to give Shakerism another chance.

Shakerism had made quite a mark in the Coös. First carried by books with Lemuel Crooker, the Shaker message flowed through the community via the Dyers' network of family and friends. Mary attempted to convert her sister, Fanny Marshall, and Sarah Curtis. The Dyers' earlier visit to the Enfield Shaker village had stimulated Joseph's belief, but the attempt to live a Shaker life far from the Shakers did not work well for the Dyers. Unlike most other religions, Shakerism demanded the complete severance of worldly ties and familial relationships. Without the support of a communal group to provide for necessities such as food and clothing, the Dyers, and others attracted to the faith, found themselves constantly challenged by continued ties to the world. In addition, the world to which they were by necessity still tied scorned their participation in the sect isolating the Dyers by distance from the Shaker community, and isolating them socially from the Stewartstown community. Jewett's and Lyon's autumn 1812 visit to Stewartstown solidified the Dyers' interest in and enthusiasm for the faith. With one-on-one attention, the Shaker missionaries convinced the Dyers to move to the community at Enfield. The missionaries' visit was profitable. In addition to the Dyer family, Sarah Curtis's parents placed Sarah and several of her siblings under Shaker care. Daniel Taylor, who had worked for Joseph as a hired hand, and his family also joined, a total of nearly thirty people.

Joseph found the doctrines of Shakerism "agreeable" but his conversion was helped along by his still-troubled marriage and growing financial difficulties. Perhaps the Shakers offered stability in Joseph's crumbling world. He bemoaned the loss of order and hierarchy in his family. His young son Orville would not obey his eldest, Caleb. His wife would not obey him and neglected work and family for seemingly self-centered interests in public preaching and long, private conversations with visiting preachers. The ideal, ordered patriarchal family in which Joseph was raised was not a reality in his own household. Joseph found himself in financial "embarrassments," his marital difficulties and an economic downturn had affected his farm's profitability. The threat of war in 1812 added an additional concern for safety for settlements on the American-Canadian border. For Mary, joining the Shakers offered the possibility for her to preach without community, or her husband's, censure. She may also have imagined that a move to a Shaker community would have removed herself from the tiring rural agricultural life that tied her to home, hearth, and husband. For Joseph, Shakerism offered a retreat from his worldly obligations and stress; for Mary, Shakerism offered an entry into a more public, visible role.

In late fall of 1812, the Shakers agreed to care for the Dyer children free from expense "out of charity considering [their] embarrassments." Although Mary saw benefits in a Shaker life, including an opportunity for preaching, Mary may have had lingering doubts about joining the Shakers. She extracted a promise from Joseph that should she decide against Shakerism, she could leave and take at least some of the children with her. With that agreement made, Joseph took ten-year-old Betsey and her eight-year-old brother Orville to Enfield. Accepting $100 to "assist us in our embarrassments," Joseph returned to Stewartstown (after a trip to Connecticut) to "turn out his property and settle his debts and thereby stop the interest and in some instances the cost of suit."[46] Mary brought the remaining three children to Enfield in January 1813. Their hired man, Daniel Taylor, drove the sleigh that carried them, accompanied by Mary's sister Betsey Tillotson. After leaving the children, Mary returned to Stewartstown to help pack up the furniture and assist Daniel Taylor's family who were also joining the Enfield Shakers. Mary returned to Enfield a month later with Miriam Curtis, Sarah's young sister, and awaited Joseph's arrival. Once Joseph settled his affairs as best he could, he returned to the Enfield Shakers in November 1813.

In Stewartstown Mary wore Shaker dress and Joseph carried the Shaker Bible, and although the Dyers had moved family and furnishings nearly 130 miles, they were not yet Shakers. First they would undergo a novitiate period during which they would learn the customs, manners, beliefs, and practices of a dramatically different way of life.

A Shaker Life

The Enfield Shaker community sat eight miles east of Hanover, New Hampshire, and the Connecticut River. Shaker missionaries first came to the area in 1782 and initially Shaker converts lived independently in their own biological families. As in the southern New England Shaker communities, in 1792 the Enfield Shakers united in a secluded community and withdrew from the persecuting world. Through trade and donations of land from new members, the growing community acquired property on the western shore of Mascoma Lake. The community was ideally situated with hills providing both soft and hard woods with fertile agricultural land below. By 1810, when the Dyers first learned of Shakerism, the Enfield community consisted of 134 members living in three communal families, or self-sufficient subcommunities, within the Enfield Shaker village. Each family had its own dwelling house, meeting space, and industries. Although the earliest Enfield Shakers met with the same distrust and fear as other early Shaker communities, by the time the Dyers arrived, the Shakers were well accepted by the neighboring townspeople of Enfield, Lebanon, and Hanover, for their growing community of productive farms and neat, ordered buildings.

While Joseph returned to Stewartstown to sell his property and break his worldly connections, Mary settled into Shaker life. She lived in the North Family that housed the novitiate. The North Family had been organized in 1810 to deal with increasing numbers of converts who were attracted to Shakerism's message that the millennium was at hand. Shakerism also presented a practical option for families disrupted by death, poverty, or other hardship. The Shakers represented the only available social service agency of its day, taking in widows, orphans, and those unable to make a living in the world. The dwelling house, where all new members slept and ate, had been completed in June of 1812, a few months before the Coös group arrived. Shakers John Lyon, Edward Lougee, Lucy Lyon, and Mary Mills served as the elders and Eldresses of the North Family, and it was their task to instruct new members in the faith, those who had come seeking salvation and those who had come because they had no where else to go.

Mary at first appeared a promising convert. She spoke at worship meetings by Shaker request and was content with her new life and the apparent fulfillment of her preaching aspirations. But by summer, six months or so after her arrival, she had grown less satisfied. A visit from a former Shaker planted the first seed of doubt in Mary's mind, warning her not to espouse Shakerism or she "should be obliged to renounce everything . . . thought to be grace."[47] This direct intervention between a seceder and a Shaker was not unusual and acted as a recruitment mechanism into the social category of Shaker seceder. Troubled by the message, Mary questioned the Shakers. She "read their books, sometimes argued against their principles, at other times for them, and applied to the scriptures."[48] This marked Mary as a troublesome novice and is reminiscent of the querying strategy apostate author Thomas Brown employed in his experience with the Shakers at Watervliet and New Lebanon a decade before. Instead of receiving instruction from the elders, Mary, like Brown, read and interpreted scripture for herself. This was in direct contradiction to Shaker practice where the ministry leaders alone provided information. With her independent spirit, Mary demonstrated to the elders all too vividly the dangers of printed texts and permitting members access to them.[49] As literary historian Etta Madden has argued in her study of Shaker literacies, published works such as the *Testimony* drew Shaker communities together by presenting a unified theology-in-print, but at the same time published works threatened to tear communities apart as individuals interpreted what they read for themselves.[50]

Joseph returned to Enfield in November of 1813, along with Sarah Curtis, who joined her siblings who had previously been sent to the Shakers. Shortly after Joseph's arrival, Father Job and Mother Hannah, the leaders of the entire Enfield Shaker community, gathered all the new members together and told them they had a "gift," or directive from God to share with the assembled group. Joseph Dyer, Daniel Taylor's family, Moses Atwood and his child, and some of the Curtis children would live as a Shaker family in the nearby village of Lebanon.[51] Mary, her son Joseph Junior, and Thomas Curtis (who was just about the same age as the young Joseph) would remain at the North Family; and Jerrub Dyer and Martha and Raphael Curtis would move to the Church Family. The Dyers' furniture would be distributed to wherever it was needed. Community records indicate that Caleb Dyer, age thirteen, and his sister Betsey, then eleven, were already living at the South Family. Joseph was agreeable to the gift, but Mary did not respond well to the directive to separate her family further. She wept for an hour and then took on a stony, resolute silence. Her actions concerned the Shaker leaders, and a few days later, Joseph returned to live at the North Family.

Mary saw herself as a Shaker, but instead of learning to conform to the faith, she tried to reform the religion to suit her needs. Mary had been reading *Testimony* and "questioning the lower orders" about belief and practice. She promoted her own ideas for Shakerism, including a concept of spiritual marriage where especially enlightened Shakers would pair up for sanctioned reproduction. This idea appalled the leadership who denied that Shakers ever had any such plan to abandon celibacy. She was not the first, nor the last, novitiate to attempt to take a direct role in Shaker theological construction, and the genre of Shaker apostate literature is filled with texts authored by individuals whose ideas for Shaker reform were dismissed.[52]

In the spring of 1814, three key events signaled that the Dyers were intent on a Shaker life, despite Mary's misgivings. Shaker records recorded an appraisal of Joseph's property that included 200 acres of land in Stewartstown (valued at $800), land in town ($250), furniture, cloth, and goods ($191.47), and notes and cash worth $191.92, for a total value of $1,433.39, a significant sum for a family a few years earlier to be found in embarrassments. This documentation suggested Joseph was coming close to finalizing its dispersal.[53] Secondly, the Dyers indentured their children to the Shakers. The Shakers would house, feed, clothe, and educate the children until age twenty-one, at which time the children could decide for themselves whether or not to remain at the Shaker village. Finally, Mary and Joseph signed the North Family articles of agreement—an agreement of intention to uphold Shaker principles.[54] These actions moved the Dyers away from the concerns of the world and the individual family and towards the communal aspirations of the Shaker village. But how much input did Mary have in these critical decisions? Mary later claimed she signed the indenture under force, and as a woman, she could not understand the legal document before her.[55] And although both had worked their farm, Joseph had ultimate and sole control of the property and could sell it at his will. More critical to Mary's concerns, Joseph also had the ultimate power over the destiny of his children and of his wife.

By mid-1814, Mary reached a point of frustration with Shakerism. She did not like being classed among the "lower order" (the novitiate). Her confession of sins disappointed the elders who urged her to reveal all of her sinful behavior. A central tenet of Shaker theology, confession was the means by which members purged themselves of the past in order to move forward to practice a Christ-like life on earth. Until the elders believed her to have fully confessed, Mary's spiritual progression was stalled. She found that life in a Shaker village was much like life in Stewartstown with daily farm and household tasks that required attention. Divided along gender lines, daily work at a Shaker village mirrored that in any agricultural community. For the men, care of animals, crops, and the manufacture of needed goods (such as barrels, buckets, and buildings) filled their day. For Mary and the women of the Shaker village, cleaning, mending, cooking, and laundry—for more than 100 people—were but a few of the tasks demanded of Shaker women. Far from an escape from those tasks in order to pursue a life of freedom and preaching, Mary found herself confined in an even greater degree than in her rural isolation. Among the Shakers, as troubled as her marriage had been, Mary could not rely on support from her husband who was striving to break his personal connection to his estranged wife. More problematic than the loss of an emotional attachment to Joseph was Mary's diminished relationship to her five children who were living among three different Shaker families.

Mary's pretensions to a preaching life had also been thwarted. On one occasion, she gained an audience with the ministry leaders, the spiritual guides for both the Enfield and Canterbury Shaker communities. During the meeting Mary explained her personal interpretation of the Shaker faith. There's no record of exactly what Mary espoused, but the Ministry did dismiss her ideas for a Shaker reform and summarily dismissed her. In the fall of 1814 Mary spoke during worship services before the assembled group of Shakers and visitors from the world. She testified that the Shakers were the people of God. But despite her public profession, perhaps an attempt to regain favor with the elders, she remained unsatisfied, and as 1814 wound down, so did Mary's commitment to Shakerism.

What prompted Mary to retreat from Shakerism? She later argued that she was never a committed Shaker at all and had simply reached the point where she could no longer live with such hypocritical and evil behavior, revealing a litany of Shaker crimes and misdemeanors. Joseph, however, told a different story and argued that Mary left disappointed in not receiving a leadership position. It would seem, as with much of the Dyer debate, the truth lay somewhere in between. Mary was anxious for a rapid spiritual progression and was impatient with the North Family elders' demands for her complete confession of sins. Her lack of input into the religion was another source of frustration. The Shakers represented one of the very few options for a religiously motivated woman such as Mary, yet she could not obtain a leading role. This was a far different situation than that which the Dyers enjoyed when they hosted itinerant preachers and ran religious meetings in their Stewartstown home. At the Shakers Mary was situated in the "lowest order" of the strictly hierarchical community, under constant watch from other members and by the North Family leadership who in turn reported to the Church Family. Mary, who had been accustomed to speaking about religion both to the public and in her private conversations with Putnam and Crooker, now found that she had no audience for her preaching and no sounding board for her ideas. And while the *Testimony* provided provocative information on Shakerism, Mary learned through her unsatisfying meetings with elders and the ministry that that information was not subject to personal interpretation nor open for debate. Mary's intelligent, independent, and ambitious spirit simply did not fit within the rigid, structured society. Although the community offered security for an individual, the tyranny of community disempowered Mary and left her frustrated, angry, and alone.

Shaker community organization was also problematic. Mary had been raised on the New Hampshire frontier that promoted independence and self-sufficiency in order to survive. Relationships were built on a network of kin to whom one would turn for support and aid. Men provided for women: a husband provided his wife with a house, food, and material goods. As a married woman, in the eyes of the world, Mary's security was Joseph, but at the Shaker village marital ties were negated, and she was directed to others for her needs. While Mary did not regret the absence of a romantic relationship with Joseph, she grew concerned that her economic and legal relationship was threatened. Although Mary was quite independent of spirit, she realized full well that without a husband, a wife had no legal power and, moreover, was a nonexistent entity in society.

But of primary concern to Mary was her children. Her children defined her, and her children were her future. When Mary described her children's future she emphasized not their individual potential but rather that in her old age they would surround her and care for her.[56] Dyer's portrait combined an emotional image of a mother's undying love with a well-understood economic reality. A mother raised her children and profited from her sons' labor later in life. As her 1852 will indicated, her economic survival and emotional support would be based on her children. But at the Shaker village, her children were scattered about the community and, once indentured, were legally no longer hers. Like a wife without her husband, a mother without her children was unthinkable, and Dyer could not imagine her future without them. As doubt and frustration grew, so did Mary's antipathy towards the

Shakers. She faced an unresolvable dilemma. She longed for self-autonomy and a religious life, yet she needed support and protection to survive. Despite her residence in a communal group, Mary was very much alone.

Deconversion

By the beginning of 1815, Mary Dyer had deconverted from Shaker belief. In her mind and heart she was no longer a Shaker, yet she felt compelled to remain physically in the Enfield community to be near her children. As many sociologists of religions have described, leaving a religious group is a multistep process where one disengages from both belief and from the community of believers.[57] Mary had left behind belief; now she struggled to leave behind the Shakers. In print, Mary described her travel from deconversion to departure from the Shakers as a series of chance events ultimately orchestrated by God. As Mary tells the story in her later publications, one early January day a "near relation" of Joseph's passed by the North Family dwelling that faced the public road running through the Shaker village. Seeing Mary at the door, he stepped up and asked about her health and well-being. Mary admitted her unhappiness. John Williams looked at her "with intention, and then said, 'Don't thee stay here because thou thinkest thee has no friends to go to.'"[58] The knowledge that she had a destination, gained only through Williams's serendipitous visit, prompted Mary to leave the Shakers.

The trope of chance occurrence leading to her rescue worked well in print to portray Mary as open to the will of God. In reality, the self-directed Mary had sent a letter, undetected, to Willliams asking him to visit.[59] Coincidence or not, the knowledge that she had a destination gave Mary confidence in her soon realized apostasy. As she told her tale, God provided the means of her rescue from near death at the Shakers and gave her the task to "bear testimony to [the Shakers'] iniquities."[60] Mary continued with the Shakers for two weeks following Williams's visit and waited for an opportune moment, in the meantime imagining her post-Shaker life. Williams's visit and her impending separation pushed her ever closer to public acts of apostasy as she reimagined herself not as a Shaker, but as separated from the Shakers.

In a Sabbath meeting shortly before her departure, Mary indicated that she had already been thinking through the consequences of her upcoming apostasy. During the meeting, Mary felt "strongly inclined" to speak out before the assembly of Shakers and many observers from the world.[61] She wanted to "declare how [she] had been deceived; also what falsehood and intrigue the Shakers used to gain proselytes."[62] Despite the intensity of her feelings, Mary resisted the urge to speak out, fearing the Shakers would keep her children. In silent protest, she did make her stance clear, refusing to kneel in prayer with the Shakers. Mary displayed her first public act of apostasy through body language. When she refused to kneel she marked herself, boldly and quite literally, as standing apart from the Shakers.

Although Mary could make her silent protest, Shaker power had prevented Mary from speaking during meeting. Mary wrote of Shaker power as a mind-controlling force not unlike hypnotism. The elders used this power to control the community, and it was this power that Mary strove to resist through private prayer and scripture reading. By the following Sabbath, Mary felt the bands of Shaker power loosening. During the previous week's meeting, Mary had stood alone among the Shakers. On this late January Sabbath she worshiped entirely alone in the empty spinshop, praying for release from the Shakers. Similar to her experience in the pesthouse years earlier, God answered her prayers and filled Mary with a "calm peace."[63] While the Shakers gathered at meeting, Mary paid a visit to her son, six-year-old Joseph, too young to attend Sunday service. Shaker James Jewett, assigned to watch the youngest children, scolded Mary for not attending the service and therefore "breaking the body of Shakers." This admonition secretly pleased Mary and gave her proof that her faith in the Almighty gave her power over the Shakers.[64] Mary later wrote that she subsequently learned "by the conversation of others" that when she prayed alone she damaged the Shaker spiritual union, "all the leading ones of the family felt the shock, and were uncomfortably affected."[65] Once again, Mary's aggressive action, this time in prayer, moved Mary closer to her goal.

Mary's deconversion came slowly and was marked by a shift in power relations. The further she traveled away from Shakerism, the less power she ascribed to the Shakers (and to the elders in particular) and the more she claimed for herself through God. During her final days as a Shaker, Mary placed herself as equal to the Shaker leaders. Her power had become strong enough to disrupt the combined power of communitywide worship. Knowledge and faith gave her confidence to leave, although she had no specific plan to put into motion that decision. In this way Dyer was very much like apostates from a wide variety of sectarian or alternative religious groups from the nineteenth century to present day. The soon-to-be apostate has decided to leave, but the actual departure is typically quite ad hoc.[66] The first step towards departure, though, was the realization that one could leave and by late January 1815 Mary Dyer had reached the point where she believed she had the power to do so.

Power, though, meant more than a force that spiritually affected Shaker leaders and followers. What prohibited Mary from speaking out against the Shakers was the reality that the Shakers had custody of her children. Mary feared the elders would relocate her children to another Shaker community, a scenario not unknown among the Shakers to help along the loosening of biological bonds. In this sense, the Shakers held power in that they controlled a mutually valuable resource, the five Dyer children. To the Shakers, the children were potential future members; to Mary, they were her reason for life and her future economic security. Using power in this sense, the Shakers were able to control members and enforce rules.

The fear that she would lose her children forever kept Mary at the Shakers. She sacrificed her health and potentially her life for what mattered most to her. But as much as the welfare of her children kept Mary with the Shakers, it was the children's welfare that in the end led her to leave. The final motivation came on the following Friday. As Mary mended mittens with young Joseph at her side, North Family Eldress Lucy Lyon burst into the room and yelled at young Joseph for some alleged misdemeanor. Mary objected to the harsh verbal discipline, but Lyon informed Mary that the young boy belonged to her and she would do as she pleased. This was the last straw. Mary now realized that in the Shaker community she would never have control over her own children. She had lost the power society routinely accorded mothers. Sensing her own spiritual morass and declining health, Mary resolved to leave immediately with her children. But how to do so?

Mary needed an audience with the elders. The next morning, Saturday, Mary refused to work, knowing the Shaker leaders would admonish her for this unShaker-like behavior. When the expected summons came, Mary took immediate control by keeping the elders waiting. When she felt herself "sufficiently composed," she approached the elders, who were waiting none too patiently for this most troublesome novitiate. Mary announced her decision and resolutely adhered to it, despite the leaders' alternating threats of eternal damnation and expressions of her potential as a future leader.[67] The Shakers wanted to retain as many members as possible. Yet despite Mary's strengths—intelligence, public presentation skills, and motivation for a religious life—Mary's obstinacy and lack of full acquiescence to Shaker life made her a "bad fish caught in the Gospel net."[68] Ultimately, the four elders consented to Mary's secession and instructed her to write a letter for some-one to come and get her.[69]

Having successfully negotiated a release from the elders, Mary then asked to speak to her husband. When Joseph arrived, Mary explained that she was ill and felt that she had to leave the Shakers. Joseph, hav-ing had little to no emotional attachment to Mary from when she had made their marriage celibate years before, also consented to her depar-ture. Up to this point the meeting had been fairly civil. The Shakers were unhappy with Mary, and she was unhappy with them; her depar-ture was best for all involved. Joseph offered to come to an "honor-able settlement" and give Mary "her full and just portion of property," effectively ending the Dyer marriage with a permanent, legal separa-tion.[70] Mary declined the offer, stating she could care for herself, but asked Joseph to honor the agreement they had made three years before. To her horror, Joseph recanted his promise to give her some of the chil-dren. He declared she was no longer his wife, and the children were no longer under his care. He went further, telling Mary that he had no obligation to provide for her, and because of the indenture they both had signed, he had no power to divide up or release any of the chil-dren. Mary was horrified: Joseph had single-handedly erased the Dyer family as a legal and social entity.

In her thoughts of a post-Shaker life, Mary's children had always been a part of that picture. Mary offered to compromise and take just the youngest, six-year-old Joseph. Again the Shakers refused. She was desperate: "to go any further from my children was dreadful; to stay was death."[71] Distress turned to anger. The civil meeting escalated into a verbal battle. Elder Lougee threatened Mary and told her if she stayed among the Shakers, she would not live long enough to ever leave again. Mary's response revealed her public plans: "All I asked of the Lord was to let me live until I could let people know what people the Shakers were."[72] Mary accused the elders of wickedness and threatened to expose them. The Shakers warned her against spreading false stories or she would suffer. When the Shakers pleaded with her to leave quietly, she refused, reaffirming her promise to God. Shocked by the unexpected turn of events, Mary returned to the North Family dwelling house uncer-tain of how to free herself from this nightmarish situation.

The following day, during Sunday meeting, Mary lingered in the dwelling house. She knew young Joseph was there, but a Shaker girl followed Mary from room to room, preventing her from seeing her son. Looking for a chance to be with Joseph, Mary chided the girl for neglecting to set out the daily meal and the girl went off with a start, leaving Mary alone. As luck would have it, a sleigh with a man and two women approached the Shaker village.[73] Mary ran out through the snowy yard and asked the driver to carry her letter. He agreed. Seizing the opportunity, Mary then announced she wished to leave the Shakers and asked him to carry her off. He consented, and Mary ran back to the house.

Mary went to young Joseph's guardian, an aged man, and told him the sleigh driver had agreed to carry her letter. To create a needed distraction, Mary requested some cider for the driver and when the Shaker brother left the room, Mary grabbed her son and fled. "This," Mary wrote, "was the only deceitful thing I done while with the Shakers."[74]

The sleigh driver in "great haste" carried Mary and young Joseph to nearby Hanover. Mary needed to find sympathetic friends, someone who could support her in her quest to leave the Shakers with her children. She urged the sleigh driver to take her to the home of John Williams, the "near relation" who had appeared on Mary's doorstep two weeks earlier. Meanwhile, the Shaker meeting was thrown into turmoil. Joseph, Sr., alerted to Mary's departure by the deceived Shaker man, rushed out of the meeting and followed Mary on horseback. A double sleigh with four Shakers followed Joseph. The driver had taken Mary to the Hanover home of Jeremiah and Deborah Towles, whom she did not know and whose home Mary had mistaken for the home of the Williamses. Mary had only begun to tell her tale of woe when Joseph arrived and snatched his son from Mary's arms. Mary cried and begged, the child screamed, and Joseph, said Mary, "was raving." The Towles, who witnessed the frightful scene on this frigid January day, concluded that Mary's "trouble appeared great."[75] Astounded at Mary's audacity, Joseph took his young son and stormed back to the Shaker village. Mary made her way to the Williamses' home; she had left the Shakers, but she had left alone.

Apostasy

By mid-January 1815, Mary Dyer had seceded spiritually and physically from the Shakers. Although her son was forcibly reclaimed, she chose not to follow. Dyer had gone to the Shakers in hopes of finding the religious excitement she had found in the Methodist meetings and Freewill Baptist revivals and the theological stimulation she enjoyed in her intense conversations with Putnam and Crooker. But as in the world's mainstream Protestantism, Dyer found there was little room for a woman's interpretation of doctrine. Although she might eventually gain a leadership position, Dyer realized she would spout traditional Shaker doctrine, not her own ideas for the faith. Classed among the lower orders of the hierarchical community, Dyer had less autonomy among the Shakers than she had enjoyed in her Stewartstown life. She could not even fall back on her role as mother to her five children. When Eldress Lucy Lyon disciplined young Joseph and berated Mary for her maternal protest, Mary realized she had no future as a Shaker. As for a future outside of the Shakers, Dyer knew she needed, and indeed wanted, her children. Forbidden to care for her children at the Shakers, Mary hoped she could help them from the outside world.

Here Mary crossed the line between Shaker seceder and Shaker apostate. Many had left the Shakers before Mary Dyer, but most put their Shaker experiences more or less behind them and reestablished their lives in the mainstream world. The apostates, however, would not or could not put Shakerism behind them and as part of their return to the world, turned around to fight the faith they once embraced. Mary needed her children, and she needed her husband's legal and financial support. In the meeting with the elders, she had asked for, and was refused, both requests. Dyer moved from a seceder to an apostate when she vowed to fight the faith that had caused her to be in such a socially untenable position. During the winter of 1815 in Hanover, Mary met local people through the Williamses and in attending local churches. Mary told them of her trials and started to work out the structure and content of her apostate tale in an oral format. She also began to create a network of support that in the winter of 1815 provided shelter and food. In the coming months (and years) this network would provide legal assistance and testimonies regarding her experiences and character. In the winter of 1815, Mary busily worked to meet her various, and at this point somewhat undeveloped, goals: retrieving her children, gaining Joseph's economic support, and exposing the Shakers.

Mary remained at the Williamses for eight weeks.[76] Joseph suspected that Mary had gained some allies and "finding that she was determined to trouble [him] as much as lay in her power," he advertised her in the *Dartmouth Gazette and Grafton and Coös Advertiser* on February 18, 1815.[77] The advertisement, a common method of publicizing marital discord, stated that Mary was Joseph's lawful wife, and since she had left his bed and board, he refused to pay any claims Mary made on his account. The advertisement acknowledged that marriage entailed certain rights and obligations, including that the wife would remain in the husband's household under his care and watchful eye. With Mary's departure from the Shakers, Joseph accused Mary of breaking the marriage contract. The advertisement publicly signaled that Mary had broken the contract, and thus Joseph was no longer accountable for his usual husbandly responsibilities that included paying for any debts she contracted in the purchase of goods necessary for survival. His statement also acknowledged that Mary had some power, specifically to attract attention to her situation and to place the Shakers under scrutiny. Joseph hoped the advertisement would restrict Mary's ability to "trouble" him further by preventing her from buying any goods on his account, thus causing her to be an economic burden to anyone who offered to help her.[78]

Mary interpreted the public notice as Joseph's signal that he would provide for her. She expected shelter, food, and clothing, and access to supplies (such as cloth or cooking materials). Protection meant she would have a role in society (wife) and that Joseph would take care to see that the role was honored and respected by others in the community. In other words, she would have a legal and social identity. According to the law, a wife's residence was determined by where her husband lived. In order to gain the benefits of the role of wife, Mary's residence would have to be with Joseph at the Shakers. With the Towles as witnesses, Mary returned to the Enfield Shaker community on March 6 and requested Joseph's support, as advertised, for a place of residence, for his care, and his protection, with the condition that she enjoy "liberty of conscience" and would not be forced to espouse the Shaker faith. After several objections, Joseph consented to provide "what the law enjoined . . . in the marriage contract, provided she would yield obedience."[79] Mary returned to the Shaker village, glad to be back near her children and feeling that she had won the latest battle. She would live with her husband at his residence, yet not be constrained by his faith. Joseph was relieved to have Mary under his watchful eye, thinking that he, too, had won the latest round. With Mary nearby he could prevent her from speaking against the Shakers. Yet the seeds of further conflict were embedded in the clashing conditions each Dyer set: Mary demanded independence, and Joseph demanded obedience. Despite Mary's return to the Shaker village, a second advertisement, published on March 21, 1815, revealed Joseph's continued difficulties with Mary. "[F]inding her mind unfriendly," Joseph warned readers not to trust her on his account and noted that this advertisement should be considered a "permanent warning."[80] The Dyer dispute was far from over.

Mary's life at the village became a contest of wills. It was highly unusual for a nonbelieving spouse to live within the Shaker community. Mary lived in a room, alone, that Joseph described as comfortable, convenient, and with free access to the highway, dooryard, and kitchen.[81] Joseph expected Mary to wash her own clothes and do work he provided, that in ten weeks' time amounted to spinning "twenty run."[82] The Shakers restricted her movements around the community. She was kept away from her children and "forbidden . . . writing or speaking to anyone who had separated from the Shakers," an attempt to prevent Mary from establishing bonds with other apostates.[83] In another recounting of this incident, Mary framed the condition as forbidden to write to anyone *but* Shakers emphasizing her allegedly forced enclosure within the community of Shakers. Both versions indicated that boundaries were drawn between Shakers and apostates, and great care was taken to make sure Mary did not cross the borders between. It seemed to Mary that the Shakers were attempting to make life so miserable she would willingly leave. In fact the Shakers repeatedly told her she could leave, but Mary stubbornly replied she would rather stay miserable but near her children, than out in the world in better circumstances. She "was willing to suffer until people were willing to have a better law" in regards to the way a husband could treat a wife.[84] Forced to stay in the Shaker community in order to survive and motivated to stay in the Enfield community to protect her children, Mary would prove Joseph's religious ideas false through the example of her own death. If she died, she reasoned, Joseph would see the Shakers as cruel and would finally "liberate the children."[85] If Mary's apostasy culminated in her death, Mary imagined she would be a martyr for the cause of Shaker-held children and mistreated wives. Her willingness to die for the sake of her children, at least as she expressed her imagined martyrdom in her books, reinforced the sincerity of her desire for her children and the ultimate sacrifice she was willing to make.

Once she returned to the Shaker village, back at the site and source of her mental anguish, Mary's health declined. Despite her continual illness, Mary carefully considered her options. When Asa Tenney, a Quaker "debilitated with consumptive habits" and one of her newly-found Hanover friends, visited on a Monday Mary made two requests: to send her some paper and information on "what liberty the law allowed me as a wife."[86] Two days later, a Wednesday, two of her new Hanover friends, likely John Williams and Calvin Eaton, fulfilled her requests.[87] These visitors and the powerful tools they brought changed Dyer's outlook and the future enactment of her apostasy.

With the paper Mary began a journal describing Shaker history and present practice. The journal provided the basis for her later published accounts. It also provided a means to authenticate her story. Dyer dismissed her critics's charges of Mary's poor or faulty memory, claiming her journal records as her source of information. Clearly, having departed from Shakerism (though still living with the Shakers), Mary had every intention of making good on her threat to let the world know what sort of people the Shakers were. In addition to the gift of paper, Mary's visitors provided her with knowledge of her rights, and with that information, she drafted a petition to the New Hampshire legislature. She understood that marriage was a contract of mutual rights and obligations. She understood that in her present position she was in a social limbo, betwixt and between the roles of wife, mother, and autonomous woman. And finally, she understood that she did have some legal rights, including the right to petition the legislature for help.

Her visitors had affected a remarkable transformation. Instead of seeing herself as captive under the Shakers' direction, Mary now understood herself to be independent of their government. Mary "took more liberty." She left her room, looked for her children, and twice took the stagecoach to Hanover. She also made trips to "different parts of the town of Enfield and other places just when she pleased."[88] At Hanover, Mary spoke to the members of the Congregational church and "let the people know of the Shakers' conduct."[89] As her story spread, outsiders began to interfere in the private family dispute, the Dyers' "domestic broils" as the Shakers termed it. Mary's story inspired a local lawyer named Gilbert to write to the Shakers and warn them to treat Mary better. A short time later, two local men went to the village and also told the Shaker leaders that Mary should be allowed to see her friends, attend meeting of her choice, do her own work, and care for her own children. These specific demands reinforced Mary's understanding of her rights. Mary's increasing independence, along with the public revelations, the visitors, and her new connections, enraged Joseph whose authority over his wife was being undercut.

Mary's new understanding of self led her to increase the public nature of her apostasy. As she gained local support, and self-confidence, Mary's interaction with the Shakers changed. Instead of the Shakers preaching to Mary, Dyer turned the table and preached to the Shakers, pointing out their religious errors. No longer a Shaker, she no longer feared the elders' repercussions. She spent time writing, putting her experiences and ideas down on paper, and honing her tale. Mary took on the preaching role she had long desired and warned the Shakers of divine retribution and "of judgements and calamities from God if they did not cease in their practices."[90] Here Mary had reversed the practice of the Shakers, who frequently wrote in correspondence between communities and told to assembled groups of Shakers these "tales of woe." In these dismal tales of death and destruction, persecutors and apostates paid for the sin of denouncing Shakerism.[91] But here, Mary warns that the Shakers will pay for espousing Shakerism. Mary claimed that after her warning, many Shakers died suddenly and strangely and that fevers ran rampant unlike the Shakers had seen in fourteen years. When the Shakers spoke of the wave of illness, Mary claimed omnisciently that "it was not unexpected to me: God would remember them."[92] Her illness apparently dissipated, and her bold behavior growing, Mary went so far as to mock Shaker beliefs with "certain expressions" she would flash to the sisters seated at the dining table. At those meals, by custom eaten in silence, Mary loudly proclaimed her thanks to God for making the grass grow and for providing food, even if it was conveyed by the Shakers.[93]

Mary's growing public support, her willful disobedience, and community disruption angered the Shakers to no end. Her apostate predecessors had had the good grace to leave the Shakers before attacking but Dyer, in fact, conducted her anti-Shaker campaign from within the Shaker village. As Joseph described the situation in the spring of 1815, Mary was "gadding from place to place" defaming the Shakers "and thus she continued in her malicious proceedings, propagating falsehoods and exciting disturbance and tumults both in the [Shaker] family and vicinity until her conduct became intolerable."[94] By late spring, the Shakers had reached the limits of their charity, and the North Family elder told Joseph to make other arrangements for Mary. Mary reported this decision as a Shaker ultimatum in which the elders demanded that Mary herself find her own living arrangements outside of the community or they would remove her children to a distant village. Her recollection of the event stressed her direct contact and interaction with religious leadership, Mary already acting independently of her husband. Another way to view this moment is as further evidence of Shaker cruelty heaped upon Mary, who, in this telling, suffered greatly in the absence of a protecting husband. Regardless who provided the order, the Shakers were expelling Mary and they wanted her gone in two weeks. But Mary had regained proximity to her children and a limited independence. She was also, after all, reaping some of the benefits of communal living without having to pay all of its challenging price. This time, Mary wrote, "I should not go out willingly."[95]

In previous altercations, Shaker threats so reduced Mary to tears that she described herself as inconsolable. In this incident, she turned her shock into action "and let [the situation] be known," contacting John Williams and Enfield judge Edward Evans. Both came to the Shakers and told the elders that they must treat her better, allow her to see her children, and made vague legal threats.[96] The Shakers and Joseph promised Mary greater freedom, but the next day, unbeknownst to Mary, Joseph went to hire Mary's board at the home of her sister and brother-in-law, Obadiah and Betsey Tillotson, in Orford, New Hampshire, twenty-six miles north of Enfield.[97] Mary learned of this new arrangement only shortly before her forced departure. Without even giving Mary an opportunity to say good-bye to her children, Joseph and Shaker James Chapman took Mary and her furniture away.[98]

Joseph tried a new tactic in dealing with his wife: distance. Living up to his end of the marriage contract, Joseph provided for Mary's board, paying the Tillotsons $1 per week. Seeking a settlement and an end to her disruptive presence, Joseph offered his wife the bed and bedding, their best furniture (valued at $50), and $5 in cash. He told Mary that contrary to the expected marital arrangement where a husband garnered his wife's wages, she could keep for herself any monies earned from her own labor. But Mary could not be so easily satisfied. She refused Joseph's arrangements, the goods, and even refused to get out of the wagon when arriving in Orford, even though Mary would be boarding with relatives. Mary arrived weeping in an open lumber wagon with only Shaker dress to clothe her. The Tillotsons pleaded with her to enter the house. Obadiah offered Joseph a room for the night, tactfully arranging "a separate bed." Joseph refused his brother-in-law's hospitality, although on previous trips he had spent pleasant evenings with the Tillotsons. Joseph and James Chapman spent the evening in a nearby inn before heading back to Enfield. Mary now resided with family, but she was far from her children. She was also far from her new, powerful, and, to the Shakers, troublesome Hanover friends.

Relocation to Orford did not silence Mary. She took the stagecoach back to Enfield intent upon convincing Joseph to let her board nearer her children. But Joseph was away from the Shaker village, and Mary returned to Orford disappointed. Mary's unexpected visit prompted Joseph and James Chapman to travel to Orford shortly thereafter. Once again the Dyers argued about their marriage and the obligations that relationship entailed. Joseph declared he was now a Shaker and no longer Mary's husband. If she wanted the protection and care of one, Joseph taunted, Mary would have to find another. Mary retorted with her quick wit, "give me one of my children, and I will dismiss all husbands."[99] Joseph made her an "immodest answer" and Chapman spoke "with vulgar talk."[100] Obadiah Tillotson, witness to this bitter argument, opened the door and told the visitors to leave.[101]

Having no success in her meeting with Joseph, Mary attempted to argue her view in a letter, a portion of which she reprinted in her 1822 work *A Portraiture of Shakerism*. This letter revealed Mary's growing understanding of her dilemma and her realization that she lacked real power. She may have found success as a thorn within the Shaker community, but outside of it, Mary knew she was very much in social limbo. She complained to Joseph that she had no money and could only obtain necessities by charging on Joseph's account, which kept her dependent on him. She had no home other than that offered by her relations out of pity or that which Joseph arranged. Mary recalled how she had always been under the care of a male and sacrificed her father's kind care for marriage and Joseph's protection. She acknowledged that Joseph held the power over her children but despite his claims that the Shaker gospel had separated them, Mary argued that their current dilemma was his doing and it was within his power to rectify the situation. Joseph, she accused, attempted to have the best of two worlds. He claimed he was no longer a husband and denied his obligation to support Mary, but at the same time claimed the authority of the husband in holding property and children.

Mary saw herself in a marital limbo. She argued that marriage was "more than a few words, or ceremonies from a man that bind us." Mary explained to Joseph that the ties between them were "sealed with the days of my youth" and also of "five children now bound to my heart, which I have bourn to you and nursed from my bosom."[102] While on the one hand she alluded to the solemnity of marriage bonds as joined by God, on the other she knew that to survive, those bonds must be broken. Mary wrote: "Give me my children, or cause me to be as before I was married; and I will say those bands will feel to me broken."[103] Both options provided Mary with an identity: the first, as a mother, the second as a single woman not subsumed by marital unity. Her letter had little effect, but she wasted no time in enlarging her web of allies. On May 22, 1815 a group of judges, lawyers, and court officials from Guildhall, Vermont, signed a group affidavit that attested to Mary's honest and virtuous character. These affidavits helped establish her credibility, particularly in her role as a wife and mother. Two of the testators bore close personal connections. Christopher Bailey was Mary's brother-in-law, husband to her sister Abigail. Moses Morrill was an old Baptist friend, a member of the group Elder Putnam converted in 1806. Although the Shakers had put distance between the children and Mary, as Joseph relocated Mary and as she traveled, her story reached further and further north, following the Connecticut River from Enfield and Hanover, to Orford and Guildhall. Word of mouth carried her tale as she told family, friends, and strangers about her life at the Shakers. Relying on a network of kin and community alliances, Dyer rallied support.

When her board in Orford expired, Dyer once again traveled to Enfield, arriving around October first. On this trip to the Enfield Shakers

Mary had the assistance of Judge Evans. They repeated a familiar scene. Evans warned the Shakers to treat Mary better and let her see her children. The Shakers refused to grant the unannounced visit. Evans urged Mary to speak her business in front of the Shakers, but Mary refused the public forum. Having realized he was in the middle of a contest of wills and there was little he could do, Evans left. It had been more than five months since Mary had seen her children, and Mary, stubbornly, sat down in the meeting room and began sewing "a nice cap." She refused to discuss her business with anyone but Joseph and refused to leave unless able to see her children. As Mary obstinately sewed and the day progressed, the Shakers' patience wore thin. Joseph steadfastly refused to meet with Mary alone afraid of what Mary might later claim he had promised; Mary refused to discuss family business in the presence of Shakers afraid that Joseph would be pressured by Shakers to turn even more against her. By 3:00 PM, Elder Lougee told Joseph to get Mary out of the house, peaceably if possible. Reflecting the commonly understood doctrine of coverture and marital unity, Lougee reminded Joseph that Mary's transgressions were his transgressions. Since she was no longer a Shaker, the elders had no authority over her. It was up to Joseph, her husband, to rectify this profane intrusion of apostate Mary into the sacred space of the meeting room. Joseph, taking a page from Mary's book of aggressive responses, and with the assistance of James Chapman, grabbed Mary around the waist and hauled her out of the house. Mary fought her rude dislodging; as they passed through a doorway, Mary clung to the casing until Eldress Lydia Merrill forcibly unclenched Mary's hands. Mary was unceremoniously dropped in the public street running through (but not part of) the Shaker village. The ensuing struggle from the house, to the dooryard, to the street, tore Mary's dress and dislodged her cap and handkerchief. The Shakers had removed Mary from the house but not from the vicinity, and her very presence still grated.

Mary, disheveled and seated in the road, "was past the power of anger or grief."[104] She taunted the Shakers asking if in this action they served Christ. After half an hour, Joseph came outside and suggested she find some place to stay. Resuming a contest of wills, Mary informed Joseph she would rather die right there in the road so he would know her end. More time passed. Now evening, one of the deacons came out and offered Mary a room in the storehouse. She again refused, stating she would stay in her husband's home, the North Family dwelling house from which she had been forcibly ejected. Once again the Shaker leaders called upon Joseph and James Chapman to rectify the standoff. They picked up Mary, placed her in a wagon and drove her across the

Shaker settlement to the Trustee's Office, the appropriate place for non-Shaker visitors. Upon arrival at the office, yet another tumultuous scene ensued: Mary accused Joseph of treating her as if she were "deranged," holding her so her arms were pinned tightly against her. Mary insisted she could get out the wagon herself. Joseph ignored her and dragged her over the wagon wheel as Mary's former Shaker brothers and sisters watched.[105]

This incident provided more grist for her anti-Shaker campaign. Mary spent the evening repairing her torn gown and writing down her latest humiliations with tools she had hidden in her clothing. Had she expected, or forced, another fight? Perhaps she feared that the Shakers, because of their previous attempts to prevent Mary from keeping records, would take away her journal unless she had kept it hidden. Perhaps, with her previous experiences as her teacher, she knew this meeting would be unsuccessful yet provide further evidence of Shaker cruelty. As she sat alone in the house, Mary recorded her thoughts and after midnight retired to bed.

The following day, the Shakers permitted a brief visit with the five Dyer children. The Shakers, in fact, did not forbid visits with biological relatives, but to maintain separateness from the carnal world and to maintain their spiritual community, they insisted that those visits be regulated in time and space. From the Shaker perspective, Mary could not simply appear and demand her children. Yet Mary (and others from the world) failed to see why that should be so. Satisfied for the moment with the brief visit, Mary returned to Orford where Joseph had paid for six more weeks of board with the Tillotsons. He advanced Mary an additional six weeks worth of board ($6.00 cash) to enable her to travel north to the Coös to visit family, but only on the condition that she not travel south to Enfield.[106] As agreed, Mary remained in Orford for six weeks and then journeyed to her mother's home in Northumberland.

After six weeks with her mother, Mary intended to return to Orford for another six weeks board. But Joseph had another idea. Instead of paying for the next six weeks board in Orford, twenty-six miles from Enfield, Joseph liked better the idea of Mary being in far northern New Hampshire, even further away from Enfield. Unbeknownst to Mary, Joseph hired her board with the Page family in Lancaster (a connection from his previous Masonic activities and relatives of one of the Dyers' former household girls), just six miles south of Mary's mother's home in Northumberland and nearly one hundred miles from the Shakers.[107] Mary learned of this new arrangement only when the Northumberland constable left notification on her mother's door. Mary was furious. Joseph determined where she would live, moving her at his whim increasingly further north and away from her children, and in this case, hiring her board among perfect strangers. Livid at this latest move, Mary canceled her board with the Pages, moved in with her mother, and resolved to claim the "just rights" that belonged to her sex.[108]

During the winter of 1816, Mary returned to Enfield to demand Joseph's support. This time she traveled with Judge Moody Rich, the husband of Mary's sister, Sally. Rich demanded Joseph provide support for Mary, and Joseph obliged, paying Rich $52.00 for one year's board. During the visit, the Shakers cautiously watched Mary. When Rich asked the elders why they permitted him to question the children, but not Mary, North Family elder John Lyon replied that "one question from Mary would be attended with more injurious consequences, than twenty from you."[109] This admission acknowledged Mary's power to produce "injurious consequences" in the form of public scrutiny of the Shakers. While Rich questioned his nephews on their education, health, and happiness, Mary spoke to her fourteen-year-old daughter, informing her that she could have a home with any of several uncles or with her grandmother. Betsey, to Mary's great sadness, stated she was well satisfied with the Shakers and declined her mother's offer.

Mary lived with the Riches in Maidstone, Vermont, for the next year. Her brother-in-law judge counseled her to place a petition before the state legislature. Along with some of his friends, he provided funds to enable Mary to do so, the $52.00 Joseph had paid Rich for Mary's board. Mary had gained another powerful ally. A year later, in February 1817, her board with Rich had expired but Joseph refused to provide anymore for her as she was "among those whom [he] considered to be [his] enemies."[110] Rich and his colleagues had boasted of their power, money, and desire to injure Joseph, and Joseph was none too pleased that his financial support funded his wife's petition against him. In yet another attempt to get Mary out of his life, Joseph met with Rich and Mary at Mary's mother's house. Joseph offered a settlement. Mary could have a parcel of land in Stewartstown if she agreed to give Joseph an acquittance for life. She refused, telling him "land would do me little good without my children." Mary made a counteroffer: Give her just one of the children and he could keep his land. Joseph refused. Mary pressed on and stated her dilemma quite plainly, that without children "a lot of wild land is of no use to me, I must hire my board or lean upon my relations. . . ." Joseph was still her husband, and Mary pointed out in conclusion that he "ought to provide for [her] a home."[111]

A home equaled mother and child(ren). Indeed, wild land was of little use to Mary. Without the help of at least one of her sons, she had little chance of clearing the land and settling. Her youngest son Joseph, for whom she continually pleaded, was now eight years old, her best bet for help. But even with the assistance of a young son, Mary's opportunities for success were slim. Rich had seen the land and judged it be worth not more than $50—a poor deal. In addition, with the informal separation Joseph had offered, Mary would have no right to sell the land. In other words, although land had monetary value, it had no worth to Mary. Further still, the War of 1812 had ruined the northern New Hampshire economy, and the region had just suffered the infamous "year without a summer," unseasonably cold weather that killed off major crops and brought snow as late as June and as early as October 1. Wild land was no bargain. As Mary pointed out, she and Joseph were still legally married yet he continued to ignore his part of the marital contract to provide a home. Without his support, Mary was forced to live with family or worse, with strangers. Without at least one child, Mary could not establish a home. Mary sought to create a family of single parent and child, an uncommon arrangement by choice, but she expressed that idea with an older, familiar language that emphasized the obligations of a husband. Mary stonewalled, Joseph stood resolute. Yet another meeting failed to resolve their dispute.

This private family dispute had reached an impasse. No doubt with the counsel of her brother-in-law attorneys, Mary turned to the New Hampshire legislature for help. With the support of her new friends, Mary began to prepare for the June session of the legislature in earnest.[112] Not without skills, Dyer sewed and by February 1817 she had saved nearly $100.[113] She wrote her petition in Northumberland and completed it on June 5, 1817, the inauguration day of Governor William Plumer, who many years before had described with curiosity the Shakers in a letter to a friend.[114] Mary collected an affidavit from her brother-in-law Moody Rich and then traveled south. She arrived in Hanover by June 11 and gathered affidavits from Calvin Eaton and Jeremiah and Deborah Towle. Wearing a borrowed dress and accompanied by her younger brother Silas Marshall, Mary headed east to the state capital, Concord, hoping the state legislature would resolve her dispute.

For all her boldness and quick retorts, Mary faced a real dilemma— she had, in fact, been a Shaker for two years and made public testimony in support of the faith. Because of that, "people will come upon me to know why I have left it . . . but I do not know how to turn it."[115] Why then should Mary expect people to support her, especially after having been warned of the Shaker threat from her former

Stewartstown neighbors? At this point, then, Mary faced multiple challenges. She sought to retrieve her children, gain a permanent residence, to provide financially for herself, to find religious satisfaction, and to reestablish her credibility among the mainstream community in which she had not lived for nearly three years. One method of achieving those goals was in the production of the anti-Shaker tale, first worked out and practiced orally, and soon to be encapsulated in a written format. By emphasizing the pain of an aggrieved mother and casting the Shakers as evil seducers, Mary Dyer began publicly to reassume her role as a mother while she also simultaneously assumed a new role as a Shaker apostate.

2

The Sympathy and Malice of Mankind

Mary Dyer sought redress when she submitted her petition to the New Hampshire legislature in June of 1817. The legislature could restore her children, sanction the Shakers, and force Joseph to support his wife. Mary and Joseph had been raised in the first decades of a new American nation and absorbed rapidly changing ideas about family roles and organization. Yet these ideas were neither uniform in their presentation nor in their acceptance, and Mary and Joseph's dispute revealed different interpretations and understandings of these roles of husband and wife. Mary's position reflected a newer, more flexible definition of marriage as a partnership of differing but equally important roles. Joseph, however, revealed a more rigid, hierarchical view of marriage. Although Joseph and Mary were locked in a bitter public dispute, they agreed on one point—both wished to alter the structure of their family.

A marital separation was one option. A variety of separations were possible in the early nineteenth century. The judicially ordered "divorce à mensa a thoro" (divorce from bed and board) would provide a legal separation and end the Dyer marriage for most intents and purposes. In this type of formal separation, neither party could legally remarry (as they were not fully divorced) but they would no longer be beholden to each other. Alternatively, the Dyers could separate and come to some equitable agreement as to support or division of the property. In this situation, the Dyers would basically have separate maintenance agreements or some other sort of legally enforceable contract between husband and wife. The separation contract, in effect, would replace the marriage contract. On the other end of the separation spectrum was an informal separation such as those caused by desertion or abandonment or from unenforceable contracts. This situation put the wife at greatest risk because she had no legal recourse if her husband vanished or made a vague, unenforceable arrangement.[1]

Joseph was intent on some form of separation. His marriage undoubtedly over, Joseph had tried to reach a settlement agreement with Mary. He had offered her land in Stewartstown, some of the household goods, and the opportunity to keep any money earned from her own labors in exchange for an acquittance for life. It was in Joseph's best interest to offer some sort of contract to bring their marriage to an effective end and to release himself from his duties and obligations.[2] But Mary could not accept a settlement. Separation would give her only a "partially new identity."[3] She would still be a wife, though one without a husband. She wanted more than a separation could give; she wanted the return of her single, unmarried status.

A divorce was an option. Since 1791 when New Hampshire established its divorce laws, both husbands and wives had the right to petition to end their marriages given certain conditions. States varied in their requirements for divorce. In New Hampshire divorce was permitted for impotence, incestuous marriage, adultery, abandonment for at least three years, and extreme cruelty. Divorce was an adversarial proceeding requiring grounds. There would be a guilty party who had transgressed the expected role of husband or wife, and an innocent party who suffered as a victim of their spouse's evil or immoral acts.[4] Although Dyer initially denied she sought a divorce, she nonetheless based her public explanation for why she sought legislative redress in the latter two criteria. Mary used these arguments to show that Joseph had failed to act as a husband should, and therefore the family should be reorganized. As legal historian Hendrik Hartog has described, "divorce was not a right, only a remedy for a wrong."[5] Mary hoped the New Hampshire legislature would right that wrong.

Failing to reach an agreement with her husband or the Shakers, Mary appealed to the public and the legislature in her quest to retrieve her children. In order to succeed, Mary had to prove that she was the innocent party in this marital disaster and that her character was spotless and above reproach. In *A Brief Statement* (1818), her first publication, Mary combined first-person narrative and affidavits to present herself as a faithful, religious wife and loving, child-focused mother while she simultaneously portrayed the Shakers as everything a mother was not—deceptive, immoral, and unable to care for children. The icon of "mother" was a strong cultural symbol, and the Dyer debate was built around its definition. Joseph defended his position in his published work,

A Compendious Narrative (1818). As head of the family he addressed his words to "any man" similar to Mary's appeal to sympathetic women. Joseph argued that he could not turn his children over "to a woman whose immorality, impiety and base conduct has far exceeded any thing I have hitherto stated." His justification for keeping the children was clear-cut. As he had "the first and exclusive right, with regard to the protection and well being of my children, vested in me not only by the laws of man, but by the Creator. . . . I cannot sacrifice this right or transfer it to Mary Dyer, even if it were in my power, without a pointed violation of my own conscience."[6] Joseph made explicit that he was the head of the family, guaranteed by Biblical argument and legal custom. Children and wife were his to control, a fact that Mary did not deny. Yet from Mary's point of view, Joseph betrayed his obligations in that role by placing his wife and children among the Shakers. In Joseph's view, he had acted according to his rights by indenturing the children to the Shakers as a solution to a family crisis brought on by the mother's failure to fulfill her role. It was up to the legislature to decide who had transgressed their role and what could be done to undo the consequences of that transgression.

This chapter follows Mary Dyer as her apostasy moves to a much more public stage; from confrontations with Joseph to accusations in front of the New Hampshire legislature and to publications for the reading public. Out of her legislative appearance grew a public curiosity about Dyer's tale and a market for information in print that dueling newspaper editors readily provided. For both Mary and the Shakers, it is an opportunity to enlarge the audience for what has become a very public performance. During this period, 1817–1819, Dyer established the framework of her printed apostate story that she used and reused for the rest of her life. Dyer's performance of apostasy, more than any of her predecessors, was widely visible. Her public appearances and statements were covered by the newspapers, an arena she exploited in combating her Shaker enemies. The newspaper also served as the vehicle for spreading her story beyond her immediate friends, family, and supporters. After leaving the Shakers, Dyer created a network of support and assistance centered around where she lived at a particular moment. Following her 1817 and 1818 appearances before the legislature, newspapers carried Dyer's story beyond her immediate geographic sphere. This began the commodification of Dyer's story as it was told and retold first across space and then time. The name Mary Dyer became a rallying cry—reified in print as a symbol of anti-Shaker activity.

Mary Dyer's dispute with the Shakers was not the first such incident
to come to the attention of Concord's reading public. On June 24, 1817,
the weekly Concord newspaper, *New Hampshire Patriot,* printed James
Chapman's *Memorial,* a response to an anti-Shaker pamphlet his wife
Eunice had recently published in New York State.[7] Mary had had several caustic run-ins with James Chapman at the Enfield Shakers, but
his Shaker story had actually begun in New York. James Chapman had
joined the Watervliet, New York, Shakers in 1812, a year after he abandoned his wife and children. When the Shakers informed James he was
obligated to uphold his marriage contract and provide for his family,
James attempted to convince his wife, Eunice, to join him at the Shakers.
Unsuccessful, and having heard that Eunice had placed his children
among the town's poor, James secretly took his three young children
into the Society's care. Eunice was furious at the loss of her children
and accused James of neglecting his family and kidnapping the children. Eunice began a vocal campaign to retrieve her children and obtain
a legislative divorce. She published two pamphlets describing her experiences with (and against) the Shakers. James Chapman's *Memorial*
refuted her accusations and placed the blame for the failed marriage
and subsequent situation squarely on Eunice and "the fatal effects of
her calumniating tongue." James's *Memorial* was published first in New
York in an attempt to gain public support for the Shakers in their legal
battles against Eunice.[8] The talk of Albany, Eunice's case was also immor-
talized in a caustic, anonymous play that cast legislators as drunken
fools and Eunice as a lustful siren.[9]

The New York dispute found its way to New Hampshire. In addition to Chapman's essay, an open letter addressed to the New York
legislature also appeared on page one of the *Patriot.*[10] In this remonstrance the Shakers outlined and defended their principles and argued
against a proposed New York State bill that would declare individuals who joined the Shaker sect "civilly dead," a position that would
then permit wives a divorce and family members an inheritance of goods
destined to become Shaker communal property. The bill was defeated
when the Shakers reminded the legislature that the dead do not pay
taxes.

Patriot editor Isaac Hill printed Chapman's *Memorial* and the
Shakers' remonstrance because although many people had heard of the
Shakers, few had read Shaker publications. Hill printed the documents
for his readers "because, as it amused and instructed us, we suppose
[readers] will be willing to see what the Shakers have to say for themselves."[11] But Hill did not publish the Shaker remonstrance simply to
satisfy his readers' curiosity. In printing Chapman's *Memorial* and the

Shakers' address to the New York legislature, Hill revealed what would be a key question in the Dyers' argument: Did the Shakers deliberately destroy marriages or did they require their members to provide for wives and children? While Shakers themselves may have chosen not to marry, did they or did they not support wider community obligations of spouses to one another? Isaac Hill was biased toward the Shakers and in printing the Chapman and Shaker defense, he told only one side of the story. This was a calculated move. On the same day the Shakers appeared in print in Isaac Hill's *New Hampshire Patriot,* Mary Dyer testified against them in her first appearance before the legislature.

A small legislative committee had reviewed Mary Dyer's petition and on Monday, June 23, 1817, recommended that she be granted a hearing before both houses of the legislature. The legislature met in a one story wooden building built in 1790. Eighty feet long and forty feet wide, the building featured a narrow stairway that led to a small gallery overlooking the assembled body of legislators. The room would have been filled to capacity; construction was still ongoing on a new, more spacious state house to replace the aged and overcrowded legislative building.[12] On Tuesday, June 24, Dyer, in her borrowed dress, presented her story.[13] Dyer sought two actions: legislative interference to force the Shakers to return her children and to force Joseph to provide for her. The *Patriot* revealed Dyer's testimony in the next published issue, July 1.[14] The *Patriot* reporter summarized the "substance of her petition": that fifteen years ago she and Joseph had married and lived together happily "and by their industry increased in goods and became easier in their circumstances." The Dyers learned of the Shakers and "they were induced to join them." Mary, upon living with the Shakers, "began to doubt their rectitude and whether they lived according to the professions which they made." Mary left and was subsequently refused access to her children while her husband "evinced he had lost the affection, which is natural from a husband towards a wife."[15] Joseph also spoke before the legislature. He complained that although Mary was a "capable creature" (a backhanded compliment emphasizing Mary's ability to perform economically valuable labor), her natural disposition was to lead, not to be led.[16] Similar to James Chapman's complaint against Eunice, Joseph blamed his marital difficulties on Mary's disposition and her tongue that he described as "an unruly member."[17] In front of the legislature, Mary blamed Joseph's failure as a husband for disrupting her domestic tranquility; Joseph blamed Mary's insubordination.

Although their calumniating and unruly tongues caused marital discord, Eunice Chapman's and Mary Dyer's ability to speak out gained them an opportunity to command attention and demand attention to their situations. Mary's skill in public speaking received special notice. Isaac Hill reported how "Mrs. Dyer appeared on the floor and told her story; and she discovered she was not wanting in talent. . . . She portrayed in strong colors the misery of her unhappy situation."[18] Governor Plumer recorded his impressions as well and described Dyer as "a woman of considerable talent, confidence, and enthusiasm."[19] Despite this praise, there was doubt as to "the sincerity of her motives to make an impression on her audience."[20] Dyer insisted to her reading public that she had asked only for "redress," but Isaac Hill (and others) suspected she really wanted out of her marriage. Plumer, in fact, recorded in his diary that Dyer requested a divorce.

Mary's performance "excited an extraordinary interest," and her Concord appearance enlarged the geographic circle in which her story was known.[21] The Dyers' argument moved from a local arena centered on Mary (Enfield to Hanover to Orford to Coös) to a statewide arena as legislators carried the interesting tale with them when returning home. More importantly, Dyer's story moved beyond her immediate sphere when Hill's July 1, 1817 article was reprinted in several newspapers including *The Yankee* (Boston, July 11), the *Connecticut Courant* (July 15), the *Berkshire Star* (Massachusetts, July 24), the *Baltimore Telegraph* (ca. mid-July), *The National Intelligencer* (Washington, D. C., ca. late July), and the *Ohio Watchman* (July 31). This dispatched her story across New England and eventually across the country.

Despite her impassioned performance, the legislature decided not to pursue her petition, unwilling to meddle in a private marital dispute and the practices of a religious sect. While many legislators were moved by Dyer's sad story, most felt there was no current law that could address the peculiar situation. Despite the lawmakers' hesitation, a committee was appointed to consider whether joining the Shakers should be a legal cause for divorce. New Hampshire's divorce laws were considered liberal by early-nineteenth-century standards, and while divorce was often a judiciary procedure, a legislative divorce was a possibility, particularly where the situation did not fit the usual statutory causes.[22] The legislature proposed to amend the 1791 divorce act to permit a divorce in situations where one spouse joined a sect, such as the Shakers, that held the marriage bond as void. The legislature passed and sent the bill to the governor near the close of the June session. Governor Plumer reflected on the proposed bill and how Dyer had stirred emotions and forced the legislature to take action. Plumer was concerned with setting such a precedent. Although "the bill was general it was in fact made for the relief of Mary Dyer. It was passed under the ardent feelings excited by her case & increased by her pathetic address, & not the result of investigation."[23] While Plumer in general did not object to modifying the state's divorce statutes, he hesitated to make a law to satisfy the unique, though unfortunate, circumstances of just one citizen. Pressed with other duties and unable to "investigate" the ramifications of such a bill, the Governor allowed the bill to die on his desk. Isaac Hill remarked that several gentlemen objected to the bill that would in effect stigmatize the Shakers. As drunkenness, conviction for theft, and other crimes were not just causes for divorce, it seemed unfair to permit divorce simply when one (or one's spouse) chose to join a specific religious sect. Such a bill would "abridge the rights of conscience."[24] Mary and Joseph had religiously "grown apart" in our contemporary parlance, yet in the nineteenth century, that was not justification for divorce. Moreover, the Dyer dispute came in front of the legislature in a period of intense debate on two other topics: the management of Dartmouth College and a religious toleration act that would eliminate the practice of state financial support for churches of some, but not all, denominations. What linked all three debates was the issue of legislative interference. How much power could (and should) a state have in the governance of a private college, of religious institutions, and of families? The Dyer dispute encapsulated these issues. Did the Shakers, a sectarian religious group with unique family practices, have the right to manage themselves, or could the state interfere in that management?[25]

For Concord's reading (and gossiping) public, two consecutive issues of the *New Hampshire Patriot* had provided information on Shakerism and its detractors. Isaac Hill was not unfamiliar with Shakerism, having an established business relationship with the sect. In addition to his newspaper, Hill operated a bookstore that sold various books, stationery, blank forms, a variety of medicines, and Shaker seeds, the arrival of which were advertised in the *Patriot*. Hill published books, calendars, and would publish the New Hampshire Shaker's 1818 remonstrance to Mary Dyer's accusations. Later in his career, Isaac Hill published an agricultural newspaper in which he frequently praised Shaker agricultural practices and products. An important man in Concord and with a newspaper at his control, Hill was a critical link in the Shakers' network of allies.[26]

Despite Hill's published pretense that he had simply happened across James Chapman's *Memorial* and the Shakers' *Remonstrance* and printed them for his readers' "amusement," Hill likely received both works from the Enfield Shaker community. Although not widely known at the time, Eunice Chapman's three children, accompanied by their father, had been surreptitiously moved from New York State to Enfield in

February 1815 and arrived at the New Hampshire community shortly after Mary Dyer had fled.[27] The Enfield Shakers were aware of Mary Dyer's impending petition to the legislature and called upon Hill to act in their defense drawing on the New York Shaker's recent legislative experience with Eunice and James Chapman. Although the remonstrance addressed the New York legislature and the dispute involved a different Shaker community, the parallels between the Chapman and Dyer disputes were obvious. Both women fought to retrieve Shaker-held children given by their husbands to Shaker societies; both would appear before state legislatures seeking a divorce and redress; both were skilled and brought their story to a public format; both had husbands who remained Shakers. In printing the Chapman-related texts, the *Patriot* effectively addressed its own New Hampshire legislative body on the very day the Dyer dispute came to a public forum.[28]

At the behest of the legislature, Dyer withdrew her 1817 petition but a year later, in June 1818, she would return to Concord for a second attempt prompted in part by yet another failed attempt at reaching a settlement with Joseph.[29] In the winter of 1818 Mary had been living in Enfield where she had taught school for the wage of one dollar a week plus board. She approached town Selectman Joseph Merrill and "made a grievous complaint" about her disrupted family life.[30] Mary complained she "was deprived of every earthly enjoyment" and thought "it proper to make application . . . to the selectmen of the town." Merrill was caught off guard by the situation that he called "a new case to me." He offered to speak to Joseph when he attended to business matters at the Shakers in a few days. Mary must have had a sinking feeling—instead of taking action as a town official, Merrill deferred to Mary's husband for guidance in the matter. Joseph, no doubt frustrated by Mary's reappearance in Enfield and continued attempts to gain assistance and himself wanting a resolution to this situation, asked Merrill to call together the selectmen and "some of the principal inhabitants of [Enfield]" to hear Joseph and Mary present their cases. Soon after, in early April, the group came together at James Willis's inn, where Dyer had boarded herself. Mary did not come without allies. In addition to the selectmen, Mary had invited several "neighborhood women" to witness the meeting. Joseph Dyer made a "long statement" detailing how they joined the Shakers and "their other difficulties." Joseph provided evidence of his support: a written record of articles provided to Mary, expenditures made on her behalf (such as board), and expenses incurred because of her actions, including defending himself against her legislative petition. Merrill recalled that Joseph's conversation "appeared to shew [*sic*] what he had done and that he had done as

much for her as he was able to do."[31] Judge Edward Evans, also present at the meeting, recalled that Joseph had but four dollars and few
cents left and that Joseph said "that Mary was capable of taking care
of herself."[32] Mary bitterly pointed out how she "thought it hard for
her to be under the necessity of calling on the selectmen for assistance"
when "she had spent the best part of her days in bringing up a family
[and] procuring some property" through her hard work. She argued
that she deserved a share of the success of that labor "as they had begun
poor [and] she had worked hard & done all she could to assist him in
his business."[33] Mary asked that Joseph provide for her and let her
have one or more of the children. Joseph once again offered Mary wild
land in exchange for an acquittance for life but he refused to give her
any of the children. Lavina Johnson noted that Joseph's "neglect was
such towards her that it caused her grief to be so great that it is unex-
pressible."[34] Merrill noted that "the interview appeared to end in confusion and nothing agreed upon or any provisions made for her by the
Selectmen or [Joseph] Dyer."[35]

Despite her failure with the Enfield selectmen, in the interregnum
between sessions, Mary gained an important ally—Eunice Chapman.
Mary Dyer's 1817 legislative petition had cited a "situation in a sister
state," an indication that Dyer was aware of the Chapman case before
it had appeared in the New Hampshire papers. She had met James
Chapman and endured his rude behavior during several of her visits
to Enfield, but she did not know Eunice. Enfield apostate Josiah Terry
provided the link between the two women. Terry left the Enfield Shakers
in December 1816. He wandered to Albany where he heard of Eunice
Chapman's troubles with the Shakers and read Eunice's 1817 pamphlet,
An Account of the People Called Shakers, James Chapman's *Memorial,*
and the New York Shakers' *To The Legislature.* Bitter at the elders'
denial of wages for his work while among the Enfield Shakers, Terry
met with Eunice Chapman and provided a lengthy affidavit (August
1, 1817) for her second publication. In his affidavit, Terry described
Shaker abuse of children and women at Enfield, including the treatment of Mary Dyer.

Having learned of Dyer's difficulties from Josiah Terry, Eunice
Chapman initiated a correspondence with Mary.[36] The women
exchanged their personal stories, expressed a mutual desire to see the
Shakers publicly exposed, and discussed their respective legislative sessions. Chapman sent Dyer a copy of her first publication and requested
an affidavit from Mary to include in her second work. Chapman published *No. 2 Being the Additional Account of the Conduct of the Shakers*
in early 1818. Dyer's statement supported Chapman's claims by show-

ing a history of Shaker neglect toward wives and children. As Dyer had experienced several interactions with James Chapman, she could attest to his vulgar language and abusive behavior. As part of Chapman's book, Dyer's story radiated out from Albany and continued the geographic distribution of her tale. But unlike the reprints of Hill's July 1, 1817 newspaper article, in Chapman's book Mary told her story in her own words. Dyer's story as told in Chapman proffered an early version of what became her 1818 petition to the legislature and Mary's first publication, *A Brief Statement*.

Chapman assisted Dyer in several ways. She promoted Dyer's case to the public and argued for legislative assistance. Chapman wrote a threatening letter to Shaker Seth Wells and others at the Watervliet community. In a postscript to her missive, Eunice stated that the best the Shakers could do would be to settle with Mary Dyer. Chapman rendered more effective assistance when she sent New Hampshire Governor William Plumer a lengthy letter and a copy of *No. 2*. Plumer read the pamphlet and accompanying letter on May 17, 1818, a month prior to Dyer's second appearance before the legislature.[37] Chapman's letter provided Plumer with additional information on Mary Dyer and Shaker abuse. It also spurred him to action. The next day, Plumer wrote to New York Governor De Witt Clinton seeking more information on the Chapman situation and specifically on the objections the New York Council of Revision had raised to proposed divorce legislation.[38] In 1817, Plumer did not have time to give a thoughtful response to New Hampshire's proposed divorce bill. In 1818, he explored all sides of the issue well in advance of the legislative session.

Eunice used her extended network of kin to promote her case in New York State and then to assist Dyer in New Hampshire. Eunice's brother, Jesse Hawley, a member of the New York legislature, also wrote to Governor Plumer and expressed his support for Dyer. Hawley urged Plumer to pass a reformation "for there is no legerdemain in true religion, and the age for its use has gone by."[39] Thus, when Dyer's second petition appeared before the New Hampshire Legislature it did not come as a surprise. On Monday, June 15, 1818, a committee was appointed to investigate the petition of Mary Dyer and a petition of Joshua Stevens (and forty-seven other Enfield village residents). Both petitions claimed bad conduct on the part of the Enfield Shakers. Once again the legislature granted Dyer a hearing. Dyer's petition and public visibility prompted action. A special committee of legislators was formed to investigate the Shakers, and in addition, a group of local physicians took it upon themselves to investigate Dyer's claims that the Shakers gave women medicine to prevent menstruation and pregnancy.[40] While the twelve-member official committee visited Canterbury, the closest Shaker community to Concord, Dyer and the Enfield Shakers pleaded their respective cases before the remaining legislators.

Dyer's connection with Eunice Chapman proved beneficial. Apostasy is a learned role and perhaps Mary learned a few tricks for performance in the theater of apostasy from Eunice. Mary rewrote and expanded her short 1817 legislative petition into a thirty-five page pamphlet, *A Brief Statement of the Sufferings of Mary Dyer*. Dyer distributed copies of *A Brief Statement* to all the legislators, a tactic used by Chapman in her dealings in New York.[41] *A Brief Statement* allowed Mary to tell her side of the story, unrestrained by time or format demanded in a legislative appearance. For legislators who had attended the previous year's session, *A Brief Statement* provided new details and restated her accusations. For new legislators, it provided a detailed introduction. The advantage of a written statement was that it could be read and reread at the reader's choosing. Distributing a pamphlet to a key but finite audience was a strategy that forced a reaction: read and decide. The New Hampshire Shakers also knew the advantage of a written tract and countered Dyer's pamphlet by distributing a lengthy *Remonstrance* to all the legislators.[42]

In addition to the experienced and powerful ally Mary had found in Eunice Chapman, public opinion provided Dyer with another source of power. Her previous legislative session had illustrated how emotion had a strong effect; her "pathetic" speech had motivated the legislators to draft a divorce bill. To excite public opinion and make some money on a hot topic, Joseph Spear, the editor of the Concord *Gazette,* published *A Brief Statement* on June 16, 1818.[43] Spear sold the pamphlet to the public at the *Gazette* office and advertised the newly available work in both the *Gazette* and in his competitor's newspaper, the *Patriot*. In response, *Patriot* editor Hill published the Shakers' *Remonstrance* as a twenty-four page pamphlet shortly thereafter, sold it at his printing office, and likewise advertised the work in area newspapers.

The Dyer-Shaker dispute was the talk of Concord. Typically, Concord newspapers did not carry much local news, instead offering articles on foreign affairs, new laws, and seemingly trivial stories from distant communities. Yet the Concord papers overflowed with information on the Dyers. This was a big story. The newspaper commented on Mary Dyer's reappearance:

The subject of the present year, as it did the last, has arrested not only the attention of the legislature, but has become a topic for general conversation. Mary Dyer has published a book containing an account of her sufferings, in which, with no inconsiderable share of talent, she has accused, and attempted to support her charges, the Shakers with high crime and misdemeanors; and the Shakers have answered in a remonstrance drawn by a person who had lived and been educated in their society ever since he was three years old:—this performance discovers talents which would do honor to the "man of the world" who had made letters the study of his whole life. "When Greek meets Greek, then comes the tug of war."[44]

Spear had timed the release of Dyer's text to coincide with her second appearance before the legislature. In addition to the weekly newspaper reports, the reading public could now indulge their curiosity with more detailed information. Perhaps to spur readers to purchase Dyer's more detailed book, and certainly to sell more newspapers, in the issue following the publication of *A Brief Statement*, the *Gazette* published on page one Dyer's 1818 petition to the legislature. Hill responded the following week (on June 30) and printed the Shaker remonstrance. The rival newspapers brought an encapsulated version of the Dyer debate into the public view. No doubt with their mutual allegations and titillating innuendos, Dyer's petition and the Shaker remonstrance spurred readers to seek more details. A clever newspaper advertisement testified to the public desire for information on Joseph and Mary's dispute. A Concord firm that carded, dressed, and dyed wool and other cloth articles titled their newspaper advertisement in large, bold type "DYERS." The notice appeared in the *Patriot* throughout the summer, often on page one. The readers' eyes could not avoid looking at this bold, eye-catching headline.[45]

In the year between legislative appearances, Dyer had modified her petition. In 1817, Mary's petition centered on the failure of her marriage and her personal disagreement with Joseph. She wrote of how he prompted the Dyers' conversion to Shakerism. Joseph "attached himself," "deluded your petitioner," and "carried her and their children to Enfield."[46] Her complaint centered on Joseph's failure to perform the duties of the marriage contract by not providing shelter and protection. The fate of her children aggravated her situation to the point of a decline in health. In sum, the 1817 petition focused on the effects Shakerism had on Mary; no health, no home, no husband, no children, and that this situation was entirely Joseph's doing.

In the 1818 petition, the Shakers took center stage as the agents of misery. Responding to the legislators who in the previous year worried about creating a law solely for the relief of one individual, Dyer downplayed her personal situation. She made clear that she was an unwilling participant in Shakerism and described how she "was induced with reluctance," deluded by her husband and the Shakers who already had taken her children. In this petition, then, Dyer did not carry her children to the Shakers, but rather, she followed them there to protect them. Answering criticism of why she joined the sect in the first place, Dyer amended her 1817 statement to make clear the transitory nature of her dalliance with Shakerism, that she was deluded into a "temporary" belief. Further, she made more vivid her abhorrence of the faith. In the 1817 petition she "realized their hypocrisy," and left. In the 1818 version she "became completely disgusted" and then left the faith. In the second petition, Dyer described Joseph as acting only under the orders of the society as "the poor deluded man has no will of his own," feminizing Joseph in a pointed reversal of the idea that wives, under coverture, had no will other than that of their husbands. The children, who were of secondary concern to the collapse of her marriage and withdrawal of her husband's support in the 1817 petition, were in 1818 painted in a more threatening scene as Dyer likened their living arrangements to convents, drawing on long-standing anti-Catholic sentiment. Her 1817 conclusion made reference to Chapman's case and asked that the legislature note the example of "a respectable sister state," who had just granted Chapman a legislative divorce. In 1818, Dyer responded to the objections the previous year's legislators had raised and buried her personal goal for a broader motive—that legislation against the Shakers would serve the entire community in preventing more women and children from entering poverty and suffering ill health because of their association with Shakers.[47]

Mary Dyer took an offensive stance during the 1818 legislative session. Her expanded network of supporters had raised her awareness of the magnitude of those affected by Shaker practices. Making full use of her expanded network, experience from the previous year, and association with Eunice Chapman, Dyer took the lead in this campaign and forced the Shakers to respond to each of her many actions. The Shakers were caught off guard. Their remonstrance rebutted her petition, but they had no detailed defense prepared to offer the public to counter *A Brief Statement*. The reading public read Mary Dyer's accusations against the Shakers and against Joseph. The Shakers offered a defense of their practices with a written remonstrance (authored by Joseph Dyer and Canterbury Shaker John Whitcher), but where was Joseph's side of the story—the details of marital collapse from his perspective?[48] Mary Dyer's planning and network had gained her an edge and showed the Shakers she was indeed, as Joseph had stated, quite "capable."

In the 1818 legislative debate, whether or not to assist Mary Dyer hinged on two key points. The first issue concerned whether the Dyer children had been legally indentured to the Shakers. As in 1817, and despite Mary's claims of being forced and tricked into signing a bond, the legislature upheld the indenture, giving state-sanctioned affirmation of Shaker membership practices.[49] A second and more critical concern addressed whether the Shakers mistreated children and thus whether or not a Shaker village constituted a proper home. Dyer argued that the celibate Shaker community was an unnatural setting. Her medical accusations focused on the unnatural biological state of the females. Her accusations had a moral tone as well, as she detailed the alleged hypocrisy in espousing celibacy while the leaders engaged in sexual relations. Dyer argued that the Shakers abused children and turned young innocents into small adults before their time with harsh work, little sleep, and a regimented lifestyle. Witnesses in support of Dyer told story after story of cruel discipline. Dyer's plea, then, focused not just on her children, but on all children living within Shaker communities. Dyer's personal campaign had shifted to a broader social reform.

Despite a wave of public sympathy for Dyer, the legislature found little to support her renewed accusations against the Shakers. When the special investigative committee visited the Canterbury Shaker village they found a neat, well-ordered community, with happy, healthy children. Thirty members of the legislature attended Sunday worship services where Job Bishop and Joseph Dyer addressed the assembly, for Joseph an impromptu venue for making his case to the legislators.[50] In addition, although not an official investigation, three local physicians who had examined the Shakers in Canterbury concluded that Dyer's suggestions that Shaker women took "certain poisons or medicines" to produce "a change in their habits and constitution, thereby inducing a state of sterility is wholly without foundation, as are also her statements of a similar character respecting the other sex."[51] As far as the outsiders could see, there was no indication of illicit sex or cruel abuse.

On June 25, the legislature reconvened and the investigative committee made their report. Caleb Stark, reporting for the committee, reported how this important case required careful consideration. Testimony was gathered from all concerned but because of the highly antagonistic nature of the case "the task of your committee has been one of no ordinary import."[52] Despite these challenges, the committee concluded there was no evidence among the Shakers "of any uncommon depravation of morals," although they recognized an earlier period of fanaticism in Shaker history.[53] The Shakers had shown a "progressive spirit of improvements" and at present did not appear to be "a serious ground of complaint from the public."[54] On the issue of abuse, the committee saw Shaker discipline as "unnecessarily rigorous" yet praised the Shaker system that brought forth obedient children who were well educated and strong in religious faith. The Committee had no praise for the communal lifestyle that broke down biological ties. Despite the Shakers' explanation for communitywide affection, the committee described communal life as "erroneous" and "fallacious."[55] Nonetheless, the committee concluded that the Shakers, although misguided in their beliefs, were a society "honest in their dealings, and industrious in their habits, and by no means an inhospitable or an illiberal people."[56] Further, they were good farmers and mechanics "and may, in this respect, furnish a useful example to the community at large."[57] As the Shakers supported their own schools, took care of their poor, and paid their taxes, the Shakers were not a burden on the community, but rather an asset. Shaker material success and community self-reliance was the very model of republican ideology, but not for women like Mary Dyer who found herself without an identity within the Shakers or within the world. The legislature once again suggested that she withdraw her petition.[58] William Plumer responded to Jesse Hawley's earlier letter and explained that "our legislature passed no law in relation to the Shakers, tho the subject was fully and ably discussed." Plumer wrote how the " . . . Shakers are wild enthusiasts." With the Dartmouth case and religious toleration debate in his mind, the governor feared that "[l]egislative interference will produce more evil than good to society." His strategy was one of benign coexistence. As Plumer reasoned, "[n]othing is more fatal to enthusiasm than toleration and neglect. It damps its ardor and cools its frantic spirit."[59] If ignored, Shaker enthusiasm will simply fade away and cease to present a problem. On July 7, the *Patriot* published the legislative committee's decision.

Dyer protested the outcome and used the newspaper to make her feelings known. In a statement addressed to "Friends of Humanity," Dyer complained that lack of money and personal contacts prevented the success of her petition. She directly addressed "You, Shakers," restated her previous accusations, and hinted at even greater crimes. She revealed plans to continue her anti-Shaker campaign. First, Dyer announced that as God directed her apostate activities, she would find no relief until she had exposed the Shakers. Second, she hinted that she would travel from town to town to gather information against the Shakers. In this same issue, Dyer placed a small advertisement addressed "To the Public." In it she announced that *A Brief Statement* had been intended solely for the state representatives and that for the public, Dyer would provide more of the "particulars" in a "history more full." Clearly Dyer had no intention of giving up the fight.[60]

Isaac Hill defended the Shakers and offered a critique of Dyer's recent performance in Concord. He suggested that Mary Dyer would have been more successful, not if she had more money, but rather if she had not written with so much emotion and such a "vindictive and angry spirit."[61] Hill's editorial relayed gender stereotypes of the day—that men were rational and thought with their heads, and women were emotional and thought with their hearts. While emotion, especially that of a mother's love for her children, was appropriate and beneficial in the domestic setting, Dyer had taken those characteristics into the public sphere where her emotion was magnified inappropriately. Further, Dyer's critics employed the image of an angry, vindictive woman to dismiss Dyer and her cause. Far from the pious, self-sacrificing woman of the home who made an argument based on love, Dyer was portrayed by Hill as motivated by anger and self-serving vindictiveness. This image reinforced Joseph's assertion of Dyer's uncontrolled (and uncontrollable) passions that destroyed the Dyer household and brought confusion to the Shakers. Where the legislature had concluded that the Shakers were a model for society, Hill's attack on Mary suggested that her outspoken, public presence was not an example to emulate.

Dyer's public apostasy continued via the newspapers, and although Isaac Hill criticized Mary Dyer, other newspaper editors supported her public campaign. *Gazette* editor Spear had connections with Boston newspapers and used them to distribute *A Brief Statement* and information on Mary Dyer. The *Boston Commercial Gazette* was sympathetic to Mary. In an article dated July 23, 1818, the editors praised Dyer as an "intelligent female" and suggested that the Shakers be "held up to public view in order that they may be shunned as a pestilence."[62] In response to the anti-Shaker sentiment stirred by the Boston papers, and as a message to Spear who headed the campaign, on September 1 an article from "A Friend" appeared in the *New Hampshire Patriot*. This article reported on the anti-Shaker view prevalent in the *Boston Gazette* and defended the Shakers.

The Shaker remonstrance had proven an effective tool in combating Mary's accusations in front of the legislature. To address the public and refute in greater detail the allegations in Mary's *A Brief Statement*, advertised in the Concord newspapers well into the fall of 1818, the Shakers published their own pamphlet, *A Compendious Narrative* (1818). At some point after the legislative hearing, Joseph approached the New Hampshire Ministry and "manifested to [them] that he thought it his duty to make some reply to Mary's impositions on the public."[63] The ministry recognized that Mary Dyer's actions had the power to stimulate "the sympathy and malice of mankind."[64] As the Shakers had nothing substantial in print to refute her accusations, their silence was taken as guilt, as the public "never heard anything to the contrary."[65] The ministry granted Joseph's request. In October, John Whitcher came to Enfield from Canterbury to help Joseph (or, as once source states, compile for Joseph) his rebuttal.[66] As new to authorship as Mary, Joseph leaned upon the more experienced Shakers for help in constructing and shaping his argument. The experience of the past few months had taught Joseph and the Shakers what the reading public wanted: details in personal statements and affidavits to support one's claims. In this public theater, the audience/readers shaped the play as much as the author. Once the text was assembled, Joseph sent the pamphlet to Concord to the printing office of Isaac Hill.

The printer's family fell ill during the winter of 1818/19, and *A Compendious Narrative* was delayed until February 18, 1819.[67] On March 9, Isaac Hill advertised the new publication under the headline "Hear Both Sides." *A Compendious Narrative, elucidating the character, disposition and conduct of MARY DYER. . . ."* sold for twenty-six cents for eighty-eight pages of "close printed matter," a much larger pamphlet than the thirty-five pages of *A Brief Statement.* Hill advertised Joseph Dyer's work from February through the April 6, 1819 issue of the *Patriot.* The public had not tired of the Dyer debate. Pamphlet collector Daniel Robinson read "both sides" of the Shaker debate, and doing so moved him to comment on what he had read. In a manuscript note on the cover of his copy of the Shaker *Remonstrance against the Testimony and Application of Mary Dyer. . . .* (1818) Robinson indicated that he also owned Mary Dyer's *A Brief Statement,* number thirty in his pamphlet collection. The *Remonstrance* was number thirty-one. After having read both texts, Robinson favored the Shaker position, and on the inside cover of the *Remonstrance* handwrote an anti-Mary Dyer poem that began "Mary Dyer, be on thy guard!" These texts encouraged a reader's response. Another reader, name unknown but who had visited the Shirley and Harvard Shakers in 1795, scribed a long manuscript message on a copy of the *Remonstrance.* The writer critiqued Mary Dyer's argument, stating that she failed to prove Joseph's intemperate behavior and the "despotic manner of the Shakers as no example is given of illegitimate children." Further, the *Remonstrance* had demonstrated that "the Shakers hold themselves open to the laws of the country."[68] Like the nineteenth-century divorce trial pamphlets legal historian Norma Basch describes, Mary and Joseph's dueling accounts of their marriage and Shaker experience were commodities for consumption, offering an "opportunity to peer through the key-hole" at a marriage in crisis and the life of a secretive sect. While they offered a peep at the private, the pamphlets conflated the "didactic with the sensational" and also offered a "cautionary tale" about the structure of the proper family. As many readers would, Robinson and the anonymous writer had read both sides, and decided which of the proffered moral lessons they would learn.[69]

A War of Words

Anti-Shaker publications damaged the Shaker public image more than any other apostate activity. Books could travel great distances and exist far beyond the life of their authors. Books had greater longevity than ephemeral newspapers or impassioned speeches before the legislature. Books could reveal greater detail, and they offered first-person accounts as validation. Anti-Shaker books often included selections from previously published apostate accounts, connecting generations of apostates over time and illustrating the longevity and serious nature of the Shaker threat to mainstream religion. With every apostate work published, membership in the social category of "Shaker apostate" grew.[70] Readers could spend time with books, mulling over arguments, and returning to the text to read and reread accusations. Long after the story had happened, far away from where it happened, and long after the author's life, books continued to broadcast their messages.

To combat Mary Dyer's pervasive accusations, the Shakers sent Joseph's pamphlet to areas in which Mary's *A Brief Statement* had circulated. In March 1819, shortly after Joseph's *A Compendious Narrative* was published, the Ministry at Hancock (Massachusetts) suggested that copies of his work be sent to Boston to counter "a very slanderous peace [*sic*] published in a Boston paper about the brethren in New Hampshire stating that Mary Dyer had unfolded their wickedness."[71] In May of the same year the Enfield Shakers sent six pamphlets to New Lebanon for distribution.[72] Correspondence between Shaker communities, newspaper advertisements, and newspaper discussions about *A Brief Statement* chart the spread of Mary Dyer's first pamphlet. Long after the Dyer dispute was the talk of Concord, Mary Dyer's anti-Shaker tract kept visible her complaints and accusations.

When Mary Dyer began her public apostasy she had little to offer in personal credentials. She was not an author, theologian, or politician. Although literate, she had not attended a formal school. Although married and having managed a farm, she did not own property or hold any assets. Having neither wealth nor power, Mary could offer only her firsthand experience among the Shakers and her reputation in the community as evidence of her credibility and the legitimacy of her claims. Her very lack of credentials offered a credential. Because, as a woman, she was naturally unfamiliar with the competitive world of publishing and politics, some readers understood her account to be a statement of truth borne straight from the heart. Yet other readers saw Dyer as the public speaker and the polished writer and wondered, given her surprising skill in these foreign venues, if her presentation was as straightforward as she claimed. Some critics doubted an unschooled rural woman could write such works and wondered who had really crafted Dyer's account. Dyer's capabilities were proving to be both assets and liabilities.

In thirty-five pages, *A Brief Statement* related Mary Dyer's version of the events that transpired at the Enfield Shaker village. She reprinted her 1818 petition to the New Hampshire legislature and included affidavits in support of her character and in denouncement of the Shakers. A Boston edition of *A Brief Statement* was published in 1819 by Charles Spear.

In the opening paragraphs of *A Brief Statement* Mary described her life in a series of short, clipped statements identifying her place of residence, family structure, and religion:

> We resided in Stewartstown, in the county of Coös, and State of New Hampshire. We lived quietly together eleven years, though there had been some disagreeable by my husband's being unsteady, and given sometimes to intoxication. We had five children and were in good circumstance. We were united in a hope of salvation, through Christ. We were of the Baptist profession; yet as there was no church established we stood as single characters.[73]

This image of a quiet family life was altered in a shift in both narrative and writing style as Mary related the town's decision to send Lemuel Crooker, the itinerant preacher, to New York to gather his family, return, and settle permanently in Stewartstown. Much to Mary's dismay, Crooker returned not with his family, but with Shaker books. Her response revealed the seeds of both religious enthusiasm and disappointment as she remarked that "this was astonishing and disappointing; and the first information I ever had of the Shakers."[74] In the opening paragraphs of her story, the arrival of books corrupts Dyer's innocence of Shaker practices. How interesting that she, too, will awaken other's naivete with the same tool.

Mary used the arrival of the Shaker books to display the difference between husband and wife. Joseph, according to Mary, "was induced to go see [the Shakers]," suggesting Joseph's inability to resist outside control, both from the temptation of alcohol and from the religious seduction of the Shakers.[75] Mary on the other hand "had strong impressions that their belief was contrary to the gospel," an illustration of her piety, caution, and suspicion of outside, or nonmainstream ideas.[76] The text provided a sharp contrast between weak Joseph (described in the passive, "was induced") and strong Mary (described in the active, "had impressions"). Although the husband controlled the household, Mary portrayed Joseph's leadership as susceptible to outside influence.

From Mary's point of view, the Shakers deceived Joseph into joining the community, and she had been made an unwilling participant. If she had refused to join her husband, he would have abandoned her and taken her children away, just as had happened to Eunice Chapman.[77] Mary felt trapped. As she reasoned, if she went to the Shakers, she would be forced to relinquish her maternal care for her children, and her family and friends would despise her for joining the strange sect. If she refused to obey her husband, she would lose her children and be left without property or protection. Mary opted to uphold her obligations as a wife and go to the Enfield Shakers with Joseph. But first she extracted a promise from Joseph for separate housing and the authority to care for her own children. He agreed and in January 1813, Mary moved to the Enfield Shakers.

Having related the tale of how her family came to know Shakerism, the setting for the Dyers' drama moved to Enfield. *A Brief Statement* revealed Mary's next disappointment: there was no separate house for the Dyers, and Mary found she had no authority over her own children. At the Shaker village, Mary was punished and abused, segregated from her children, and continually harassed. Here for the public, for the first time in print, were the details of Mary's experience among the Shakers.

Mary Dyer's affidavits supported her assertions. Affidavits provided corroboration of the events Mary described and also attested to her reputation as a good wife and mother. Twenty-five individuals provided affidavits. The first affidavit was recorded on May 22, 1815, an early indication of her plan to pursue a legal resolution to her marital difficulties. Subsequent statements were recorded on January 25, 1816, three in early June 1817, and a final group in late May and early June 1818. Dyer also included several undated statements.

The affidavits took three forms. In the first format the affiant made a broad claim of acquaintance with Mary Dyer. Following a statement regarding the length of time an individual had known Mary, the affiant provided a description of her character. Betsey Tillotson, for example, swore to having known Mary for twenty-four years. Affidavits stated that Mary was "ever considered . . . to be a person of good character, . . . strict truth and veracity." Others remarked that they had never "known or heard of immoral or irregular conduct or behavior"; a reflection of the very same accusations Mary and other anti-Shaker writers had leveled against Shaker founder Ann Lee, repeating decades-old rumors and allegations Mary had learned through oral tradition.

The first ten affidavits (representing nineteen individuals) followed the format of length of acquaintance/statement of character and were undated, with the exception of a six-person group statement from Guildhall, Vermont. Affiants in this first grouping included former neighbors from Northumberland, where Dyer was raised, and Stewartstown, where she raised her children. To the reader unfamiliar with the northern New Hampshire locale in which this drama occurred, the affidavits provided one level of credibility. But to the reader personally acquainted with the characters in this debate, a second reading was possible based on the interrelationship of the actors, obscured in the text by different surnames. Betsy Tillotson, for example, was Mary's sister; Christopher Bailey, who led the Vermont group affidavit, was her brother-in-law; and Elisha Dyer was Joseph's cousin. For those readers familiar with the Dyer/Marshall families in Coös County, Mary Dyer's first affidavit was perhaps the most interesting. It was from Joseph Peverly, the town clerk of Northumberland and the father of Joseph Dyer's deceased first wife, Elizabeth. Not only were townspeople and family supporting Mary's cause, but Joseph's own former father-in-law, who had no consanguineous ties to Mary, supported her as well.

The second type of affidavit focused on specific contested events at the Enfield community. Jeremiah and Deborah Towle, with whom Mary stayed after her departure from Enfield, confirmed Joseph's promise to divide the children if Mary left the Shakers. Moody Rich reported that the Dyer marriage was happy until Joseph joined the Shakers and declared his marriage contract was dissolved, reinforcing Mary's claim that it was the Shakers who disrupted her family tranquility. Calvin Eaton and John Williams, both of whom claimed to have seen Mary at the Shaker village, described her poor health and miserable condition while at the Shakers. Thomas Tillotson (Mary's brother-in-law's father) recounted how Joseph neglected Mary and how he had refused to pay a bill of her making. These affidavits served to illustrate that

Joseph broke both his marriage contract and his agreement regarding the division of the children. The affidavits indicated that he also broke a community contract by refusing to pay a bill. They identified Joseph's connection with the Shakers as the root cause of his antisocial behavior. The affidavits in this second group were recorded in June of 1817 (Rich, Towles, and Eaton) and in 1818 (Tillotson in March and Williams in May), immediately prior to each of Dyer's legislative appearances.

Former Shakers living near the Enfield Shaker community provided the third and final group of affidavits. These statements indicated how Mary used the loosely connected web of Shaker apostates. Three statements attacked the Shakers for a variety of wrongdoings (dated between May 27 and June 3, 1818). Two statements described founder Ann Lee and her early followers' conduct, repeating charges of intemperance and naked dancing made in several previously published apostate accounts. John Heath complained that when he left the Enfield Shakers he received limited compensation for land he had brought to the community when he first joined, a complaint, again, shared by several earlier apostates. These final affidavits cast doubt on the behavioral and business propriety of the Shakers.

The entire corpus of affidavits appeared as an appendix following the main narrative and portrayed Mary as a quintessential American woman: pious, faithful, economical, industrious and concerned with her family. Affidavits emphasized Dyer's productive (and reproductive) labor as a member of her household, family, and community. Mary, her supporters insisted, did the work that led to personal and community success. Joseph's actions, instead of supporting his household and wife, disrupted Mary's world of home and family. The Shakers, her enemies, were depicted as liars and licentious. As Joseph considered himself a Shaker, he, too, held that character. The affidavits began with descriptions of Mary's character (where length of acquaintance equaled knowledge of her character), shifted to the specific impact of Shakerism on the Dyers, and concluded by displaying the alleged immorality of the Shaker movement at large. This sequence paralleled the opening sections of *A Brief Statement* where Mary began with statements of her position in society, then turned to the Shaker intrusion on the Dyers' lives, and finally moved to an indictment of Shaker life and theology. *A Brief Statement* was read widely because in the experience of one rural New Hampshire family, readers saw a warning for the country as a whole: forces that challenged family stability, challenged national stability.

Male affiants lent an authoritative voice to her claims. Her supporters included town clerks, lawyers, and numerous justices of the peace. The three female affiants merely echoed statements made by the men. Despite their authoritative voices, Dyer's affidavits came under suspicion and were soundly attacked in Joseph's *Compendious Narrative*. The argument over the veracity of her texts ran deeper than measuring truthfulness; it forced the reader to choose between conflicting images. The affidavits at the close of her treatise provided information by which the reading public could perceive Dyer as a dutiful wife, concerned mother, and Christian woman. Anti-Shaker statements, in the form of affidavits attacking Ann Lee, provided a contrasting female image making the difference between good and evil all the more clear. While Mary was the quintessential mother, Ann Lee and the Shakers were anti-family and "without natural affection."[78]

In *A Compendious Narrative* Joseph Dyer picked apart Mary's arguments by offering alternate interpretations and contrasting images. Joseph cited specific page numbers from Mary's book so curious readers could compare texts. His technique encouraged curious New Englanders to read both works and decide between the two versions. The book's format also reflected a legal strategy the Shakers employed to discredit their detractors. Joseph questioned Mary's version of events, cast doubt on the legitimacy of her sources, and, most devastatingly, attacked her character. Similar to his wife's text, Joseph's work included an appended section of affidavits to supplement his claims. Joseph's argument rested on two points: he was the rightful head of the family and Mary was an unfit mother.

Joseph began his tract "with reluctance and deep regret that I now undertake to disclose to the public that *refractory and imperious disposition* which Mary, my wife, retains."[79] And sharing a similarity with divorce trial pamphlets, Joseph stated plainly that discussion of family matters in public was repugnant; only out of a sense of duty to the public did he respond to Mary's misleading attack.[80] Joseph and Mary both cited duty as the motivation for writing their texts. Mary combined her personal duty to protect her children with her duty to society in her revelation that the Shakers duped unknowing novitiates and the public; Joseph felt it was his duty to enlighten the public about Mary's deceptions.

Joseph began his text with a statement of the Dyer marriage nearly identical to that in Mary's version: "In the year 1799, I, Joseph Dyer, was legally married."[81] While Mary focused on their experiences among the Shakers (where for her the difficulties began), Joseph focused on family life prior to Shaker involvement. This strategy diverted attention away from the maligned Shakers and towards Mary. Joseph's discussion of Mary as wife and mother revealed his expectations for his marriage. Joseph sought a wife who was his friend and helpmeet. When Mary refused him in bed he bemoaned that he had "no one to converse with upon retiring."[82] He expected his wife to care for the children, milk the cows, and obey her husband's will. Joseph's world was one of duty. He obeyed duty when he lent a saddle to a poor woman, duty when he provided for his family, duty in defending his new Shaker family, and duty owed "to the candid part of mankind" in his revelations of his side of the story. For Joseph, the roles of husband, wife, mother, and children were clear-cut. His problems began shortly after their marriage when Mary moved beyond her expected role.

Joseph portrayed Mary as domineering, willful, and cruel from the beginning of their marriage. He related numerous incidents where in a battle of will against will, Joseph determined the best course of action was submission. He was caught between a rock and a hard place, between living "in a state of perpetual uproar, or else condescend to let her do just as she pleases and yield an implicit obedience to her in all things." As Joseph "always abhorred quarreling," he wrote how he "submitted to the latter and thought at the time, that of the two evils I had chosen the least, but I have since doubted it."[83] To admit such a reversal of roles—the insubordinate wife, the condescending husband—was humiliating. Controlling his household was what provided a man with his social and political role. To lose that control over the family was, as legal historian Hendrik Hartog has described, "a disaster, a source of overwhelming shame."[84] Joseph carefully suggested that his submission was not a sign of weakness on his part, but rather, that this stance protected Mary from the injury she would cause herself if not given her way. Joseph depicted himself as the protector of his family who dutifully watched over his spouse, even to the point of self-sacrifice, a quality more often associated with mothers than with fathers.

Joseph's critique of Mary's ability and interest in motherhood formed the crux of his rebuttal. Where Mary had called her children "promising," Joseph described them as "peevish and cross," faulting her child-raising skills. Joseph complained that Mary's refusal to nurse babies and provide for the older children forced him to step into the maternal role, another reversal and a duty he clearly never expected to perform. Mary allegedly told Joseph, "Here! Take your brats and take care of them. I do not want the trouble of them and you need not have had the trouble of them, if you had not been a mind to. It is all your doing."[85] Far from the self-sacrificing mother depicted in *A Brief Statement,* Joseph portrayed Mary as selfish, egocentric, and unconcerned with the needs of her children and husband.[86]

Although children were the object over which the parental dispute occurred, neither parent's work offered any specific information about the five Dyer children as individuals. Both Mary and Joseph were more concerned with issues of child-rearing and discipline. Joseph claimed Mary disciplined to the point of abuse and described her whipping a child until she raised welts. Mary accused the Shakers of placing her son Orville in a darkened closet, an incident Mary related as evidence of the Shaker's inability to raise children. To Joseph, Mary disciplined in order to break a child's will, a position aligned with an evangelical view of child-rearing guided by "love and fear."[87] On the one hand, Joseph took a more moderate approach and suggested that the Shaker closet punishment was harmless since it caused no physical harm and Orville did not even remember it. On the other hand, he did not discount whipping as a punishment. In his recollection of the incident, he observed the whipping but claimed he did not want to question Mary's maternal role as disciplinarian, although he did question the severity of the beating. Mary described her children as blank slates, in need of the maternal guidance through their childhood that good republican mothers provided. Joseph offered little information on his personal view of children. In Mary and Joseph's texts, the children were not important per se. How Mary and Joseph acted in association with children, in their roles as a mother and as a father, was the important message.

Joseph argued that the Shakers were more moderate in their child-rearing strategies. Children were provided with education (even arithmetic for the girls, noted Joseph), were trained in a practical trade, given plenty of food and adequate rest. By his description, the Shakers molded children by "love and duty," a more flexible position that emphasized reciprocal obligations as necessary for the continuation of family and community. For the early-nineteenth-century public, Joseph presented an image of children being prepared for a future of their individual choosing. In the Dyer debate, methods of child-rearing appeared secondary to the character of the child-rearer, a reflection of the basis for custody decisions in the early nineteenth century. Joseph wrote how he doubted the sincerity of Mary's public expression of her desire to be a mother "for she has not performed the duty of a mother towards her children."[88] Mary attacked the Shakers, rather than Joseph, because they reared the children—a further reminder of Joseph's lack of authority.

Joseph also assaulted Mary's performance in the role of wife. Contrary to Mary's claim, Joseph insisted that it was Mary who broke the marriage bond by initiating a celibate relationship three years prior to moving to Enfield. Further, he lobbed the ultimate accusation against a spouse: adultery. Joseph accused Mary of having two extramarital affairs, the first with Elder Benjamin Putnam. Joseph stated that while Putnam was in their Stewartstown household "to have intimated that I doubted [Mary's] chastity would have been unpardonable," but since Mary had begun this war of words with her "unprovoked and audacious insults" her intolerable behavior had forced Joseph to lay bare the truth. Mary's desire for celibacy, Joseph alleged, was merely a means to get Joseph "out of the way" so that she might be with Putnam.[89] Yet when Putnam announced his plans to marry, Mary's anger replaced her prior sentiments and shortly thereafter Putnam left town. Shortly after, itinerant preacher Lemuel Crooker arrived, and Mary embarked on her second extramarital liaison. Joseph blamed Crooker, in part, for his wife's alleged infidelity, stating that Crooker flattered Mary "which took her feelings captive." "At length," Joseph wrote, "they became so familiar together and capriciously fond of each other that some of our Baptist brethren were seriously tried on account of their conduct."[90] Despite this egregious insult to his manhood and household, Joseph portrayed himself as a forgiving man having told Mary that "[i]f she would live with me as other women did with their husbands, I would overlook all that was past and would go no more to the Shakers." But Mary replied: "Joseph Dyer, you need not think to bring me to this. I will *die* before I will do it. Whether you go to the Shakers or not, I will never do it."[91] And "it," then as today, referred to sexual intercourse. It was Mary, Joseph revealed, that had ended the Dyer marriage, long before they joined the Shakers.

Joseph continued his attack when he combined what he described as Mary's "common deportment" with her frequently changing religious views. Joseph claimed Mary attempted to instigate a new system at the Shaker village, a system that would permit sexual relationships. In *A Brief Statement* Mary claimed that North Family Shaker John Lyon had been selected to follow and, she implied, do something horrible to her. In his narrative, Joseph accused Mary of lustfully chasing after Lyon whom she had selected as her potential mate simply because he was likely to be the next elder, an alignment that would bring Mary quickly to the top of Shaker leadership. Joseph justified his accusations. "Perhaps," Joseph wrote, "some may think that I have carried these things too far; but as Mary has called upon us to let her know what her unseemly conduct is, I felt it my duty to tell the truth as far as modesty will admit."[92] In other words, she asked for it.

Modesty did not prevent Joseph from leveling his final accusation of Mary's impropriety, although he did find it necessary to refer the reader to a Bible passage rather than state outright Sarah Curtis's revelation that Mary made a sexual advance towards her while at the Shaker village, an abuse of expected gender relations, of age, and of class, as Sarah had been Mary's household help and was considerably younger than Mary. Joseph took all of Mary's charges against the Shakers and pointed them back towards her. Having portrayed Mary as "entirely blind to that modesty which becomes one of her sex," Joseph depicted Mary as the opposite of everything a woman should be.[93] Mary, Joseph argued, did not leave the Enfield Shaker village because she was abused; Mary left because she was denied a leadership position and was unable to run things her way. Mary's insubordination—to her husband, to the Shaker leaders—was linked to a wider problem of the sexual control of women. Mary, while out of her husband's control both within and then outside of their marriage, was quite literally a "loose woman" whose, Norma Basch writes, "legal aggressiveness was translated into unregulated sexuality."[94]

The tension between Shaker celibacy and marital sexual relations formed a broad area of conflict in early nineteenth-century society. To Mary and her supporters, the Shaker stance on celibacy was contrary to the laws of God and nature. Mary argued that a celibate life was unnatural and made Shaker women (and men) unsuitable to raise children. At the same time, Mary accused the elders of hypocrisy and profligacy when she alleged that the elders and eldresses enjoyed what they denied to the common Shakers. Joseph's parry portrayed Mary as the sexual deviant, first in his accusation of her extramarital affairs, then in her avoidance of sex with her husband, and finally, in a veiled allegation that Mary made a sexual advance towards a woman. Joseph's accusations not only ran counter to the notion of woman as naturally moral, but also counter to the idea of woman as sexually passionless. Thus for Mary to be so overtly sexual was as unnatural as Shaker celibacy. As the Dyers argued about degrees and direction of sexual behavior, they made their accusations against a normative background of married, monogamous relationships with sexual intercourse as an act necessary for reproduction.

A Compendious Narrative included twenty-one affidavits in support of Joseph's assertions. Like Mary, Joseph included statements from former Stewartstown neighbors, as well as from two former house girls, Susanna and Sarah Curtis, who had each worked for the Dyers just prior to their involvement with the Shakers. These affidavits indicated that Mary expressed the initial and more zealous interest in Shakerism. The Curtis girls also reported that Mary was an unwilling mother and unfaithful wife.

Shakers provided the majority of Joseph's affidavits. These included devastating statements from Caleb and Betsey Dyer, the oldest of the Dyer children. Caleb and Betsey, then ages 18 and 16 respectively, stated they were happy to be with the Shakers and considered the Enfield community their home. Betsey's only regret was watching her mother's actions towards her father, disappointed that Mary's actions had wreaked havoc on Betsey's biological family and the Shaker family that replaced it. Joseph Dyer's kin provided affidavits as well. Betsey Tillotson and Elisha Dyer, who had also provided statements to Mary, made supporting statements for Joseph, too.

In *A Compendious Narrative,* twenty-one affidavits attested to Joseph's kindness and Mary's obsessive behavior. The affidavits were detailed eyewitness accounts whereas those Mary included were based more on hearsay. Her statements described what petitioners had *not* heard, rather than what they *had* heard, an observation that Joseph did not fail to make. As Mary's text included her petition to the New Hampshire legislature, Joseph reprinted the Shaker *Remonstrance,* concluding Joseph's work with a reiteration of the Shaker philosophy of living a Christ-like life and Mary's refusal to live by those tenets.

Joseph argued backed by the laws of God and the laws of man. In a letter to Mary, included in his book, Joseph reminded her that the legal expenses she was accruing were being paid for out of their property, not from Shaker coffers, and warned her that if she persisted in her claims, there would shortly be no property left to support her. Joseph's veiled threat hinted at Mary's potentially dismal economic future: no support, no property, and no children. Married, separated, or divorced, there would be no source of support.

In placing petition and remonstrance before the legislature and parallel pamphlets before the reading public, Mary and Joseph invited the public into their personal drama. Divorce, writes Norma Basch, is a "form of moral theater," and although neither Joseph nor Mary had yet petitioned for divorce, the construction of their testimony and their printed tracts clearly revealed their cognizance of the prevailing standards of guilt and innocence.[95] While contemporary readers see room for fault on both sides—a demanding husband, an ambitious wife— nineteenth-century viewers looked for a guilty party and an innocent victim. In this either/or context, Mary and Joseph framed their stories. The children were little discussed because they were not the central issue. The key point was this: Was Mary a proper wife? Was Joseph a proper husband? Whoever neglected their role was the one that destroyed the Dyer family.

As Mary Dyer's attack broadened beyond her personal history to an all-out attack on Shakerism, the voice of the Shaker response shifted from Joseph to the Shaker leadership. Joseph's pamphlet, however, continued to be read and utilized in the Shakers' ongoing battle with Mary. The Harvard (Massachusetts) Ministry requested a copy of *A Compendious Narrative* to present to an inquirer "as Mary Dyer's Books is handed round about here . . . I want Joseph Woods . . . [to have] an opportunity to read and hear both sides."[96] A second edition of *A Compendious Narrative* was published in 1826 with a new preface to counter renewed agitation, especially in western Massachusetts. Joseph Dyer's *Narrative* was still in use to refute Mary's allegations in 1847. But in 1817 and 1818, Mary Dyer's battle with the Shakers had only just begun.

3

The World Worked Up to Some Purpose

Although her legislative appearance, books, and newspapers had brought Mary notoriety and general sympathy for her plight, the legislators and publications did little to help Mary retrieve her children. Now Mary needed to turn "tender feelings" into direct action from sympathetic supporters. In 1818 and 1819, Dyer motivated the residents of Enfield, New Hampshire, to come to her aid in three dramatic events: a mobbing at the Shaker village, a forty-seven person petition to the legislature, and a lawsuit against Joseph Dyer. These three events brought Enfield residents to the forefront of Dyer's quest, and each event defined the boundaries of Enfield's communities—town and Shaker enclave—and reaffirmed expected behaviors from men, women, husbands, and wives. As family stability portended community stability, the breakdown of the Dyer family and the unique nature of the Shaker family provided a warning of the dire consequences of challenging social norms.

Although ostensibly helping Mary Dyer, the actions of men in these events reflected a male agenda and the public sphere in which they traditionally moved. In the mob at Enfield, the town selectmen and local officials acted (to varying degrees) on the behalf of Eunice Chapman and Mary Dyer who they understood as women in need of protection, that which their husbands had failed to provide. Chapman received support from men throughout the five day mob event and achieved some success. During the same event, Dyer's support faded and she was disappointed in her quest. And although the local officials worked to help the women retrieve their children, their real agenda was to keep the town peace by forcing adherence to community standards. Similarly, Mary interpreted Joshua Stevens's petition to the New Hampshire legislature (requesting assistance with the problem of wives displaced by Shaker husbands) as support for her cause. Yet Stevens and his forty-seven cosigners were more interested in a quiet community and avoiding a heavier tax burden than they were with the plight of a bereaved mother. And finally, when James Willis sued Joseph Dyer for a debt Mary contracted, he brought to the forefront her need for protection and support. Yet again the bottom line was economic: Joseph's refusal to pay a debt of his wife's abrogated standard community practices for the buying and selling of goods. Men and women worked together in these events, but they worked toward different goals.

The Mob at Enfield

The mob at Enfield brought violence to the Shakers. In 1818 Mary Dyer, with Eunice Chapman, mobilized a network of supporters and made a show of strength in a mob attack. This strategy was more physical and direct than endlessly debated legislative petitions and quietly read books. Yet print culture played an important role in this event. Prior to the mob, Eunice Chapman sent her books to Enfield for general distribution, familiarizing local residents with her situation and priming residents for action. The books "were read, and excited indignation against the Shakers, and spread terror amongst them."[1] After the mob, the incident became a central event in subsequent publications, including those of Mary Dyer and of Abram Van Vleet, an anti-Shaker supporter in Ohio.

Mobs were part of a long tradition of acts of public disorder. Although in current usage the word "mob" carries with it the idea of an uncontrolled frenzy, research from the perspectives of history and social science has shown otherwise. In fact, mobs contained an order, distinct behaviors, and goals.[2] Raising a mob against the Shakers was one of the earliest and most violent forms of anti-Shaker activity. Frightful mobs harassed, threatened, and injured Shakers throughout founder Ann Lee's proselytizing journey across New England (1781–1783). In the eighteenth century, a mob gathering reflected the prevailing cultural ideology of a corporate community. An attack against the Shakers signaled that the local populace viewed the Shakers as a threat to the welfare of society as a whole.[3] The anti-Shaker mob's goal was to remove physically the Shaker leaders from their towns and thus prevent further conversion to Shakerism. During Ann Lee's journeys, the early Shaker missionaries were stoned, beaten, and chased out of town. In an early nineteenth-century attack on the Turtle Creek, Ohio, Shakers, a mob burned the platform on which the Shakers practiced their religious dances in an attempt to stop Shaker worship services.[4] The mob effectively replaced the public performance of Shaker worship with their own public performance of anti-Shaker activity.

The action of the 1818 Enfield mob shared similarities to public protests against other religious sectarians. Yet unlike the eighteenth-century anti-Shaker protests, in the Enfield mob the concern was not theology per se but rather the Shaker treatment of women and children. The participants in the mob included townspeople from Enfield from a variety of social levels including judges, a state representative, and the town selectmen. In general, the mob sought to force the Shakers to provide better treatment for nonbelieving wives, and specifically, the mob attempted to obtain the release of the children of Eunice Chapman and Mary Dyer. The participation of local authorities reflected the still accepted belief that a mob was a tolerated bending of civil law to fight against, in this instance, the Shaker assault on natural law.

The Enfield mob of May 1818 did not erupt spontaneously. It was a planned action that grew out of face-to-face discussions between Mary Dyer and Eunice Chapman, who had secretly traveled from New York State to New Hampshire. In March, Eunice had received a legislative divorce from her husband, James, and had received guardianship of her three children. But at that time, she did not know their location. Acting on a tip that her children were hidden in New Hampshire, Eunice traveled to Enfield and arrived in mid-May. Although she traveled undercover, local residents discovered her purpose and sent for Mary Dyer. This was the first meeting of Chapman and Dyer, although the two women had corresponded with one another for several months. Eunice and Mary stayed at James Willis's inn in Enfield Center and made their plan, confiding only in those who could help them. The initial plan called for Dyer and several women to travel to the Shakers and request a visit with the Dyer children. Once admitted, the group would request to see Chapman's children as well. At that point Eunice would take the Shakers by surprise, bursting in on the group and taking away her children. One of the Dyer-Chapman confidants, however, alerted the Shakers to the impending visit and this forced Mary and Eunice to alter their strategy.[5]

The mob event provides a good example of how Dyer and Chapman gained access to power despite the legal limitations accorded their gender. Male authorities responded to the bereaved mothers and took up their cause. Dyer and Chapman used the symbols of mother and children and their own gender to reinforce their helpless position. They understood themselves as powerless and in need of assistance to achieve their goals. When local authorities moved to action and took control, they reinforced the idea of a public feminine submission. Dyer and Chapman, in effect, used powerlessness to gain power.

On Monday, May 25, the Shakers learned that Eunice and Mary "with their forces" (supportive townspeople) planned to come to the village the following morning at 8 AM Several of the male leaders and Joseph Dyer were absent from the Shaker village, and the remaining community members had good reason to worry about the gathering mob. In an attempt to preempt violence, the Shakers sent Judge Edward Evans, who on previous occasions had assisted Mary Dyer, to speak to Eunice and Mary and reach a compromise on visiting the children. Chapman refused to bargain as she intended not to go to the Shakers unless she could take away her children. Evans agreed to escort Chapman to the Shakers the following morning.

On Tuesday morning, May 26, Evans returned to Willis's inn to escort Chapman but arrived to find a disturbance. Joseph Merrill, an Enfield selectman and justice of the peace, was in the crowd, and the two attorneys argued with one another. Merrill had visited the Shaker village the day before, and the Shakers had quizzed him about the gathering mob and pleaded with him as "an officer of the peace" to quell the attack. Instead, Merrill supported the notion of a show of town strength. Evans argued that the Shakers would not respond to such a large crowd coming to visit the children, and he drew up a list of proposed visitors that he carried out to the Shakers. But as Evans returned to the inn with the Shakers' counterproposal, Dyer and Chapman were already headed towards the Shaker community with an entourage behind them "some on gigs and some on horseback."[6] His attempts at mediation having failed, Evans decided to return to town.

At the Shaker village both the mob and the Shakers attempted to gain control of the volatile situation. The Shakers did not want to expose the Chapman and Dyer children (eight children in total) to such a large number of excited visitors, fearful that, as had happened at other Shaker villages, the mob would simply surround the children and take them away. The Shakers agreed to permit Chapman and Dyer along with selectman Merrill, Jesse Fogg (Enfield's representative to the legislature), and their wives visit the children in the Dwelling House. Chapman refused this offer and insisted the children be brought to her in the Trustee's Office. This standoff was the first phase of the extended event. Merrill and Fogg and their wives decided to visit with the children at the Dwelling House. Next, Dyer went down, and finally, after a two-hour standoff and a personal invitation from her thirteen-year-old son George, Eunice Chapman made her way to the Dwelling House. The Shakers gained the first victory in forcing the visitors to go to the Dwelling House—a private Shaker setting as opposed to the more public (and worldly) Trustee's Office.

The visit was difficult for both women. Eunice had not seen her children in over two years. When she saw her daughters, she wept uncontrollably—joyful at the reunion but fearful of the changes in their manner. Her youngest daughter, Julia, refused to sit in her lap, and Susan, age twelve, became alarmed when Eunice removed her Shaker cap. Although Eunice had brought a gift of a "handsome" doll, her young daughter did not want it. Both girls stated that they wished to remain at the village. Mary's visit was equally distressing. Betsey and Caleb intervened between Mary and their younger siblings and insisted that they were all well cared for and that none of them wished to leave. Mary's recollection of this day focused on young Joseph, now nine years old, whom she held in her lap. In a clever use of Shaker phraseology, Mary asked Joseph if he would like to come and live with her "if it was the gift." The "gift" indicated a God-directed, elders-sanctioned action, and thus young Joseph, fully socialized into Shaker life, responded "Yes." At this point, Caleb, Betsey, and Shaker Deacon Nathaniel Draper whisked the youngster out of the room, angry at Mary's cleverness. The Shakers attempted to keep an aura of civility in the proceedings and served supper to the six visitors before they returned to Enfield. Although Eunice, the Shakers recorded, spoke rudely, the Merrills and Foggs appreciated the Shakers' hospitality. This concluded the first phase of the mob event.

In private correspondence the Shakers described Eunice and Mary in terms of their language. Mary's tone was "very high" and Eunice's was "very haughty." A Shaker diarist who recorded the events of this tumultuous week made a point to note some of Eunice's threats. To Shaker James Pettingill she warned, "I will scare you yet and make you tremble, it is a mercy you are not all dashed to pieces, you know what I have done in the state of New York." When Pettingill replied insultingly, "You do look some scarrish," Eunice responded with another threat: "Scarrish! I could scare you to non-existence. I have scared six smarter men than you are." Pettengill concluded that "it [was] a pitty [sic] . . . that the United States are so reduced as to be stirred up by two old women running up and down the streets."[7]

The second phase of the mob event occurred the following day, Wednesday, May 27, and indicated the rapidly shifting power relationships. Towards the end of the day, Mary Dyer with six or eight women traveled to the Shaker village. Compared to Chapman, Dyer had the weaker claim to see her children. She did not have legal custody, and thus local authorities hesitated to interfere in what was still seen as a marital dispute between Joseph and Mary. Her appearance at the Shakers without the accompaniment of authorities, or even any men, underscored her weaker position. On the previous day, the Shakers permitted Dyer a visit out of courtesy and in a controlled situation with important witnesses present. This day, the Shakers refused to let Mary enter the community, and this encounter ended with Dyer's threats of greater action against the Shakers. The warning rattled the Shakers and James Chapman, fearing a night attack, hid his children.

The next afternoon, Eunice Chapman returned with local resident Samuel Cochran and his wife. She demanded to see her former husband but James could not be found. The Shakers invited Eunice into their building to wait for his return, but Eunice made good on her threats and instead stood in the road "hailing everyone that passed along, and telling them how bad the Shakers used her."[8] This continued until six in the evening. News of the ruckus traveled back to town and by evening Squire Merrill, Samuel Cochran, and twelve to fourteen men arrived at the Shaker village and demanded to see James Chapman. Merrill and Cochran led the group. Merrill made a long speech with many threats directed towards the Shakers. He began with an assertion that the group did not come for a riot, nor for the Dyer children. They sought the Chapman children and insisted upon a meeting with James, whom they implicitly recognized as possessing the power to release the children. Merrill asserted loudly that James Chapman had escaped the laws of New York by fleeing to New Hampshire. James's escape from justice, and the Shakers' refusal to help Eunice, had "stirred up" people's minds. Merrill declared that the treatment of Eunice, and by extension Mary, was "contrary to the laws of God and man," and the group would not leave until "satisfaction was given."[9] As darkness fell, more townspeople gathered at the Shaker community. One Shaker estimate recorded that more than one hundred people surrounded the village. Some patrolled on horses, and others hid under fences. Shaker John Lyon asked Merrill as an officer of the peace to disperse the crowd, but Merrill refused.

After dark, James Chapman appeared and met with Eunice in the North House shop. The meeting was quite volatile and lasted until 11 PM. James and Eunice argued about the truth of her publications and a division of the children. Eunice suggested James could keep George, to which she acknowledged he had some claim, but she pleaded for the girls. The Chapmans could not come to an agreement regarding the division of the children, and Eunice and Merrill threatened to bring 500 people to the village the following day. While this lengthy argument dragged on into the night, Mary Dyer worked in the background and found a way to remove James Chapman from the debate. At 11 PM town officials produced a warrant for the arrest of James Chapman for previous abuse to Mary Dyer—the incident when James Chapman and Joseph Dyer forcibly dragged Mary out of the North Family Dwelling House and deposited her in the street. Some of the gathered crowd returned to their homes, but others interpreted James's arrest as the removal of the last obstacle to obtaining the children. When Eunice announced she would not leave the Shaker village, the crowd took matters into their own hands and searched the village for the children. Around 1 AM Enfield resident Moses Johnson discovered George hidden in a barn. The rest of the mob broke up. Although she had hoped to retrieve her daughters as well, Eunice immediately fled New Hampshire with George and returned to New York State. First, George represented tangible proof that James had removed the children from New York State. Upon her return to Albany, Eunice could receive a writ of habeas corpus to acquire, without a mob, her daughters. Second, Eunice realized that the aggressive means by which she ultimately recovered George shaded on an illegal procedure, and it was best to absent herself from the fallout of such an action. Finally, and most importantly, George was unwilling to leave. When Eunice placed him in a carriage, he attempted to run back to the Shakers. Eunice wrote how "he came near to dragging me out [of the carriage] head first upon the ground, but I did not quit my hold." Eunice found she had to hold him in the moving carriage, so that he would not jump out. Eunice wrote how she " . . . had to lay my commands upon him, told him he must go with me and stay until he was 14, [then] he could choose for himself."[10] To prevent his return to the Shakers, either by his own volition or by a Shaker attempt to retrieve him, Eunice placed as much distance as possible between George and Enfield and made a rapid return to Albany.

The following morning, Friday, May 29, the Shakers lodged a formal complaint with Judge Blaisdell of the nearby village of Canaan. Blaisdell called together the principal mob participants including Joseph Merrill, the Shaker leaders, and Mary Dyer. He rebuked the group for such a disorderly proceeding and especially castigated Merrill for permitting the unlawful search of the Shaker village. When Blaisdell described Eunice Chapman as a "very bad character," Dyer argued that women like herself and Chapman were helpless against Shaker husbands. Blaisdell urged Dyer to petition the legislature. Although Mary portrayed this incident in her writings as evidence of Blaisdell's support, in reality Blaisdell urged the resolution of disputes through legal measures, rather than mob action.[11]

The mob at Enfield combined elements of the eighteenth-century public disorder tradition as well as elements more prevalent in the nineteenth century. Particularly reminiscent of efforts to enforce community standards in the eighteenth century was the practice of charivari, a noisy clanging of pots, pans, and other objects used to serenade a newly wed couple, or to disturb the sleep of someone who has transgressed community norms. In the Enfield incident, charivari took the form of guns firing night and day to keep the Shakers on edge. The mob event did not aim to annihilate the Shaker faith, as had been the goal of anti-Shaker mobs in the eighteenth century, but rather to force the Shakers to treat mothers and wives more in-line with community standards. The local authorities played a supporting role. Evans worked to keep the situation from exploding with a plea to Eunice to be calm and not cause trouble. He offered to accompany Eunice to the Shakers as she was a stranger in town. Given her attempts to rile up local residents through her books and secret presence, her initial plan to suddenly storm the Shakers and grab her children, as well as her stubborn refusal to compromise, Evans reasoned that alone Eunice was a loose cannon likely to explode. His presence would serve to prevent a potentially dangerous confrontation. But when Eunice and Mary took control, and Evans met the mob headed towards the Shaker village, he realized his attempts at a peaceful compromise were in vain and he absented himself from the event.

Merrill took a more active role and spoke on the behalf of the townspeople. When he threatened to raise a larger mob, it may well have been a bluff. At the Shakers, Merrill took control of the situation. His lengthy speech focused the demands of the mob on securing the Chapman children. Merrill addressed his speech more to the large crowd than to the Shakers. In asserting that James Chapman was a fugitive from justice and should be removed from New Hampshire, Merrill focused the crowd's wrath on one individual, instead of Shakers in general. In arguing that Eunice had been badly treated, Merrill kept the restoration of her children in the forefront, rather than an assault on Shakerism. Merrill's speech united the large crowd and prevented random mob violence by focusing attention on specific goals and by providing a time period in which hot tempers could cool. Most of the mob heeded his words and when James Chapman was arrested and removed, most of the local residents also departed. Consistent with nineteenth-century patterns of mob action, as a local authority, Merrill worked to enforce religious tolerance while still attending to local concerns. His refusal to disperse the crowd showed solidarity with his constituency and ultimately prevented the collective group from degenerating into one hundred angry individuals. His efforts maintained religious tolerance and maintained order in society.

The mob event presented a public performance of power. The local participants demonstrated what they felt was their right to define and enforce community standards of behavior. This belief was supported by the lack of opposing action on the part of local officials. Residents enacted their power by presenting a large gathering and in harassing the Shakers by patrolling the community borders and by firing guns. The Shakers, Dyer and Chapman, and local residents all called upon the power of local officials. The Shakers wanted the officials to stop the event. Dyer and Chapman sought allies to use power on their behalf, and local residents looked to authorities for support. Merrill used his position to speak for the crowd and simultaneously to the crowd, controlling the potentially dangerous situation. While Merrill controlled a good portion of the mob event, in the end Eunice Chapman's power superceded his.

Mary and Eunice used cultural and social powerlessness to gain access to power via Merrill and Evans, as well as through local male residents. Additionally, they used women's powerless position as part of their initial plan to retrieve the children. They had planned to travel to the Shakers in a group of women, an attempt to catch the Shakers unaware and use the power of perceived powerlessness to grab the children. At the morning meeting at Willis's inn, Eunice and Mary seized control when they refused to wait for Evans's return from the Shakers and led the crowd themselves to the Shaker village. Eunice also took control from Merrill after James Chapman's arrest. Refusing to leave the Shakers without her children, Eunice incited the crowd to search the village.

Dyer and Chapman succeeded in stirring up the town of Enfield to come to their defense. Eunice in particular garnered the support of authorities as her claim to her children was backed by the New York legislature. This legitimacy provided the basis for Evans's initial offer to escort Chapman to the Enfield Shakers and Merrill's subsequent assistance. On the other hand, while the town sympathized with Dyer, the authorities refused to interfere in her situation and promised the Shakers they would make no attempt to take the Dyer children. Unlike Chapman, Dyer's petition to the New Hampshire legislature had not become law. Evans did not offer to escort Dyer. On Mary's subsequent visit to the village, several women, not men, accompanied her.

News of the mob at Enfield traveled fast. Towns as far away as Boston to the south, Salisbury, New Hampshire, to the east, and Champlain, Vermont, to the northwest were aware of the event and offered support to residents of Enfield against the Shakers. Like many of the anti-Shaker mobs, a few principal actors interacted with the Shakers while the large crowd formed a menacing background. Although the potential for violence was very real, once a goal was attained, the mob dispersed.

The *Dartmouth Gazette* carried the news of Chapman's successful retrieval of her son, George. James left Enfield in October 1818 in an attempt to retrieve George, but once he arrived in New York State, he was advised there was nothing he could do unless the legislative act that granted guardianship to Eunice was repealed. He had left his daughters at Enfield although the Shakers insisted he indenture them to a person from the world so that they would have a defender should another mob event occur. The following year, Eunice returned to Enfield and, armed with a writ of habeas corpus, legally retrieved her daughters.[12] But before she retrieved her daughters, Eunice Chapman guaranteed the mob event would gain wider notice when she wrote to Abram Van Vleet, an anti-Shaker ally who made both Chapman's and Dyer's stories public.

Van Vleet was the editor of the Lebanon, Ohio, *Western Star* and had taken it upon himself to fight the Shakers. He was acquainted with the Shakers because of his close proximity to the seat of western Shakerism, Union Village, Ohio and had taken a strong stance against the Shakers' dealings with families. Van Vleet frequently published articles on the Shakers, both articles he had written about local events and those he republished from other newspapers. When Chapman informed him of her difficulties, as well as those of Dyer, Van Vleet saw an opportunity. In the summer of 1818 he wrote to Dyer and requested information on her situation. Dyer responded quickly and sent Van Vleet a copy of *A Brief Statement*. On July 11, Van Vleet published in his newspaper extracts from letters from Eunice Chapman and Mary Dyer and selections from Eunice's pamphlet. He announced plans to reprint Chapman's work. Van Vleet republished Chapman's *No. 2* in Ohio and included Dyer's statements as an appendix. Chapman's report on the mob was also included in Van Vleet's publication and served as a literary link between Chapman and Dyer's stories. Advertisements in the *Western Star* indicate the pamphlet was ready for sale by February 1819 at a cost of thirty-seven and one-half cents.

Van Vleet was a formidable force in western anti-Shaker sentiment. As the editor of the *Western Star* he had the means to distribute information throughout the area of the western Shaker settlements. Shaker correspondence frequently commented on his troublesome activities and power. The publication of Van Vleet's compendium of anti-Shaker materials reinvigorated anti-Shaker sentiment around Union Village. In 1819, the Union Village ministry reported that although local persecutors had been quiet, "[s]ince Eunice Chapman's & Mary Dier's [*sic*] false publications and false witnesses have been reprinted at Lebanon here and circulated through the whole country, the world has worked up to some purpose."[13] Residents of Ohio and nearby Kentucky, the site of the Pleasant Hill and South Union Shaker villages, could do nothing practical to help Dyer. Still, Van Vleet's actions spread the women's stories and connected eastern and western anti-Shakerism, both ideologically and by introducing eastern anti-Shakers to western anti-Shaker readers. His opportunism in publishing their tales served his own agenda as well: making money and advancing his own anti-Shaker cause in Ohio, a battle he had waged in his newspaper.

The eastern Shakers sent pamphlets out west, both Mary's and Joseph's, to inform western Shaker leaders of their dispute. They queried various western communities as to whether such information had arrived independently by way of anti-Shaker supporters. In a long letter to Union Village, the New Lebanon ministry described Chapman and Dyer. Chapman was an "audacious wicked little creature" and Dyer "seems to be a more finished instrument of the devil than Eunice."[14] The New Lebanon ministry felt that Eunice would eventually lose her supporters because they would become ashamed of her allegedly drunken behavior in the streets of Albany and her arrest for assault. Dyer, however, was another story, and the New Lebanon ministry warned the western leaders that if they had not heard of her yet, they would shortly because "she and Eunice and the apostates in Ohio have considerable correspondence together in writing."[15] Their advice to their brethren in the west was to reprint Joseph's *A Compendious Narrative* and James Chapman's *Memorial* as needed. The Ohio Shakers did not immediately publish the tracts but decided to "wait and see what effect [Mary and Eunice's] slanders & lies would have on mankind." A few months later, the Union Village Shakers announced they had decided the time had come to publish against the anti-Shaker writers.[16]

The Shaker entry into this print war took the form of a detailed rebuttal from Union Village Shaker Richard McNemar. McNemar wrote and published *The Other Side of the Question* in the fall of 1819.[17] The prolific McNemar used this work to vindicate "the character of Mother [Ann Lee] and the Elders." McNemar's book was organized in three parts. The first described the proceedings of Eunice Chapman with the New York legislature. McNemar printed part of Eunice's allegations and then countered with James's *Memorial*. In Part Two, McNemar focused on Mary Dyer and printed some of her accusations followed by Joseph Dyer's response. Part Three concerned the publications of Abram Van Vleet against the Union Village Shakers. McNemar argued that the Shakers deserved the chance to refute the remarkable and strange stories that had been circulated in Ohio for the past two or three years, stories that emanated from Van Vleet's newspaper, the *Western Star*. McNemar stated how the Shakers were glad to expose the occasional bad apple in their midst, but that alone was not a cause to dismiss the entire religion. Further, the crimes that had been alleged as a society-wide practice had grown out of the Chapmans' and Dyers' "domestic broils" and were thus hardly a true indication of the faith.

McNemar included several affidavits. One was from Josiah Terry, who having left the Enfield Shakers and the Albany area, had made his way across the country to the Union Village Shakers where, as surprising as it seems, he sought another privilege, or opportunity, to be a Shaker. Terry reported that he regretted providing an affidavit for Chapman and that when he spoke to her, he had no intention of making his statements public. He also described his experience with the Enfield Shakers as comfortable until he gave up the faith during his final two years at the village. Terry had realized the errors of his way and wanted once again to live with the Believers.[18]

McNemar also attacked the character of anti-Shaker author Thomas Brown who had written a statement in support of Eunice Chapman that had appeared in Van Vleet's work. McNemar considered Brown "a cypher," a nonentity, and explained that since Brown never lived with the Shakers, but only nearby, he had no true knowledge upon which to base his 1812 book. Finally, McNemar included depositions from current Shakers that stated their satisfaction with the faith and a statement from James Smith, the son of Colonel James Smith who earlier (1810) had published two anti-Shaker pamphlets on behalf of his daughter-in-law. James Smith reported that his father's allegations of child abuse among the Shakers were simply untrue.

Through the efforts of Van Vleet and McNemar, Dyer's story had spread to the western Shaker regions. Included as a part of McNemar's multivocalic tract and Van Vleet's anti-Shaker tome, Dyer's work was connected in the minds of the public to a web of apostates stretching across the country. Apostate Absolem Blackburn, writing in the 1820s, applauded James Smith, Dyer, Chapman, and Van Vleet's activities and saw himself as the heir to their campaign, aligning himself with the apostate network. He, in fact, had first learned about their anti-Shaker activities through Van Vleet's text.[19] Having been resident at both Union Village and the ill-fated Busro, Indiana, Shaker communities, Blackburn had access to McNemar's work as well. Blackburn had the opportunity, as New Hampshire booksellers had urged, to "read both sides." When he later had reason to fight the Shakers, Van Vleet's text taught Blackburn about anti-Shakerism, introducing him to its latest leaders, training him to be an apostate, and perpetuating anti-Shaker claims. This power of print to educate readers on the scope and methods of anti-Shakerism was, as the Shakers had phrased it, a considerable "stumbling block" to the continued existence of the Shakers.

The Petition of Joshua Stevens, et al.

Eunice Chapman had primed the Enfield residents for battle when she sent ahead copies of her anti-Shaker pamphlets. Riling up the crowd in print and then in person, Chapman and Dyer garnered support and drew clear boundaries between the various communities of people who lived in Enfield: those who were Shakers, and those who were not. And while the town of Enfield supported in spirit the mothers' quest to retrieve their children, Mary's and Eunice's very public protest of Shaker treatment led Enfield residents to petition the June 1818 session of the New Hampshire legislature for assistance. Their written complaint revealed concerns beyond that of the Dyer and Chapman children. Residents of Enfield wanted the legislature to enact laws which would, in their ultimate effect, maintain community peace and prevent an undue tax burden.

Joshua Stevens represented forty-seven male residents when he requested that the 1818 legislature force the Shakers to provide for the wives and children of male converts. He accused the Shakers of being "destitute of human feeling" and suggested that children brought into Shakerism "were taken away by violence from their mother's arms." These "distressed females" had been "imposed upon" and "abused in a most disgraceful and shameful manner." The petitioners requested an unspecified law to be passed, "similar to a law that has been passed in the State of New York." Failing passage of a law, the residents urged the legislature to "take some other measures to relieve [women] and all others in a similar situation. . . ." They also wanted the legislature to relieve "the community from hearing the cries of those distressed women." The last phrase is key: Enfield residents wanted quiet.[20]

The petition asked for a law to help women such as Mary Dyer, who is, briefly, named specifically, but also revealed that concern was not really toward the ill-treated women but rather for the residents of Enfield who complained of frequent disturbances "time and again" from women "crying in the streets and going from house to house mourning about their situation," the same language (noise-making women in the streets) Shaker James Pettingill used to insult Dyer and Chapman. Both Pettingill and Stevens focused on the women's public display of emotion. To Stevens and his petitioners, the recent mob indicated the social disorder that resulted from the Shaker annulment of marriages. Stevens and others feared the taxpayers of Enfield would be forced to support the wives and children of Shaker husbands as the new town poor. Worse yet, these noisy women were "from a distance," outsiders that the town should not be obligated to support. But a wife's residence (and hence jurisdiction of difficulties) was determined by where her husband resided so in the situation of spouses estranged by Shakerism, worldly wives were forced to turn to the local officials of the town in which the Shaker village sat. To the residents of Enfield, this placed an unfair burden on the town. Economics and the desire for social order was at the heart of their petition. The petitioners placed blame squarely on the Shakers who "by their conduct . . . are disturbing the peace of the community at large." The Shaker disavowal of marriage, their celibate lives, and communitywide bonds of brotherly and sisterly love challenged the early-nineteenth-century definition of family and forced the residents of Enfield to hear crying women in the streets.

Shakerism disrupted the family and upset traditional gender roles. When Shakerism divided a family, vulnerable, pious women who refused to join the sect were left without their husband's protection. Joseph had neglected the expectations of husbands, but Mary transgressed the boundaries of a woman's proper behavior. Some women, like Dyer and Chapman, stepped into a public and vocal role disturbing the peace with their call to arms. Far from the revered domestic early-nineteenth-century woman, these wives of Shaker husbands with their high and haughty tones made a public display of the limitations of coverture. Their private domestic lives were made shockingly visible in the public sphere and both the Shakers and the residents of Enfield would agree, this had, as Pettengill remarked, "reduced" American society. The distressed women went from "house to house" threatening the petitioners' own domestic tranquility with this noisy display. The Shakers' unorthodox life created the situation, but who was responsible for the solution? The townspeople of Enfield pointed to the Shakers, the Shakers pointed to the women's husbands. To put order back into society, an order where women remained in their private domestic sphere and not in the public street, and where husbands and families took care of their own, Enfield turned to the legislature.

The legislature ultimately dismissed the petition of Joshua Stevens on the grounds that the occurrences of women being denied visits with their Shaker children were not, in fact, common. As the Shakers had demonstrated during the mob event, both Chapman and Dyer were permitted visits under controlled circumstances. The legislature reaffirmed the Shaker right to arrange their family any way they so desired, as long as reasonable concessions were made to the needs of biological families left behind. Although a more or less peaceful relationship between the Shakers and the town of Enfield had been reestablished, simmering tensions between communal group and neighboring village remained. In 1828, two hundred petitioners, led by James Willis (in 1828 Enfield's representative to the legislature), complained to the legislature that the Enfield Shakers forced husbands to violate the marriage contract, taught husbands to hate their wives, and by presenting false information prevented children from making a rational decision whether to remain with the Shakers or leave. The boundaries of communities were once again sharply drawn. After a lengthy series of delays and extensions, the legislature dismissed the petition. Both at Enfield and other Shaker sites, flare-ups between Shakers and surrounding communities continued throughout the antebellum nineteenth century, each social drama highlighting tensions between changing societal norms and the communal experiment.[21]

Willis v. Dyer

Mary Dyer was not as fortunate as Eunice Chapman in retrieving her children. After her second petition to the legislature was dismissed Dyer traveled across New Hampshire during the summer and fall of 1818, speaking about her experiences and collecting affidavits for a third petition to the legislature and for her second book. Drawing on an ever-expanding network, Shaker apostates carried her from town to town and introduced Mary to others who could provide information or assistance. With a divorce bill yet to be made, Dyer's living arrangements were unstable, and Joseph bounced Mary from boardinghouse to boardinghouse at his will. Mary accused Joseph of moving her whenever he felt the rooming housekeepers sympathized with her plight, an accurate complaint. Mary boarded with the Paynes of

Lebanon from October 1818 to January 1819. Joseph then moved Mary to the Lebanon home of Rhoda Flood where Mary remained during the winter. Mary returned to her mother's in Northumberland for four weeks in the spring of 1819.

The New Hampshire ministry, with cautious optimism, described Joseph as "firmly established in the faith and . . . a useful man altho' he has been greatly afflicted in consequence of Mary's malicious conduct."[22] Part of those afflictions were legal; in June 1818 Mary Dyer acted upon Judge Blaisdell's suggestion to resolve this dispute through the courts.[23] James Willis sued Joseph Dyer for failure to pay Mary's board and other expenses she had accrued while living with his family in the spring of 1818. Mary, legally unable to sue her husband, was clearly behind the suit even to the extent of traveling to the nearby village of Wilmot, New Hampshire, to collect affidavits from witnesses. The mob had failed, the legislative petitions had died; perhaps the court could force Joseph to support Mary.

In addition to four weeks board at the Willis's, Mary had made several purchases from James Willis, who was identified in court documents as a trader. The ledger sheet recording Mary's purchases, a total of $20.22 from April through early June 1818, revealed her ambiguous social position. Mary purchased ribbon, thread, and fabric, enough yardage to make a new gown for the Concord 1818 legislative hearings. She bought cambric with which she made handkerchiefs for her four sons, each embroidered with their names. Mary was capable of producing her own clothing, yet still under the necessity of charging such goods in Joseph's name. At the same time, Mary purchased a silk handkerchief for $1, a comparatively extravagant purchase. One dollar was Mary's pay for one week of teaching school or the cost of one week's room and board. The purchase suggests that Dyer was concerned about her public appearance in Concord. A new dress and a silk handkerchief were a vast improvement over the borrowed gown she wore in 1817 and spoke to her resilience and ability to survive on her own. It also spoke to her keen sense of self-presentation, wearing class-appropriate garb to meet with Concord's leading citizens and rally their support, while at the same time bemoaning that she was unable to provide on her own such things as appropriate "for a person of her age and standing in life."[24]

Willis filed his complaint in June 1818 and the trial was scheduled for the following September term of the Grafton County Court of Common Pleas. Willis and Joseph Dyer gathered depositions from those who would be unable to travel to the trial. The trial began in September and carried over to the February term, 1819. The jury awarded Willis

$5.73, Mary's board plus seventy-three cents. Joseph appealed the decision and the Grafton County Superior Court heard the case in May 1819.

The trial threw into sharp relief the dilemma of the Dyers's estranged relationship and the crumbling philosophy of coverture. Dyer's 1817 and 1818 petitions to the legislature for redress had failed, and she remained Joseph's wife. As a wife Mary was entitled to protection and support from her husband, including a place to sleep, food to eat, and materials for life (such as cloth for clothing). These things, Willis's attorney argued, Joseph had failed to provide forcing Mary to contract debts. If Mary was successful via Willis's suit in forcing Joseph to provide for her, the Shakers would be forced to provide similarly for all nonbelieving wives, effectively quieting the "crying women in the streets" of which Joshua Stevens and his fellow petitioners had complained.

Testimony focused on Mary's clothing. Clothing indicated social status and material wealth and reflected the degree to which Joseph provided for his wife. How many gowns did she own and of what fabric? How many petticoats, caps, and pairs of shoes? What was in Mary's traveling trunk? Mary could not testify against her husband, but others could. Witnesses described how after leaving the Shakers Mary had no clothes but the simple, Shaker dress that had changed little in the forty-five years since the sect was founded. She was forced to clothe herself and to do so by the sympathy of others, namely friends and sisters who gave her dresses, a bonnet, and an overcoat during cool weather. When the seasons turned again, James Willis gave Mary clothing, a task her husband should have undertaken. When Mary returned to Enfield in the spring of 1818, she had but three gowns, one of bombazette, one of blue nankeen, and one of silk. Female residents described the gowns as "much worn" and "very poor" and not appropriate for "a person of her age and standing in life." Her skirts were flannel and "considerable worn" as were her shoes. Although she owned a "handsome cap," two others were merely "common." And in her "very empty" traveling trunk, just some old silk and some articles of little consequence. Here was a woman without the means to dress, and live, as she should.

Willis's attorney argued that Mary was impoverished and in need of assistance; the Shaker attorneys praised her industry and capability. They argued that Mary Dyer was not destitute as she arrived at the Shaker village "very well clothed" with "seven white cambric handkerchiefs," including the very ones she had made for her children.[25] The handkerchiefs, judged the Shaker witness, were "nice" and estimated to be worth fifteen cents each. In addition, witnesses for Joseph recalled how he had provided board for Mary at the Tillotsons and the Riches, that he had given her the bed and bedding, and that Joseph, acting against the usual marital norm, permitted Mary to keep earnings from her own work. Timing seemed to be key: witnesses for Joseph testified that while Mary may have been poorly dressed immediately after her departure from the Shakers in 1815, when she taught school in Enfield three years later she was decently, though not richly, dressed. Joseph's support must have been adequate.

Mary's apparent survival was echoed in the testimony of one of Enfield's selectmen and in Joseph's defense against Willis's claims. When asked why the town selectmen did not offer Mary town assistance he replied that since she had not asked directly for their help, they assumed she had found support elsewhere. Joseph's defense included testimony about Mary's teaching salary, her industrious activities in sewing (both for herself and for others), and her ability to make a very large donation ($2) to charity while in Concord. Joseph described how many times he had offered a settlement, and how often Mary had refused his offers.

Mary's ability to provide for herself by seeking and gaining the support of others had weakened her claim. She was trapped in a nightmarish bind. To gain the court-determined power to manage herself she required the assistance of others to provide food and shelter as well as to file a petition. But when she used that assistance, she was deemed in no need of the court's help. To gain the court's support, she would need to be totally destitute and without any help, a situation that would render her voiceless, and entirely unheard. But Dyer had not gone unheard. With her clothing analyzed and her post-Shaker work and living arrangements scrutinized, Joseph's attorneys successfully convinced the court that Joseph had provided adequately for Mary. The court affirmed that Joseph could provide for his wife in any manner he pleased as long as Mary was not a drain on society, as long as society could not hear her crying in the streets. With her respectable clothing, ability to work, and nice gifts for her children, clearly Mary was not about to become a member of the town poor.

But this suit was between James Willis and Joseph Dyer, and while Mary's life provided the backdrop for the question of support, the key legal question was whether or not James Willis knew that Joseph had advertised Mary in the newspaper. During the appeal at Superior Court, Joseph's attorneys offered the court copies of the newspaper advertisements in which Joseph had posted Mary. This evidence was not part of the lower court trial, but here at Superior Court, the advertisements provided the conclusive evidence of Joseph having followed the customary procedure. Witnesses for the defense confirmed that not only did James Willis know that Mary had been posted, he willingly disregarded the notice and stated boldly that he would help her again, and sue Joseph again. Joseph won his appeal.[26] James Willis had willfully ignored the standard community practice of dealing with estranged wives, and he would suffer the consequences for his transgression. Willis was forced to pay Joseph's entire court costs, $123.05.

The suit was a close call for the Shakers. Three days after the trial, Joseph offered Mary a "a quiet home near [her] children."[27] Although frightened that she might once again be held prisoner, and against the advice of her friends, Dyer agreed to go with Joseph. Joseph promised Mary could come and go as she pleased and could attend religious services of her choice. The house would be separate from the Shakers, and Mary would provide her own cooking and do her own work. Joseph would live there with her, although, of course, celibately. In other words, Joseph would live up to the expectations of the role of husband in providing a house, goods, and his protection. Mary consented to go with Joseph, hoping her husband would finally provide for her, while fearing that if she refused the offer the Shakers would make it known publicly that Mary had ignored their assistance. Aware of her own public claims and image, Mary consented to the arrangement.

Joseph deceived Mary. Once she had agreed to go with Joseph, a second Shaker brother appeared. Mary's cautious concern changed to outright fear, and she insisted that Polly Clifford, a local girl, accompany her to guarantee the Shakers provide what Joseph had promised. Clifford and Mary spent the night in the Shaker dwelling house. The next morning, Mary learned that no house had been prepared for her. When she attempted to leave, the Shakers barred her path. Mary "screached [sic]" and attempted to crawl out the window.[28] Clifford was frightened to the point of immobility. The Shakers quickly ushered the frightened girl out of the village.

Dyer described this cruel deception as her third captivity and wrote how Joseph locked her alone in a room. The Shaker offer of a home was not based on upholding Joseph's husbandly responsibilities; it was a means to circumscribe Dyer's activities. As in her previous stays at the Shaker village, Dyer's health declined precipitously. At first she feared the Shakers were attempting to kill her. But when she was beset by continuous vomiting and prepared herself to die in peace, the Shakers made every attempt to heal her and brought six individuals from the world to witness their efforts. When Dyer's health improved, Joseph agreed to a settlement but later reneged. Fearing that among the Shakers she was doomed to a "dreary life," Mary escaped by pulling the nails from a door. So intense was her fear of confinement that despite her desire to see her children, she hesitated to return to the Enfield Shakers even when accompanied by others. Dyer's printed works, like many apostate texts, may have exaggerated the dire nature of the situation. But one extant manuscript revealed Dyer's quite genuine fears. In August of 1819, she left a note at the home of a prominent local judge, Mills Olcot. In the note she begged for Olcot's protection and pleaded that if he should hear she was at the Shakers, to come and rescue her.[29]

❧ ❧ ❧

Mary Dyer's apostasy stimulated the mob at Enfield, Joshua Stevens's petition, and *Willis v. Dyer*. Although each event assisted Dyer in her desperate situation, community standards and concerns ultimately motivated the (primarily) male participants. Embedded in, and even superceding, these arguments about Shaker practices and the treatment of a particular woman, were concerns for issues of social propriety—the treatment of wives, the bonds of motherhood, the satisfaction of debts. Historian Isabelle Lehuu describes the efflorescence of popular print culture in the antebellum period as presenting a "collective spectacle," a site for contesting values and revealing social tensions. Similarly, the pamphlets, legislative appearances, mobs, and court dramas presented an anti-Shaker spectacle, a "carnival" on and off the page for the reader/viewer's consumption.[30] In this public theater of apostasy, Dyer continued her campaign.

Dyer's apostate activities from 1817 through 1819 were not isolated events. Her actions built on a foundation of anti-Shaker activity that had stretched back to the eighteenth century. Her pamphlet, legislative appearance, and mob attack all had predecessors in earlier apostates. Several features made Dyer's activities unique. Dyer's gender framed her experiences. As a mother, she fought aggressively and instinctively for her children. Her emotion-filled pleas captured the sympathy of the public in a way the male apostate authors were unable to duplicate. Dyer's lack of access to power because of her gender in effect gave her more access to it as male authorities responded to the bereaved mother and took up her cause. Her gender also refocused apostate writing from Shaker theology to Shaker practice. For Dyer, Shakerism's evil lay in its lived experience, more than in its theological discourse.

Dyer was much more visible than earlier apostates. Her story appeared in multiple, simultaneous venues including pamphlets, newspapers, and the legislature. Improvements in printing technology and transportation helped carry Dyer's story rapidly across the country. Once codified in a book, Dyer's experiences had the potential to survive beyond the life of the event and of the author. The tale of Dyer's experiences traveled across the country to Ohio and Kentucky where the public was moved to anti-Shaker action by a woman they had never met. Mary Dyer and her story became two separate entities. Mary's charismatic presence inspired action and so did her sad story.

Dyer's actions also signaled a change in apostate connections. In the eighteenth century, the apostate members of the Rathbun family supported each other when they provided introductions and statements of support in one another's apostate works. In the nineteenth century, the connection of Dyer and Chapman took apostate cooperation to a new level. Eunice and Mary combined their resources. Chapman's New York supporters, such as her brother Representative Jesse Hawley, assisted Dyer in her legislative appearance when Hawley wrote to Governor Plumer on her behalf. Likewise, Dyer's Enfield supporters assisted Eunice in retrieving her children. The experiences of the two women became linked during the mob at Enfield and subsequent publication of Van Vleet, which in turn linked eastern and western anti-Shaker activists. Together, the Dyer-Chapman example indicated that the suspect Shaker treatment of wives went beyond a single example in a single community.

A final characteristic that marked Dyer's anti-Shaker campaign was her tenacious spirit. After apostatizing, the male apostate authors vented their anger, justified their temporary participation in Shakerism, and then for the most part went back to their lives.[31] Amos Taylor wrote a pamphlet about his wife, Thomas Brown a book on medicine. But unlike the Rathbuns, Amos Taylor, or Thomas Brown, Dyer was simply unable to do so. Without a husband, she had no means of support and survival and without her children, she had no reason to live. Dyer refused to give up her fight for her children because she simply had no other option. She fully recognized the desperate nature of her situation as did the public who could not dismiss pleas for help. Dyer's tenacity was born of necessity.

Joseph had tried, and failed, to reach some sort of agreement with his wife. In August 1819, Joseph "called witness of the world and told Mary that there where he resided was the only provision he should make for her support but he should no longer keep a constant watch over her as he had done."[32] Mary abandoned the board Joseph offered, and with half a quire of paper she had purchased from James Willis, and for which Willis had sued Joseph, she returned to the Coös to work on her next venture, a large volume of anti-Shaker material.[33]

4

A Spectacle for Remark

The 1820s brought Mary Dyer to the very center of the anti-Shaker world. In this, her most active and visible decade, Dyer published books, pamphlets, broadsides, and newspaper essays. She continued to receive the support of the local Enfield community who once again petitioned the legislature for assistance with, as they claimed, the socially disruptive Shakers. As Ann Lee had traveled throughout New England seeking converts to Shakerism in the late eighteenth century, so too did Mary Dyer travel in the nineteenth century, seeking adherents to anti-Shakerism as she sold copies of her books, made public appearances, and continued to collect information and solicit support for her cause. Dyer would suffer the death of her child in this decade, but moved beyond her own tragedy to fight for all women and children whose lives were endangered by Shakerism.

A Portraiture of Shakerism, Mary Dyer's largest and most complex book, formed the foundation of her anti-Shaker proselytization. She worked on her manuscript on and off for four years, describing her frustration with illness, lack of finances, and continued persecution as being like "a pelican upon the house top—a spectacle for remark in a land of strangers."[1] Having abandoned Joseph's support, during the period of bringing *Portraiture* to fruition, Dyer had to manage her own survival. Dyer lived in a succession of boardinghouses and supported herself by taking in sewing. Producing and selling *Portraiture* brought Mary new challenges: marketing her book, distributing the book across New England, and responding to criticism the work generated from both the Shakers and the public.

By the 1820s, Shakerism had grown numerically and geographically with roughly 3,500 members, spreading from New England to Indiana. Shakerism's rapid success brought with it difficulties, and the nascent sect faced a period of stress and tension. Mother Lucy Wright, the leader of the Shaker movement, sought from her headquarters in New Lebanon, New York, to achieve a unity among disparate Shaker communities. Where previously verbal communications of beliefs and practices had sufficed, size of the movement, distance between communities, and a new generation of Shakers stimulated a move toward written codification. The *Millennial Laws* (1821) lay out the expectations for behavior in areas of dress, diet, and daily life. The *Millennial Laws,* a manuscript text copied by hand for distribution within each Shaker community, sought to establish a cohesiveness to the Shaker movement as well as reign in members, particularly the younger Shakers, who evinced great variation in their understanding and following of the Shaker mission.[2]

In addition to attempts at better control of those within Shakerism, Shaker leaders also struggled to maintain their image to the world. Since the first decade of the nineteenth century, Shakers had found print culture an effective means of defending their faith and promoting their principles. But print was a double-edged sword. For as many individuals were inspired to join the Shakers after reading their principles, others used Shaker books as a basis for attack. Print culture was a powerful means of dissemination of the anti-Shaker message as well. Printed works permitted those who had never even seen a Shaker to attack the faith. To fight the persistent rumors of Shakerism as a new branch of Catholicism, allegations of excessive drinking, and accusations of lewd behavior, Shaker leaders actively promoted Shaker philosophy through print. This aggressive campaign of image control sought to attract new members, resist restrictive legislation, and to establish and maintain a market for Shaker goods.

Following the failure of her second petition the Shakers remarked that Dyer was "far from being satisfied with the decision of the legislature."[3] But Dyer still had some support for her situation. When a group of legislators told Dyer that more evidence of Shaker abuse would increase the likelihood for a law of protection for women, the knowledge spurred Mary to gather more affidavits testifying to experiences similar to those she had endured. Dyer was now quite experienced in public presentation, and she had learned valuable lessons about the power of print to stimulate the sympathy and malice of mankind. During the summer of 1818, Dyer spent "several weeks" at the home of Weare, New Hampshire, judge and Freewill Baptist Joseph Philbrick, where she "arranged her papers for a book."[4] Dyer's papers, zealously protected by Mary's roominghouse owner Rhoda Flood when the Shakers came looking for Dyer's journal in early 1819, included ninety-five affidavits, previously published apostate accounts, a theological history of Shakerism, and an expanded version of her personal experience.

Dyer selected Sylvester T. Goss of Haverhill, New Hampshire, to publish her new work. Goss, who had previously published books and pamphlets in Boston, published a variety of works including sermons, political statements, and exciting narratives such as those penned by shipwrecked sailors and Indian captives. In April of 1821, Dyer advertised across New England for subscribers to the forthcoming work and described her impending tome as a history of the Shakers "with a particular notice of the Principal Fathers and Heads of that community . . . exposition of their Religious and Moral Doctrines . . . [and] a concise relation of her own trials and sufferings, while resident with that people, and since she left them."[5] In addition to her assertion that her knowledge came from experience gained "while resident" with the Shakers, Dyer advertised that her work was "fully substantiated by undoubted testimony and historical facts."[6] The advertisement did not contain any directions on how to subscribe to *Portraiture,* although the advertisement alerted newspaper editors that those "friendly to the cause of justice" who inserted the advertisement into their own papers would receive a free copy of *Portraiture.* Despite the advertising efforts, the Shakers reported in March 1823 that the book was "stopped in the press for the present—perhaps for want of money to help it through."[7]

In addition to dislocation, illness, and lack of funds, Dyer, in a published explanation for the delay of *Portraiture,* cited copyright difficulties as another factor in the postponement. Joseph Spear, the publisher of *A Brief Statement,* had copyrighted Dyer's first work and thus prevented Dyer from reissuing the work within *Portraiture.* Ironically, copyright may have slowed the spread of her anti-Shaker message as the copyright prevented other printers from reprinting and distributing *A Brief Statement* as well. In a newspaper article, an anonymous author called the copyright restriction on *A Brief Statement* regrettable as it prevented disseminating Dyer's argument. The writer suggested that distribution of more copies "might be the means of breaking up the impious Society."[8] According to copyright law, the author or designated individual had to file a statement with the district clerk and pay a fee to register the copyright. Additional copies of the certification of copyright were an additional fee. In addition, the copyright statement had to be published in area newspapers for four weeks. This was an additional source of expense for Dyer's already strapped resources. The more important lesson for Dyer, though, was learning that she did not even own her own story, a further source of legal and social invisibility. *Portraiture* itself provides another example. To prevent Joseph from owning her story (and reaping any profits from her book), Dyer's brother Samuel entered the copyright. Despite the numerous problems, *Portraiture* was published in June 1823.[9]

Dyer had amassed 446 pages of information about and against the Shakers, the largest and latest work in a line of apostate accounts that stretched back forty years. Dyer directed the sale of her book. She appeared at a Concord bookstore to "attend to the sale" and in October of 1823 Dyer began a lengthy book selling trip that continued for several months.[10] From Concord, Dyer traveled to coastal New Hampshire and then turned south following the Massachusetts coastline to Newburyport, Ipswich, Essex, Beverly, Salem, and Lynn. As the Shakers of the late eighteenth century had traveled New England and spread their Shaker message, so Mary Dyer traveled New England spreading her anti-Shaker message. During 1824 Dyer sold books in the vicinities of the Harvard, Shirley, and Hancock, Massachusetts, Shaker villages and later she brought her anti-Shaker message to villages near Shaker communities in New York, Maine, and New Hampshire.

As she traveled throughout New England, Dyer saw herself as a bookseller and business woman, describing her activities as her "business" and noting with pride that in one town she sold $70 worth of books. Dyer took care with the presentation of her book. *Portraiture* was available in two bindings: full leather, and green paper with a leather spine. The spine had four tooled gold lines and a black label with the title worked in gold. Before the book was bound, several typographic errors were caught and corrected by hand. A copy of *Portraiture* in the collection of the American Antiquarian Society, valued at $1.25 at the time it entered the collection in 1825, provided the clue that the errors were corrected before the book was bound. This copy contains, by mistake, two copies of the same signature (that is, a duplicate set of the same grouping of pages). Both signatures contain the manuscript corrections. If the corrections were made after binding, only one set would have had the corrections, for after correcting the errors on pages 149 and 155, the individual making the corrections would have put the book aside not expecting (naturally) duplicate copies of those pages in this particular book. In some copies of *Portraiture,* an errata sheet was pasted onto the back flyleaf.[11] When her supply of books ran low, Dyer returned to New Hampshire to restock and to defend herself from any charges the Shakers had leveled against her. While some reported that

Dyer's book met with a "cool reception," newspaper articles and Shaker correspondence indicated that Dyer once again excited a strong public reaction.[12]

Dyer's book and speeches inspired visits to Shaker communities. Concord resident Mary Clark visited Canterbury and reported in a letter to a Boston friend that "everything we saw and heard tended to confirm M. Dyer's assertions respecting them."[13] Clark, who identified herself as "a kind of nominal half-way Quaker,"[14] could not find the words "to express [her] abhorrence of their delusive, pernicious, and abominable principles—to say nothing of their practical conduct."[15] Perhaps to help her friend understand her shock, Clark sent her copy of *Portraiture* along with her letter. A month later, Clark wrote again and enclosed clippings from the local papers regarding Mary Dyer and the Shaker rebuttal to *Portraiture*. She noted how "various causes have combined to make whatever relates to [the Shakers] interesting in this vicinity."[16] A year later, Clark had the opportunity to meet Mary Dyer when she visited Concord and found her "an extraordinary woman."[17] Not everyone agreed with Clark's assessment. Susan Bramley, a recent convert to Shakerism, wrote to a worried friend. Bramley reported that among the Alfred, Maine, Shakers she was as "happy as any one can be in this world. . . ." and that she had been there "six months, long enough to know if those horrid stories of that despicable creature called Mary Dier [*sic*] is true but I call them the most horrid lies that ever tongue could utter. . . ."[18]

Dyer's activities in Boston (ca. 1823-1825) illustrate how she crafted a support network to meet her daily needs and used gender segregated presentations to achieve her anti-Shaker goals. In Boston, Dyer presented herself as a mother in mourning for the loss of her Shaker-held children, especially her daughter, Betsey, who had died from consumption in January 1824 at the age of twenty-two. Dyer's personal story of deception and the deadly consequences of Shakerism moved women, especially when Mary related the sad story of how she learned of Betsey's death only by reading the newspaper. Once again clothing revealed Dyer's tragic situation. Mary wrote of how several of her new Boston-area friends presented her with gifts including a mourning coat and gloves, necessary attributes for a bereaved mother whose desperate situation denied her even the dignity of proper mourning. Women provided sympathy, companionship, and reaffirmed Mary's role as a mother, despite the absence of her children. Women also provided crucial links to their husbands and neighbors who held positions of influence, a socially acceptable route to make important connections.

It was important that Mary's associates be considered respectable. The Shakers attacked the veracity of *Portraiture* by attacking the behavior, morals, and respectability of its author. Dyer was careful to display her respectability through her clothing and her associates. Respectability and its close cousin gentility were hallmarks of the rising middle class in America. To be a respectable woman was to be moral, virtuous, and above reproach. Signaled by clothing, accessories, and actions, respectability and gentility together imbued a specific type of authenticity. Dyer noted repeatedly that she met with respectable women and stayed with respectable families. This authoritative claim appears in *Portraiture* for affiants, particularly the women, who the certifying judges described as respectable.[19] Because Mary was a woman without a husband's protection—and here protection meant of her social reputation—she was forced to take great pains to illustrate that she was not a loose woman, despite the loosening of her marital ties. Dyer's alliances with respectable Boston women reflected her own virtue.

Mary's respectable Boston friends provided emotional support, as well as material goods. But more importantly, these women offered connections to important men of the community, including publishers and legislators. Boston city directories indicate that the women Dyer mentioned in her text all lived in the same affluent neighborhood. Dyer identified the women with whom she visits in Boston, yet not their important husbands. This is a good strategy in print to present herself as a respectable lady herself, moving in the appropriate feminine circles especially as a stranger in Boston. So readers learn that while in the city, Mary visited with a Mrs. Willis, who, as it turned out, was the wife of *Boston Recorder* publisher Nathaniel Willis. Either through Dyer's own persuasive powers or that of Mrs. Willis, Nathaniel Willis published an anti-Shaker article in the *Boston Recorder.*

Other women provided connections to their politician husbands. In the Boston area these government officials included local selectmen, the mayor, and both the former and current Massachusetts governors. From her male audience, Dyer sought action. A persuasive speaker, she placed less emphasis on the loss of her own family and instead concentrated on the threat the Shakers posed to the institution of the family, and by extension to the stability of society. Dyer's presentation proved effective. Mayor Josiah Quincy promised that the Shakers "would have no poor children from that city."[20] In nearby Medford, Dyer visited former governor Brooks and then traveled to Roxbury at the request of Governor William Eustis. Eustis had met Betsey Dyer while attending a Shaker meeting at Enfield the year previous. He noticed Betsey appeared ill and offered to provide some assistance, which the Shakers refused. When Mary informed the governor of Betsey's death, Eustis provided Dyer with an affidavit of support for a law to protect women and children.

From Boston, Mary headed west. In the area of the New Lebanon, New York, and Hancock, Massachusetts, Shaker villages, Dyer traveled with the assistance of William Eliphas Davis who carried a letter of introduction from Stephen Pope, a Quaker whom she may have met through John Williams of Hanover. Dyer also carried a letter from Silas Churchill, a local minister, who verified several statements in *Portraiture*. Churchill had lived in the Pittsfield, Massachusetts, area since 1795 and was acquainted with several early anti-Shaker leaders. Her extended trip was sustained by the visibility *Portraiture* generated. Dyer lived and traveled in the vicinity of Shaker villages through 1826, moving from one to another to sell books and gather testimony against the Society. The apostate network provided practical support with food, shelter, and transportation, as well as affidavits and further contacts. In March 1827 the Shakers reported that Dyer had returned to her mother's home in Northumberland, and she stayed in New Hampshire the remainder of the decade.[21]

Dyer's newfound role as anti-Shaker spokesperson and bookseller was an extension of a lifetime of exhorting and preaching. In northern New Hampshire where the Dyers had farmed, revivals and itinerant preachers stimulated Mary's religious interests. She conversed at length with visiting preachers and, in an area without a settled church, preached herself. The possibility of a preaching life drew Mary to the Shakers but also drew her out. The Weare, New Hampshire, town history reports that in 1823 there was a small revival among area Freewill Baptists and Mary Dyer was one of the visiting preachers who "put their shoulders to the work . . . of the searching, powerful time."[22] Several of these Freewill Baptists had been key supporters in her network, including Judge Philbrick with whom she had resided in 1818 and who had helped Dyer craft *Portraiture*. Dyer saw herself as a spiritually empowered individual, having a "gift" to preach. Her description of her decision to apostatize from the Shakers was couched in terms of a shifting balance of power between that of the elders and that of God working through Mary. When Dyer's power was sufficient to "shake the elders," she departed. Now she used that power to shake all of Shakerism.

Dyer's anti-Shaker campaign was ecumenical in its approach. In Boston Dyer met with leaders from several area churches including the Methodists, Baptists, Congregationalists, and Quakers. To this audience Dyer presented herself as a fellow Christian, denouncing Shakerism as popery and arguing that children within its grasp were being raised without knowledge of God. Dyer could draw on a wide variety of personal religious experiences among the Methodists, Freewill Baptists, Quakers, Shakers, and Congregationalists in her quest to form a united anti-Shaker force.

Although Dyer frequently protested in her writing that to be in public was a "trial," her bookselling tour, while a unique statement of anti-Shakerism, had precedent in the numerous careers of itinerant women preachers. As historian Catherine Brekus has illustrated, in the late eighteenth and early nineteenth centuries dozens of female preachers traveled across the country. These women, predominantly from sectarian groups such as the Methodists and Freewill Baptists, drew large audiences. While more traditional Protestant groups, such as the Congregationalists, urged women to obey St. Paul's edict of female silence in the churches, sectarian leaders supported women's efforts as these newer faiths struggled to gain a foothold in American Christianity.[23]

During the 1820s, Dyer traveled and preached a message of anti-Shakerism. With her increased visibility, Dyer gained a significant following and among apostates was a linchpin of activity. The Shakers frequently commented about Dyer in the company of others, for example, noting the whereabouts and actions of "Mary Dyer and her coadjutors," "Mary Dyer and her disciples," and Dyer as "that modern Jezebel and her false swearers."[24] Dyer both symbolized Shaker cruelty and acted as a teacher of apostasy. The Alfred Shakers noted in 1825 how Dyer had come to Maine to instruct other apostates in preparation for a court battle.[25] The interaction among the network of apostates suggests that participants replaced the community experience of Shakerism with a community experience of apostasy. Instead of defining themselves as Shaker, the apostates defined themselves as distinctly not-Shaker, and as more apostates joined the select group, group identity, validity, and solidarity were enhanced.

Dyer's multifaceted presentation was not a conscious strategy of deception to meet personal ends. Dyer's itinerancy reflected the multifaceted world in which women of the early nineteenth century lived. Dyer clearly understood the gender segregated world as reflecting, and enforcing, differences in power and potential. *Portraiture of Shakerism* reflects her understanding of the variety of ways to gain power. In Part One, Dyer used intellect and history to make her case. In Part Two, she drew upon sentiment and sympathy.

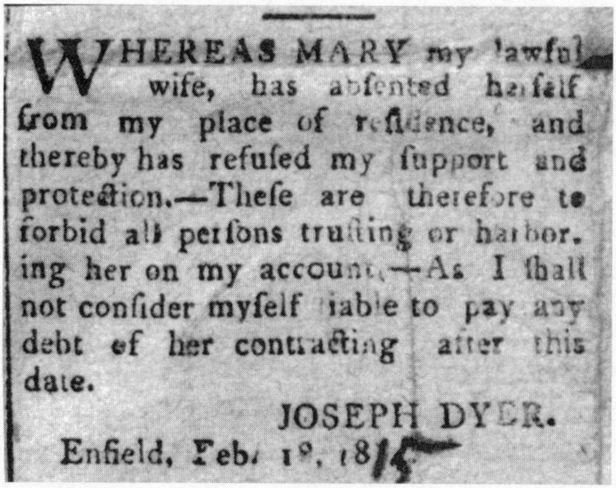

WHEREAS MARY my lawful
wife, has absented herself
from my place of residence, and
thereby has refused my support and
protection.—These are therefore to
forbid all persons trusting or harbor-
ing her on my account.—As I shall
not consider myself liable to pay any
debt of her contracting after this
date.
                            JOSEPH DYER.
Enfield, Feb. 18, 1815.

Figure 1. Advertisement, *Dartmouth Gazette*, February 18, 1815. When Mary Dyer left the Shakers, she effectively abandoned her husband's support. Following common early nineteenth-century practice, Joseph posted a public notice to alert townspeople that he was no longer responsible for Mary's actions and well-being. Courtesy, New Hampshire Department of State, Division of Records Management and Archives.

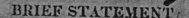

A

BRIEF STATEMENT

OF THE

SUFFERINGS

OF

MARY DYER,

OCCASIONED BY THE SOCIETY CALLED

SHAKERS.

WRITTEN BY HERSELF.

TO WHICH IS ADDED,

AFFIDAVITS AND CERTIFICATES;

ALSO,

A DECLARATION FROM THEIR OWN PUBLICATION.

[COPY RIGHT SECURED.]

BOSTON:

PUBLISHED BY WILLIAM S. SPEAR.

1818.

Figure 2. Title page, *A Brief Statement of the Sufferings of Mary Dyer,* 1818. The first of Mary Dyer's publications stirred public sympathy for her quest to retrieve her children from the Shakers and to gain financial support from her husband. Author's Personal Collection.

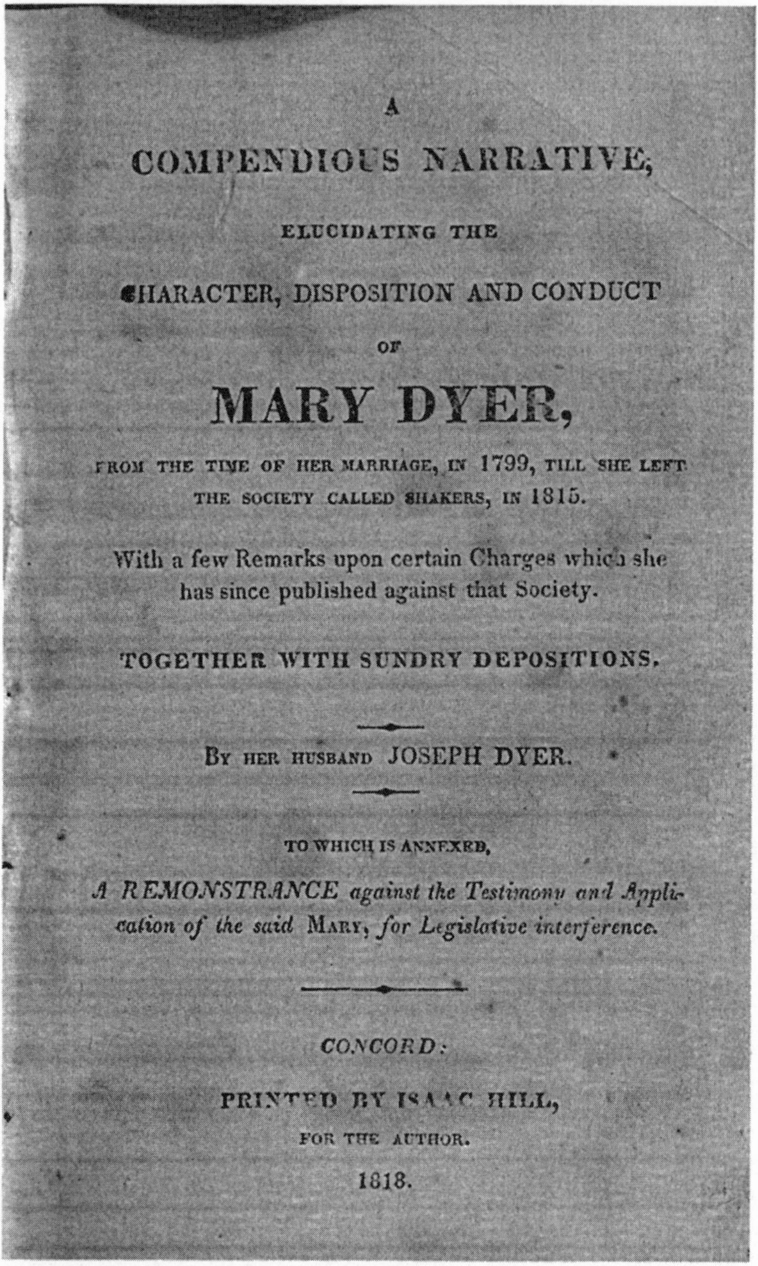

A

COMPENDIOUS NARRATIVE,

ELUCIDATING THE

CHARACTER, DISPOSITION AND CONDUCT

OF

MARY DYER,

FROM THE TIME OF HER MARRIAGE, IN 1799, TILL SHE LEFT
THE SOCIETY CALLED SHAKERS, IN 1815.

With a few Remarks upon certain Charges which she
has since published against that Society.

TOGETHER WITH SUNDRY DEPOSITIONS.

By HER HUSBAND JOSEPH DYER.

TO WHICH IS ANNEXED,

A REMONSTRANCE against the Testimony and Application of the said MARY, for Legislative interference.

CONCORD:

PRINTED BY ISAAC HILL,

FOR THE AUTHOR.

1818.

Figure 3. Title page, *A Compendious Narrative*, 1818. Joseph Dyer's rebuttal to Mary Dyer's *A Brief Statement* presented Joseph as the long-suffer-
ing husband of a willful, disobedient wife. As publishers had encouraged, the
public was eager to read both sides of this titillating dispute. Author's Personal
Collection.

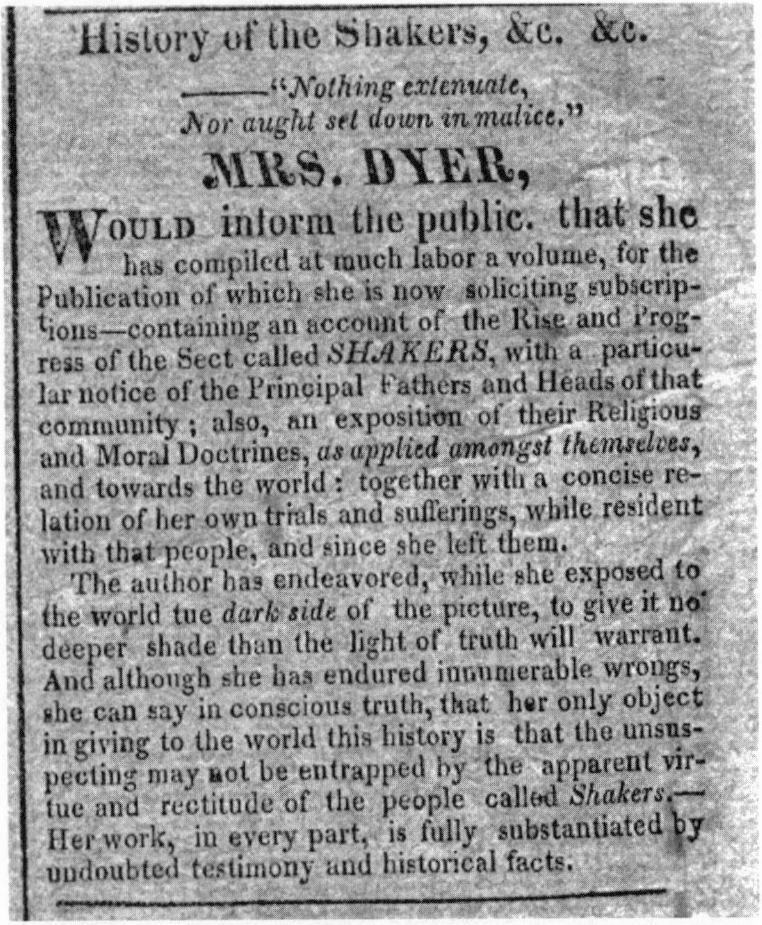

History of the Shakers, &c. &c.

———"Nothing extenuate,
Nor aught set down in malice."

MRS. DYER,

WOULD inform the public, that she has compiled at much labor a volume, for the Publication of which she is now soliciting subscriptions—containing an account of the Rise and Progress of the Sect called *SHAKERS*, with a particular notice of the Principal Fathers and Heads of that community ; also, an exposition of their Religious and Moral Doctrines, *as applied amongst themselves,* and towards the world : together with a concise relation of her own trials and sufferings, while resident with that people, and since she left them.

The author has endeavored, while she exposed to the world tue *dark side* of the picture, to give it no deeper shade than the light of truth will warrant. And although she has endured innumerable wrongs, she can say in conscious truth, that her only object in giving to the world this history is that the unsuspecting may not be entrapped by the apparent virtue and rectitude of the people called *Shakers.*— Her work, in every part, is fully substantiated by undoubted testimony and historical facts.

Figure 4. Advertisement Soliciting Subscriptions to *Portraiture. The Observer* (Woodstock, Vermont), April 17, 1821. Unhappy with the New Hampshire legislature's failure to intervene in her problems with the Shakers, Mary Dyer continued her assault with her largest work, *A Portraiture of Shakerism.* Although Dyer advertised for subscribers in 1821, *Portraiture* was not available until June 1823. Author's Personal Collection.

The Whirling Gift.

Figure 5. Illustration of "The Whirling Gift," from David Lamson's *Two Years Among the Shakers*, 1848. Apostate author David Lamson capitalized on renewed public interest in Shaker practices during the revivalistic period known as "Mother's Work." In his illustrated text, Lamson provided readers with an inside look at Shaker life. Author's Personal Collection.

FREE LECTURE TO THE LADIES.

MRS. MARY MARSHALL,
Formerly MARY M. DYER.

Authoress of the "Portraiture of Shakerism," "Shakerism Exposed," &c.

Being in this city on a visit to her friends, has consented, agreeably to their request, to give a FREE LECTURE ON THE FOUNDATION AND EFFECTS OF SHAKERISM, in Franklin Hall, (Mr. Smith Dyer's Building,) Main Street, opposite Albion Court, this Evening, at 7 o'clock.

Mrs. M. is, and always has been of undoubtedly good reputation, has lived with the Shakers two years, and has been parsonally acquainted with them nearly 40 years, and probably knows more of their practices and creed, than any other person out of that sect. She has given many such Lectures, to good acceptance, in New Hampshire, New York, Vermont, &c., and feels it to be her duty to expose by all practicable means, the cruel and unnatural practices of that secluded and cunning sect.

Your attendance with the ladies of your family is respectfully solicited.

Charlestown, Mass., Wednesday, Dec. 25, 1850.

Figure 6. Advertising Handbill, "Free Lecture to the Ladies," December 25, 1850. Despite her advanced age and few successes, Dyer continued to speak out against the Shakers in a series of free lectures held across New England. Courtesy, American Antiquarian Society.

Figure 7. Carte de Visite, Caleb Dyer (1800–1863). Mary's oldest son became a prominent leader of the Enfield, New Hampshire, Shakers. In a strange twist of fate, Caleb was murdered in 1863 by an aggrieved father attempting to reclaim his Shaker-held children. Author's Personal Collection.

Figure 8. Carte de Visite, Orville Dyer (1804–1882). Like his siblings Caleb, Betsey, and Joseph, Jr., Orville remained among the Shakers for life. An Enfield ministry leader, Orville briefly replaced his murdered brother as a trustee for the community. Author's Personal Collection.

A Portraiture of Shakerism

In *A Portraiture of Shakerism* (1822), Dyer recombined traditional elements of the anti-Shaker genre to create a new format for apostate writing. She divided her main text, which followed a short preface, into two parts. Part One detailed Shaker religious beliefs and history. Previously published anti-Shaker texts, such as those of Daniel Rathbun, Eunice Chapman, Thomas Brown, and James Smith, provided the majority of the textual material. In addition over one hundred pages of affidavits formed the main narrative. Although the affidavits served initially as part of the legal strategy for her New Hampshire legislative hearings, in *Portraiture* Dyer reinscribed the affidavits as a literary device to tell the personal story of Shakerism from the perspective of those who had lived it. Dyer provided editorial commentary and citations to religious texts in footnotes. In some instances, Dyer rephrased passages from religious texts to better suit her needs. For example, on page nineteen of *Portraiture* Dyer extracts a passage from *Buck's Theological Dictionary* in describing European antecedents to Shakerism. Where Buck described "these prophets," Dyer inserted instead "misguided persons." In Part One, readers heard Dyer's voice only in the footnotes and in a few brief passages that connected other writers' texts. Further diminishing Dyer's voice and to distinguish the notes from the main text, the footnotes were set in a smaller typeface. In several places the footnote affidavit had no direct relationship to the main text. Thus, in the first part of *Portraiture,* many voices denounced Shakerism, and in some places more than one voice spoke at the same time. Like the mob at Enfield, Part One offered a chorus of anti-Shaker song.

Portraiture made its case along distinct gender lines, a clever and effective strategy. This dual-gender persuasion allowed Dyer to argue in what we might call a masculine mode and a feminine mode, a technique male apostate authors did not exploit. Dyer was highly aware of the relationship between the gender and power of her readers. In the preface to *A Brief Statement* she called on father's tender feelings for assistance in her plight. In Part One of *Portraiture,* in one of the very few places her voice is heard, Mary Dyer offered a two-page observation signed "Author." She wrote how "the power of the law rests in the judgements of men" and called on those men with "a measure of true patriotic spirit" to restore rights "to the defenceless [*sic*] injured."[26] Women had rights, but it was up to men to provide them.

To help men restore the rights of women burdened by the consequences of Shakerism, in Part One of *Portraiture,* Dyer used materials with which men were familiar in order to make her case. Further, she appropriated male voices (through the stories of male apostates and religious scholars) to help her make her point. The masculine mode of Part One spoke the language of those in authority: male lawyers, legislators, and judges. The documentation Dyer exhibited (for example, affidavits, citations) was exactly the evidence such men needed in order to make a law. While it was not impossible for a woman to write on the subject of religion or law, for Mary it would have been unwise in light of the accusations the Shakers and Joseph leveled concerning her desire to preach and lead. Thus, in *Portraiture*, her male authorities, through republished texts and affidavits—spoke for her, a more appropriate male voice in the legal and religious arenas.

In Part One Dyer drew heavily on previously published anti-Shaker accounts, including those of apostate Daniel Rathbun (1785), and the anti-Shaker works of James Smith (1810) and Eunice Chapman (1817).[27] Rathbun's eighteenth-century work remained a strong apostate account—personal, engaging, and specific. As a direct address to Elder James Whittaker, Rathbun delivered a written sermon to a preacher— a religious argument to a religious leader that Dyer could never have undertaken. Rathbun focused on the destruction of his family from a (former) Shaker's perspective. For Mary Dyer's purposes, Rathbun's account relayed how her husband Joseph (as a male Shaker) would have been taught to feel towards her. When Rathbun wrote "my wife and children were all dead to me," his authoritative voice (male, eye-witness to Shakerism) reinforced Mary's claim that the Shakers destroyed families.[28] Apostate texts, like affidavits, corroborated what Dyer claimed and provided evidence for Shaker abuses over a greater span of time and geographic space. For example, by reprinting Daniel Rathbun's eighteenth-century anti-Shaker account, Dyer's complaints extended back four decades; by including James Smith's Ohio tract, Shaker crimes were extended from New England to the western frontier. *Portraiture* alleged that Shakerism threatened the early American republic by destroying the family and turning the social order upside down, that this threat was not new, but was increasingly pervasive and dangerous.

Dyer also included selections from Eunice Chapman's anti-Shaker narrative, providing a female voice in Part One of *Portraiture*. The specific sections of Chapman's work that Dyer chose to reprint make clear the reason for her prominence. The selections from Eunice Chapman's texts described in detail the legislative proceedings in New York State, a battle that resulted in the Chapman divorce and the return of the children to Eunice. Dyer reprinted the legislative testimony, Chapman's affidavits and the resultant "Act for the Relief of Eunice Chapman." Including these specific sections from Chapman's texts in Part One of *Portraiture* reinforced Dyer's own case. Part One was constructed as a lawyer would present an argument. The numerous affidavits in Part One provided the additional evidence for which the New Hampshire legislators had called, and the Chapman account, with the voice of the powerful New York State legislature, provided legal precedent for Dyer's New Hampshire situation. In her 1817 petition, Dyer detailed the specific effects Shakerism had on her. In *Portraiture* she widened her argument to show that Shakerism was not simply a local problem, it was a national problem "subversive of Christian *morality*" and "detrimental to the *well being* of *society.*"[29]

In Part Two, Dyer presented a more feminine argument based on her experience as a mother. Where Part One concerned the public arenas of law and theology, Part Two emphasized the domestic arena and the emotional aspect of Dyer's experience. Dyer designed Part One to solicit legislative action and Part Two to gain sympathy. Dyer employed sentiment—the affections of the heart—not simply to cause tears, but to provoke a response leading to action. Sympathy, it was widely believed, signified a civilized people. Dyer's illustration that the Shakers were unsympathetic to her agony as a mother showed the Shakers to be uncivilized and immoral and unfit to raise children, including Mary Dyer's. Hymn verses were scattered throughout the text, providing evidence of Dyer's Protestantism and offering an appropriate background "soundtrack" to her community of similarly pious, Christian women readers.[30] Unlike Part One where Mary relegated her voice to a few footnotes, in Part Two Dyer's voice dominated the text in which she appropriately molded emotions and sentiment, as well as words, in her presentation of the effects of Shakerism. Part One and Part Two of *Portraiture* took two different paths to the same goal: Stimulate individuals to action.

In Part Two, "Treating Particularly on the Sufferings of Mary M. Dyer in Consequence of the Deception and Cruelty of the Shakers," Dyer detailed her experiences before joining and among the Enfield Shakers as she made her case for a law to protect women from the Shakers. Dyer summarized her story of how her children were taken and she found she had no defense against "the power of a husband" who used "falsehood to injure." Dyer's desire was plainly stated: "a law of preservation for the defenceless part of the community, that they may be protected from sorrows and wounds of the deepest dye."

Subscribing herself "a well wisher to the publick, the female part in particular," Dyer, as historian Jean Humez has described, reinvented herself as an avenger of women wronged by the Shakers.[31]

Dyer structured Part Two as a captivity narrative, a literary structure that connected Dyer's work to previous apostate texts. The Shaker apostate account finds its literary origins in the captivity narrative. In the apostate rendition of the captivity tale, the individual mistakenly joins the Shakers, fooled by elders' seductive words. Eighteenth-century apostate author Valentine Rathbun described how Shaker leaders, to gain converts, " . . . sometimes use great severity and sometimes great flattery, to frighten on the one hand and allure on the other."[32] Once converted, the novice endured suffering and humiliation: in the 1780s Daniel Rathbun saw his family separated, two decades later Thomas Brown was forced to abandon reading, and apostates in the 1840s claimed they were vistims of mesmeric control. Ultimately fate, chance, or God intervened and the individual escaped, or was rescued, from captivity, and then, despite personal danger, denounced Shakerism and dutifully published as a warning to others.

Mary Dyer could use the captivity narrative format particularly well. In addition to the broader structural similarities between Shaker apostate narratives and traditional Indian captivity narratives, perilous tales of trials at the hand of savages and the rewards of ultimate trust in God, Dyer could draw on the content of the traditional tale. Further, captivity narratives offered one permissible venue for temporarily overstepping the narrow boundaries of female authorship. Women wrote many of the important examples of this fundamental American genre.[33] Dyer, who cast herself as a captive to the Shakers, wrote of her experiences as a series of tests of individual strength, guided by God. "In my deepest and most severe trials," Dyer wrote, "I have never lost confidence in God as my friend, my troubled mind at all times rests in the bosom of hope. Knowing that his power, has the preeminence and will render a just reward."[34] Like Mary Rowlandson, whose 1682 Indian captivity narrative *The Sovereignty and Goodness of God* established the format for subsequent versions of this genre, Mary Dyer expected God to deliver her from the savages. In addition to describing her own escapes from the Enfield Shakers (each of which she referred to as a "captivity"), Dyer returned to Eunice Chapman's narrative and incorporated additional sections of Eunice's tale in Part Two of *Portraiture*. Chapman explicitly compared her experience with the Watervliet, New York, Shakers to Indian captivity drawing on the content of the tales. Forced to leave her crying child, Chapman recalled how similar her situation was "to those mothers who have had their children forced from their arms by the savages."[35] To these authors, both Indians and Shakers erased a mother's role.

The use of the captivity format presented to the reading public a well-known dramatic tableau. Whereas historical and theological arguments failed to gain legal redress in New Hampshire, Dyer's description of the loss of her children in the guise of Indian captivity did not fail to elicit sympathy. Like white children abducted by Indians, Dyer's children were taken from her and given to someone else to raise. As a "captive" to husband Joseph and the Shaker elders, Mary Dyer relied on God for her redemption. And like women captivity survivors before her, Dyer published her experiences as a testimony to faith in God.[36]

In actuality, it was neither a literary convention nor a celibate sect that held Dyer captive but antebellum American society where economic resources determined not only power but mere survival. Dyer realized success with *Portraiture* because she attracted the curious with her description of life within Shaker walls, attracted the inquisitive with the titillating details of the Dyers' marital discord, and struck a cultural nerve when she lambasted Shaker communalism and American society for a system that left women helpless and dependent.

The Dyers' failed marriage illuminated a conundrum in legal and social practices. What happened when a marriage fell apart? Would an increase in divorce lead to the breakdown of society? What were the proper boundaries of behavior of mothers? Did the Shakers, or other communal experiments, constitute a proper family? These fundamental institutions—motherhood, marriage, and family—formed the backbone of society and the celibate, communal Shakers and the estranged, independent Mary Dyer challenged the social norm. Although neither the Shakers nor Mary Dyer would concede the point, they shared similar positions on the borders of society.

Portraiture, the Shakers recorded, "excited great enmity in the public mind; especially among strangers."[37] Stung by the specific and pointed accusations in *Portraiture* and concerned with the public uproar, the New Hampshire Shaker leaders took it upon themselves to respond to Dyer. First, they investigated Dyer's affidavits. On March 9, 1824, Shaker John Whitcher and the New Hampshire ministry leaders traveled to Enfield to visit, and interrogate, Mary Dyer's deponents.[38] The Shakers concluded that most were "mere forgery" and that "several of the deponents have given counter testimony, denying that they ever made such statements."[39] The New Hampshire Shakers published this countertestimony in the newspapers as a duty to the public "in order to show in some measure this woman's treacherous audacity and deception."[40] The Shakers strove to defend themselves in print before the general public, just as Dyer had attacked them in the same medium. Dyer, distressed by the Shakers' renewed assault, reportedly ran from "house to house to find friends but could find but very few in Concord, except some female who felt a little pitty [*sic*] on account of her deplorable and wretched situation."[41] The Shaker rebuttal had sown some seeds of doubt.

The New Hampshire Shakers, in their quick response to Dyer, had jumped the gun and neglected to follow the traditional procedure of informing the Parent Ministry in New Lebanon of their plans and soliciting their advice. Especially in putting information in print, the Shakers realized it was important to keep a unified front. In May 1824, a month after the Enfield leaders had obtained and published the countertestimony, the ministry penned an apologetic letter to New Lebanon and explained their failure to discuss their plans with the Parent Ministry. The New Hampshire Shakers described how they had not wished to "bring any unnecessary burden" on the lead Shakers.[42] The ministry explained how their public actions were a "very disagreeable task" but unavoidable. There was simply "no way to get by it, in justice to ourselves and mankind; as many of those charges were of a criminal nature, and against our moral character, otherwise we should not have made any reply."[43] The last phrase is instructive in understanding the ministry's response. If Dyer had confined herself to a theological attack or general accusations, her work may well have been ignored. But her attack was aimed at specific individuals, and it forced the New Hampshire Shakers to mount a defense to avoid possible legal action, the collapse of business relationships, and to rebuke Dyer's stinging accusations. The New Hampshire ministry had learned from their previous experience—the long Shaker silence following Dyer's publication of *A Brief Statement*—and knew that they needed to move fast.

The Shaker countertestimony in the *Patriot* had stirred interest in the veracity of Dyer's claims. The Shakers continued their offense by printing the countertestimony in a pamphlet entitled, *A Review Of Mary M. Dyer's Publication, Entitled "A Portraiture of Shakerism"* (Concord, June 1824).[44] The publisher, Jacob B. Moore (Isaac Hill's brother-in-law), inscribed and sent a copy of the work to Isaiah Thomas at the American Antiquarian Society, placing Shaker claims in that venerable institution. A copy of *Portraiture* was presented to Thomas the following year.[45] For the general audience, the Shaker strategy was to provide *A Review* at low cost (wholesale seven to ten cents, retail twenty cents) and to circulate them quickly in areas in which Dyer's books had appeared. This was not using print as a general promotion of the faith; this was a targeted response to Mary Dyer. In fact, the text of *A*

Review did little to promote the principles of Shakerism. Instead, it encapsulated the Shakers' anti-Dyer campaign.

The Shakers circulated *A Review* in areas in which Dyer's books had appeared, often where Dyer herself had sold them. A Shaker deacon from the Harvard community carried one hundred copies to Massachusetts after a visit with the Canterbury Shakers.[46] But the Shakers were careful not to unwittingly bring Dyer any new attention. New York Shaker Seth Wells, for example, decided to wait out the public storm. He reasoned that since "neither Mary Dyer nor her stories have appeared in the [Albany] public papers," it would be best to keep still unless her name came up. If the Shakers distributed the countertestimony there, then "everybody will be anxious to see and read this *wonderful book*—this *Portraiture of Shakerism* which has given the Shakers *such a terrible blow*. And if they can not get it with out, they will send away to N. H. to Mary D.—and one call from Albany will be sufficient for her to send on a whole cargo of her books, and we shall soon have business enough to attend to."[47] This strategy, reasoned Wells, would prevent "newspaper bubbles about *Mary Dyer and the Shakers*."[48]

A Review refuted Dyer's accusations with thirty-one affidavits, two supporting letters, and additional commentary. Shaker apostates, the Enfield and Canterbury trustees asserted in a unified defense, blamed the Shakers for their own bad conduct. In regards to Mary Dyer, the Shakers considered her *Portraiture* to be "a defamatory libel calculated to excite enmity and sedition among the ignorant and uninformed."[49] Dyer's sources, wrote the Shakers, consisted of persons who only occasionally visited the Shakers and opposed a life of purity, and, those who had apostatized from the Shakers or were expunged for bad conduct. Dyer had in several previous instances criticized the Shaker defense for providing affidavits drawn principally from the Shaker membership that she argued constituted a biased source. In *A Review,* the Shakers presented witnesses from outside the Society, and pointedly asked "therefore, should any pretend to deny what they have here stated, what dependence can be placed on their testimony in any matter whatever?"[50] Since Dyer would not accept Shaker testimony, the Shakers offered her non-Shakers supporting the sect.

Affidavits in both Mary Dyer's *Portraiture* and the Shakers' *A Review* formed the crux of the contested material. In *Portraiture,* Dyer's affidavits formed the text's main narrative, provided evidence that Mary's experience among the Shakers was not unique, and justified the anti-Shakers attempts at social control of the Shaker experiment. The affidavits with their eyewitness accounts gave Dyer's text an authenticity and authority that previous anti-Shaker accounts had not managed. Nonetheless, the Shakers strongly contested her affidavits and claimed Dyer falsified the statements to produce nothing more than libelous slander. Did Dyer falsify her affidavits? To what extent were the allegations crafted to form a cohesive tale, and what role did the affiants play in the social construction of the Shaker evil?

Dyer's later writings and Shaker correspondence tell us her method for gathering the testimony. Following the legislative hearing of 1818, Dyer immediately began to travel throughout New Hampshire, gathering testimony from apostates, their families, and neighbors. Dyer would listen as her affiant told a tale of abuse, family separation, and misery. She would then write down the story and later return the account to the source for review. Local judges or other officials would read the tale to the affiant who then certified that it was the truth. The story and the certification were then published in *Portraiture*.

As in contemporary debates between sectarian groups and their detractors, there is little doubt that both opponents and proponents of Shakerism exaggerated or bent the truth. Dyer had a distinct agenda: to retrieve her children and to discredit the Shakers. With the assistance of Judge Philbrick of Weare and Judge Gale of Gilmanton, Dyer crafted *Portraiture* to achieve those goals. It should come as no surprise that she selected those affidavits that best supported her claims and mirrored her own experience. Her data source was extremely narrow: disgruntled former Shakers. As a number of her affiants were connected in a loose web of kith and kin, and had no doubt shared their stories before Mary Dyer appeared, it is not surprising that the ofttold tales took on a familiar, almost formulaic pattern with stock phrases and scenes. One can imagine a very likely scenario where Dyer, having gained a good deal of public notoriety, comes into town and is introduced to the local group of apostates who sit around and relate, in their community of apostasy, the shared experience of Shakerism. As part of the process of acceptance back into mainstream society, it is necessary for individuals to absolve their connections to the former group (the Shakers) and reassert alignment with current community norms. Telling tales of abuse and suffering are not only a good vehicle for stigmatizing the Shakers, it is also a good way to illustrate just how far one had traveled along a Christian path of suffering. And if that path was exaggerated ever so slightly while one held the center of attention as an authority on the mysterious Shaker experience, what would be the harm?

The harm came when *Portraiture*, delayed several years, actually came to print, and the public began to discuss the experiences contained within. For apostates who had rebuilt their lives, having their stories displayed in print and in the papers was not in their best interests of maintaining a position in society. In these cases, it is not hard to imagine that outside of a supportive community of apostates who asserted the Shakers duped them into joining, the public thought the affiants strange for ever dallying with the suspect sect in the first place. One apostate informant addressed this tenuous public standing, admitting that "[p]eople may think it is strange, that any person of sense should believe such things. But the Shakers had a strange effect. . . ."[51] Assigning the Shakers a power to dupe individuals relieved the apostate-victim of agency in having joined the group. In addition, some apostates had family members who remained Shakers. Whether out of loyalty or fear, affiants may have had second thoughts upon seeing their statements in the cold black-and-white type of the press. In the publications following *Portraiture* we see a good deal of retreat in the statements from those who, for whatever reason, suddenly chafed at the idea of being in the limelight.

The Shakers took advantage of the affiants' embarrassment and surprise at finding themselves in print. The Shakers, too, had an agenda: stave off external and internal attack. For decades the Shakers had fought off the dogged rumors of holding children in bondage, drinking to excess, and lewd behavior. The retractions published in the Shakers' *Review* do not outright dispute the previous allegations as much as they clarify words and actions, shifting the affiant further away from agency (and hence from public scorn). The Shakers, quite skilled in verbal parry, actually rewrote several statements from Dyer's *Portraiture* to better suit their needs, telling readers that this is what the affiant really meant to declare.[52] Much of this word war was splitting hairs, but it indicated how strongly the Shakers were stung by the persistent accusations and how aggressively they mounted a defense to recast themselves in a better light than Mary Dyer. The apostates did point out irrefutable facts. The Shakers did separate families both in those cases where a spouse did not join, and internally as biological bonds were broken in favor of communitywide ties. The Shakers were celibate and their lifestyle, including communal living and methods of child-rearing, was significantly different from the mainstream norm. The public called for a defense, or at least an explanation, for the Shaker way of life.

Dyer, the apostate affiants, and the Shakers exaggerated, manipulated, and reformulated words to reflect either what they believed to be true or what they wished others to believe was reality. How well these statements reflected some subjective "truth" will never be known. The more important point is that at least a portion of the public *believed* the statements to be true because the accusations reaffirmed shared values, exposed fears, or supported previously held beliefs about the dangers of difference—in both gender roles and religious practices. Further it is important that not only were various accusations believed, but that these beliefs legitimated and motivated continued anti-Shaker activity.[53] Whether the statements repeated previously heard oral tales, confirmed preexisting beliefs about the sectarian group's challenge to the social order, or offered a means for the apostate's acceptance into the mainstream community, the affidavits were accepted as fact by anti-Shaker factions. Likewise, the Shaker statements about Dyer's character were believed to be true by another segment of the population who were quick to agree that a woman so eager to step out of the home and into a public arena, probably stepped away from other aspects of traditional behavior as well. Ultimately, what is fascinating about this extended debate is not so much the truth of any one statement, but rather how the perception of the validity of the affidavits worked to define acceptable boundaries of community behavior, whether inside or outside a communal enclave. The public interest in the Dyer-Shaker debate encapsulated two different defenses of and attacks on the social order. Mary Dyer, her affiants, and the Shakers all participated in the social construction of reality. For the opponents of Shakerism, the reality of communalism was evil; for the Shakers and their proponents, that same reality was good.

The Shaker countertestimony accused Mary of manipulating her affiants' words. For example, Joshua Fletcher, whose statement first appeared in *Portraiture,* stated that Dyer had "misrepresented and coloured in a high degree" his earlier affidavit.[54] Similarly, in *A Review,* Josiah Watson admitted that his initial statement to Dyer was unreliable hearsay, an indication of how earlier, in a more private setting, Watson may have supplied an appreciative and encouraging Dyer with what she wanted to hear. Several affidavits attempted to disprove accusations Dyer made in *Portraiture.* For example, Betsy Foster, who in *Portraiture* blamed the Shakers for a painful separation from her children, admitted in *A Review* that she *willingly* left her children at the Shakers despite the pain that decision caused. The Shakers teased apart several of Dyer's affidavits and revealed errors in geography and chronology, especially regarding allegations that Shaker founder Ann Lee had appeared in Concord, New Hampshire, during the 1770s as a fortune-teller.

A Review included devastating testimony from Mary's children. Caleb (then age twenty-four) responded to a May 3, 1824, *New Hampshire Statesman* article in which Mary claimed the Shakers held her children in captivity and ignorance. Declaring satisfaction with his Shaker home, Caleb emphatically asserted that the Shakers neither kept children in bondage nor denied them knowledge of the world beyond their enclave. Orville echoed his older brother's sentiments regarding their alleged captivity and urged his mother "not to put herself to that trouble about us, as there is no law to compel me to live with the Shakers, contrary to my choice, I do not wish to have one made to compel me to leave them contrary to my choice." Orville concluded wittily that he was old enough to decide for himself "as I am in the twentieth year of my age, and am six feet and two inches and an half in height."[55] Jerrub (age nineteen) and Joseph (age sixteen) agreed that the Shakers had treated them kindly, and that they did not wish to leave.

Dyer responded to this crisis with new testimony and a new pamphlet. In her *Reply to the Shakers' Statements* (Concord, 1824), Mary countered allegations that she had falsified the affidavits with a detailed description of how she had gathered her information and published *Portraiture*. And as the Shakers had investigated her affidavits, Dyer checked theirs and revisited many of her *Portraiture* affiants. Some, such as Joseph Stanley, stated in Dyer's *Reply* that the Shakers had visited and attempted to force a retraction of his earlier statement. Others clarified or expanded on statements made in their *Portraiture* testimony. The dynamic quality of this protracted, printed debate is seen with several individuals who appeared in both the Shakers' *A Review* and Dyer's *Reply* each time altering the circumstances of their original oath.

Consider the example of Sarah Curtis Straw. Sarah was in a unique position as an affiant, having assisted Mary with household chores in Stewartstown, and having shared a room with Mary at the Shaker village. In Joseph Dyer's *A Compendious Narrative* (1819), Sarah provided a lengthy affidavit in which she stated that Mary's conduct was so abhorrent that Sarah requested the elders to move her to another room.[56] In *Portraiture* (1822), Sarah provided a letter in which she related how the Shakers had forced her to sign the affidavit that she did not fully understand.[57] In the Shakers' *Review* (1824), Sarah stated that in 1819 she had made a few brief remarks to Mary Dyer "in order to get rid of her repeated persuasions" but had not written the letter printed in *Portraiture*.[58] In Dyer's *Reply* (1824), a statement from Lemuel and Tryphena Dow indicated that Sarah regretted her former conduct towards Mary and wanted to provide a written statement to counter her earlier allegations. The Dows' statement revealed that Lemuel had actually penned the *Portraiture* letter *for* Sarah who examined it and then signed it.[59] This exchange highlighted the power of printed words to capture (or cover) a particular meaning. It also spoke to the potential of published works to perform as actors themselves in this drama, pulling opinion one way or the other as the reader was invited to partake of this extended conversation.[60]

The public debate between Mary Dyer and the Shakers continued in 1825 and 1826 via a series of handbills, single sheets of paper with text printed on one or both sides. Like her previous publications, her handbills stimulated a Shaker response, a public response, and further assistance of the growing apostate network. In this abbreviated format Dyer tightened the presentation of her major accusations: that the Shakers deceived the public, stole property, and separated families. Her demand was straightforward: "Give me my children, I ask no more." She directed her anger towards the elders. Their "subjects," she stated, were "honest," a useful assertion to facilitate her reintegration into mainstream Protestantism, to protect the reputations of her five Shaker children, and to distance herself from the fact that she herself had been a Shaker for two years.[61]

Dyer published her 1825 handbill in New Lebanon, New York, the seat of Shaker power. She lambasted the Shaker faith as having been "founded on fraud, deception, and blasphemy" and attacked founder Ann Lee for drunkenness, naked dancing, and other conduct "more recoiling to modesty and common decency."[62] This accusation formed a preamble to Dyer's inquiry regarding an incident at Whiting's Pond where, Dyer had been told, Shaker James Farnham had watched Shaker women bathing nude. Dyer bragged in her handbill that she had enough proof to "shut mouths" of those who tried to deny her accusations and that she had deposited seventeen affidavits with a local minister to support her statements.[63]

Dyer had good success in the New Lebanon area. In addition to being the seat of the Shaker faith, and more pertinent for Dyer's purposes, the area had a long history of antagonistic relationships with the Shakers, especially in the eighteenth century when the Shakers first arrived. When Dyer inquired about interactions with the Shakers, she found many local residents who were willing to discuss the days of mobs and to repeat the old accusations concerning Ann Lee's behavior. The Shaker response to Dyer was rapid and two-fold. Three Shaker leaders published a statement denying Dyer's accusations in the August 25, 1825, Pittsfield (Massachusetts) *Sun*. In October, James Farnham published his own handbill addressed "To The Public." In it Farnham lashed out at Dyer's "proof," "the testimonies of malicious slanderers" and "stale calumnies and thread-bare stories . . . printed and reprinted and scattered in every direction."[64]

Dyer's allegations scattered across New England, but so did the Shaker response. The handbills were printed in New Lebanon and then distributed to Shaker communities as needed. The New Hampshire Shakers printed 480 copies to circulate in Northern New England in addition to those already sent from New Lebanon. When acknowledging the receipt of the New Lebanon handbills, the New Hampshire ministry warned their New York brethren that Mary Dyer was likely "plotting mischief somewhere—therefore we have counseled the deacons to be on their watch."[65] A few months earlier, the New Lebanon ministry passed a warning along to West Union cautioning the western Shakers to beware of "that wicked woman" who had "great influence on such as are unacquainted with her & who want occasion against the way of God."[66] Ironically, Dyer influenced Shaker behavior as well. In a letter that described Dyer as "that modern jezebel," the Shaker author suggested that "if we are as zealously engaged to do our father's will, as Mary Dyer is to do her father's will, that we shall be able to stand against all the storms of persecution that have arisen or may arise on her account."[67] The Shakers used Dyer's campaign as a mirror to gauge the strength of their own resolve to fight.

Dyer responded to Farnham's rebuttal with a second handbill, "To The Public," dated March 2, 1826. To counter Farnham's "outrageous and wanton attack," Dyer offered an expanded version of her first handbill, continuing her attack on the Shakers for the sake of those in captivity, including her own "wretched family." Dyer's handbill made its way to the editors of the *Boston News-Letter and City Record* who commented upon it in the April 29, 1826, edition. The editors held mixed feelings about the Shakers. On the one hand they praised the neat dwelling houses, productive land, and fine new New Lebanon meetinghouse, but on the other hand the editors called Elder Farnham an "autocrat" whose alleged actions were "enough to destroy all confidence in the purity of their morals and personal conduct."[68] By the late 1820s, this mixed attitude of praise and personal condemnation gained prevalence. Perhaps the Shakers weren't as entirely evil as Dyer had depicted?

Nonetheless, Mary Dyer's visibility through her books, appearances, and circulars acted as a springboard for additional apostate activity. In the fall of 1825, Dyer's writings stirred anti-Shaker sentiment in southern Maine. A group of apostates worked together for a year to agitate the public in preparation for a court battle over wages with the Shakers at Alfred and Sabbathday Lake, Maine. The Alfred Shakers described Dyer's role in the organization and preparation of the apostates for their "most desperate struggle." They began their campaign "by collecting all the rediculous [*sic*] stories, which could be gathered from the scum of the bottomless pit." Then "Mary Dyer and her deciples [*sic*] and every enemy [*sic*] of Believers was now collected . . . having been at school, or training for more than a year past to learn how to use their weapons to . . . crush the Shakers and break their institution."[69] Despite the concentrated apostate effort, the suit was unsuccessful and the "reprobates and their party began to feel poorly indeed."[70]

Back in New Hampshire, residents of Enfield and surrounding villages once again took up Dyer's cause, this time filing three petitions to the legislature representing a combined total of nearly 200 individuals. Similar to Joshua Stevens's 1818 petition, these petitions argued that the Shakers disrupted local society by forcing husbands to violate the marriage contract and to hate their wives and by neglecting to provide children with enough information about the world in order for them to make a rational decision whether to stay with the Shakers or leave. The impetus for this round of attacks was the Folsom family. Stephen Folsom had joined the Enfield Shakers in March 1828, but his wife refused to join him. Fearing for her family's safety, she hid her children and some household goods and gained a good deal of local support. There was so much interference from the local community that Stephen Folsom posted an advertisement, "To the Public," castigating the "meddlesome neighbors" who were disturbing the peace of his Shaker family, a reversal of the claim Joshua Stevens's petitioners had made in 1818, when they claimed that the Shakers disturbed their peace. Folsom emphasized that he still provided for his family, as the Shakers supported the "sacred duties of domestic life."[71] Dyer's complaints that the Shakers destroyed families were still very much alive.

Attorney Philip Carrigan, who helped craft Dyer's 1818 petition to the legislature, represented the Enfield residents and filed their petitions to the legislature in June 1828, but then asked for (and received) a postponement until the November term, in order to make arrangements for testifiers to come to Concord. In November, Carrigan asked for another extension, effectively postponing the hearing until the following June. The Shakers objected to the postponements and pointedly argued that "[i]t is well known that this is not the first time of exhibiting complaints to the legislature against the Shakers." Further, the Shakers argued, these complaints were merely rehashed versions of Dyer's old allegations—they "contained nothing new."[72] The Shaker remonstrance to the petitions indicated Dyer's hand working in the background: "[w]hereas certain evil disposed persons, have for a number of years past strove, and still continue to strive, either directly or indirectly, to molest the peace of the . . . Shakers."[73] The legislature had little patience for the petitioners' delays and lack of preparation, and although they understood the accusations to be serious, the specially appointed committee favored the Shakers who had twice arrived at the appointed day prepared, despite the expense and difficulty a legislative hearing presented. The legislature allowed the petitioners to withdraw their petitions, effectively silencing their campaign.

Throughout the 1820s, Dyer's most visible period, the Shakers closely monitored her movements. In July 1825, the New Lebanon ministry warned western Shakers that Dyer had made plans, apparently never realized, to travel out to "Ohio &c after she has overthrown the Mother Church." With the dry wit present in so many Shaker letters, the ministry continued: "If she does not go till she has effected that work, you will not be troubled by her person, if you should be with her books."[74] The Hancock ministry reported in March 1826 that "Mary Dyer the Abominable is in these parts, she has crept over into Lebanon Hollow and like a sitting goose or turkey-buzzard is brooding over her nest of lies, and generating them into life by her lasivious [*sic*] pen. She is still now, and probably will be during her incubation."[75] Dyer had been in the New Lebanon area for a year when the Parent Ministry sent a July 1826 update to the western Shakers and noted how "it [was] astonishing to see what influence [Dyer had] over the minds of mankind."[76]

In the mid-1820s, Dyer continued to collect affidavits in the towns surrounding the New Lebanon and Hancock Shaker settlements. Dyer's circulars, proximity to the Shaker headquarters, and a planned second edition of *Portraiture* prompted the Shakers to publish a second edition of Joseph Dyer's *A Compendious Narrative* (Pittsfield, 1826). The second edition included a new preface, signed by Joseph Dyer but written by Seth Wells.[77] The shift in the Shaker response from Joseph Dyer to Wells reflected a change in the Shaker perception of Mary's campaign. Her argument and the public reaction to it had gone beyond domestic broils. The Shakers understood her actions as an attack on their way of life. Underlying Dyer's accusations was the reality that Shakerism did indeed separate families when spouses differed in their commitments to the faith. Although Shaker practice declared that husbands "provide" for their nonbelieving wives, as the Dyer situation had illustrated, the vague policy led to a state of cultural limbo for the wife, a less than total religious commitment from the husband, and legal and public relations difficulties for the Shakers. Without a divorce, a Shaker spouse retained marital ties and obligations that, despite pretensions to the contrary, continued to hold the novice Shaker in the world. The shift in the preface of *A Compendious Narrative* signified the change in Shaker response from Joseph Dyer's personal rebuttal to an organizational defense.

Likewise, despite her plaintive demand to return her children, Dyer had shifted her own understanding of her anti-Shaker campaign. No longer did she fight solely for the release of her own children who by the end of the decade had reached adulthood. She now fought to erad-icate the faith and free all Shakers whom she believed were held cap-tive and deluded by the elders' "erroneous principles, base deceptions, and pious frauds."[78] Like those who attacked the Catholic Church and the Masons in the same period, Dyer broadened her argument to awaken the public to the danger Shakerism posed to American society.[79] This shift in her anti-Shaker campaign foreshadowed much of Dyer's later public work as she took up additional reform causes including aboli-tion and temperance.

Despite her high visibility and prodigious publication efforts, by 1827 public interest in Mary Dyer had waned. The New Hampshire min-istry reported that in terms of Mary Dyer's public reception, people were more interested in "seeking favor instead of fighting."[80] The sec-ond edition of *Portraiture* never materialized. A more positive public assessment of Shakerism, a glut of information in print, and other extra-local concerns lessened public focus on the Shakers. Apostate Benjamin Green reflected on the poor sales of his own apostate narrative and explained that by 1830 potential customers had grown more savvy about published narratives. "Most people," Green offered, " . . . seemed to think all such efforts were made for the bare purpose of gouging them out of their money." Further, his tale, "depicting the horrible gloom of Shakerism," was published too late; "the public mind was then agi-tating the subject of masonry which seemed to be the all engrossing topic of the day."[81] Anti-Shaker activity continued, but the massive and complex argument of *Portraiture,* by the end of the decade, had already become dated.

※ ※ ※

Since 1815, Mary Dyer had begged Joseph for the power to govern a home of her own, near her children. Although her anti-Shaker cam-paign had faded from public view, at the end of the 1820s Dyer achieved her goal of independence. In addition to highlighting flaws in Shaker dealings with families, Dyer's campaign had highlighted a problem with New Hampshire divorce statutes. The restrictive laws were based on a philosophy that lenient divorce would destroy the family by letting individuals out of their bonds too easily. But without a divorce, women such as Dyer were left without resources or a social and legal identity, potentially a drain on society as the new town poor. Mary's legislative petitions of 1817 and 1818 had spurred the New Hampshire legislature to investigate a change to the divorce statutes. Although the legislature had not offered direct assistance to Mary Dyer in 1817 and 1818, her unfortunate situation had made an impact on the legislature. In 1824, a new law permitted divorce when one spouse joined a sect that negated the marriage bond.[82] With this addition to the law, Mary Dyer now had grounds for divorce. Near the end of the decade, Dyer sold the last of her books in New Lebanon and returned to New Hampshire.

Given Dyer's antagonistic relationship with the Shakers, it is not surprising that the divorce was contested, and the suit dragged on for two years. In May of 1828, Dyer filed a petition requesting "that the bonds of matrimony between them may be decreed null & void."[83] Her request was based on the new law: that Joseph, "wholly disregarding the marriage contract," joined the Shakers in 1811 and has lived with the Shakers ever since, that the Shakers believed the marriage bond to be void, and that Joseph refused to cohabit with Mary. The Superior Court ordered a copy of the petition to be served on Joseph thirty days prior to the next court term. In preparation for court, both Mary and Joseph gathered depositions. By law, each spouse could be present while depositions were taken on behalf of the opposition. In addition, both Mary and Joseph (or their attorneys) had the opportunity to challenge the deponent's statements. Both Mary and Joseph took full advantage of this practice, drawing out additional information from testimony to help make their best possible case and weaken that of the other. The suit was contentious and continued from term to term, until November 1830 when it was finally heard in full.

Dyer's six-page manuscript deposition detailed the destruction of her family by Shakerism. Although it was "oppressive" to Dyer's feelings to "produce facts against one" she expected to be a "companion," "friend and protector," Dyer offered the story of her marital woes. As in *A Brief Statement,* in her deposition Dyer portrayed herself as a faithful, loving, hardworking wife. She had had no complaints about Joseph until he found the "Shaker Principle." At that point, he refused to cohabit with Mary and told her that to "incumber himself with any more family" would be a sin. Crooker's arrival signaled another downturn. Mary wrote how neither "tongue nor pen [was] able to describe my distress," as Joseph insisted on moving the family to the Shakers, with or without Mary. Mary described how Shakers took away her children, how Joseph was "confederate in the cruelty," and how her "trouble was more than I could bare [sic] and at times I lost my reason." Considering it her duty to help her family, Dyer told how she left the Shakers "to seek asylum among strangers" in hopes of getting assistance to free her children.

Dyer emphasized her captivities at the Shakers and Joseph's failure to provide for her. She related the advertisement incident, where Joseph first posted Mary as his "lawful wife," but then repeatedly denied that she was his wife, claiming the Shaker gospel had separated them. Dyer illustrated how she had turned to selectmen, attorneys and the legislature for assistance but to no avail. She pointed out how in *Willis v. Dyer*, "Mr. Dyer got beet [sic]," only to be overturned in the appeal because of Shaker lies. Mary described the Shakers' slanderous publications, including Joseph's *Narrative*, and to Mary "it seemed doubly cruel to have my husband assist in it when he was my only protection or defense." At this point, Mary relayed to the court, she "was now fully convinced that there was no protection for a wife of a Shaker . . . and that power which is allowed a husband for the protection of a wife is by a Shaker used to abuse and destroy her." Mary offered that she would rather have died with her own "true character," than to live with the stain Joseph's actions had brought upon her family. She asked the Superior Court, the "only authority remaining," for the "power to protect" herself. Her husband had no intention of doing so.

The very act of Mary suing Joseph for divorce was an example of how Mary challenged Joseph's authority, here forcing him into the defendant's role. Joseph Dyer defended his actions with example after example of how Mary neglected the role of wife and how Mary had made their marriage celibate. Joseph repeated his accusation of Mary's involvement with Lemuel Crooker, doubly problematic because all three had just joined the Shakers. He found that Mary and Crooker were "more formilliar [sic] together than I thought our faith would admit of," and this made Joseph jealous and his life disagreeable. Joseph offered Mary a deal. He would give up Shakerism if she would live with him as a wife usually did. She "positively denied it." Both he and Mary, Joseph testified, wanted to go to the Shakers, and when the War of 1812 loomed, the decision was made to move to Enfield. Interestingly, Joseph told a new version of how the Dyers joined the Enfield community. He related that the Shakers preferred that the Dyers live in their own home nearby the village but Mary refused this. Seeing "how set she was," the Shakers somewhat reluctantly agreed that the Dyers could join the society if both agreed freely to do so. Despite Mary's insistence, Joseph recalled, she soon "became discontented and ran away and has made me a great deal of cost and trouble until my interest has been consumed." Joseph still considered Mary his lawful wife and considered himself "bound by law to take care of her and her property"—and here Joseph adds a condition—"when she puts herself and property under my care in that obedience which a wife ought to be to her husband."[84] Joseph had tried to do his duty but Mary was disobedient, unwifely, and therefore not the innocent party she pretended to be.

Who had broken the marriage rules? Marriage was a contract both public and private " . . . that defined obligations between husband and wife, bound their union to the political order, and shaped constructions of gender."[85] Joseph's story of Mary's willful disobedience replayed a standard nineteenth-century format legal historian Hendrik Hartog found in autobiographies, memoirs, and trial transcripts.[86] Yet Mary's duty to obey Joseph was contingent on his upholding the duties of a husband.[87] Depositions from friends, family, and Shakers provided evidence to support one version or the other of this tale of marital failure. Testimony included descriptions of the Dyer wedding, their life in Stewartstown, and Joseph and Mary's behavior towards one another. Mary had rallied the support of several former Shakers, including the perennial deponent Sarah Curtis Straw, who recalled their own experiences of Shaker-induced marital separation. Shakers, including Caleb Dyer, asserted that Joseph had tried to provide for Mary and that the elders never demanded that husbands neglect their wives. Mary cross-examined the deponents, including Joseph who asserted, in response to Mary's somewhat surprising question, that he was willing to live with her and provide for her if she would act like a "dutiful wife." He would not, however, cohabit with Mary.

But the court was not particularly interested in what Joseph had done, or failed to do, but rather what the Shakers believed. The statute would grant the divorce if two criteria were met: if one partner joined a sect that did not believe the marriage bond to be valid, and, if they had remained with that sect and did not cohabit with their spouse for three years. If the party involved had joined the sect prior to the passage of the 1824 act and remained with the sect for six months following the passage of the law, still refusing to cohabit, then a divorce could be granted. The testimony from friends and family had proven that Joseph and Mary had forgone cohabitation in 1808 and that Joseph had joined the Shakers in 1813 and had remained with them since. The court then tackled the issue of whether or not the Shakers believed the relation between man and wife to be void. Mary's witnesses, former Shakers, adequately demonstrated that the Shakers profess no special bond, and no cohabitation, between husband and wife.

The Shakers did not deny this point. Joseph's witnesses demonstrated to the court's satisfaction that the Shakers believed it important to uphold the legal ramifications of the marriage contract with the believing husband providing for his unbelieving wife, and the wife "bound on her part to conduct herself in a discreet and seemly way." Shaker John Lyon, who had traveled to Stewartstown twenty years before this suit to help convert the Dyers and their neighbors, cited specific pages from Shaker publications to document the Shakers belief and practice. To the court it was "clearly proved" that the Dyer case met the provisions of the statute: "[T]he husband has declared that he considered it a sin to cohabit with his wife and that it was against his faith so to do." In addition, the court had "the affidavit of the wife, [which stated] that she has been desirous to cohabit with her husband, and . . . that he has constantly refused to cohabit with her." Of Mary's desire to cohabit with Joseph the court saw "no reason to doubt the fact."[88] As Hartog described, litigants in a divorce case molded their selves in ways recognizable in the law in order to best make their case, and certainly here Mary Dyer is no exception.[89] But her molding worked. Joseph may have been a negligent husband, and Mary may have been a disobedient wife, but the court saw only a refusal to cohabit. The Dyer family would never again be (re)productive. Mary Dyer was granted her divorce and regained her status as a single woman.

Dyer fades from public view after having received her divorce. Dyer wrote how having "realized the inhuman treatment I had received from my husband, I thought I would not wear his name. . . ."[90] She successfully petitioned the legislature for the return her maiden name, Mary Marshall. Although the divorce statute entitled Mary to her real estate and alimony, there is no evidence she received any settlement. Fifteen years of legislative and court battles, publication costs, and intermittent boarding expenses had drained the Dyer marital estate dry. Following the divorce, Mary lived with her sister's family in Orford and joined the Congregational Church. She boarded a while with the Purmorts of Enfield until "by her industry and economy, she . . . obtained for herself a home and property sufficient for her support."[91] With a letter of recommendation from the Congregational Church of Orford, Mary joined the Congregational Church in Enfield.[92] She would live, not far from the Shaker village, in a small cottage on Mount Calm, watching over her children until her death.[93] Mary had lost her children, but she had won her freedom.

❦   ❦   ❦

Mary Dyer and women like her pushed the boundaries of female behavior at a time when idealized gender roles were shifting. Despite sympathy for her situation, the public had difficulty reconciling Mary's desire for the domestic sphere with her public adventures. Dyer's attempts to merge public and private dimensions left her "a spectacle for remark." Similarly, Dyer's claims that the Shakers were uncivilized contrasted with the visual evidence of neatly ordered Shaker villages. Within the hierarchical view of social evolution, a society could not be both physically ordered and morally disordered. As the *Newburyport Herald* reported, those who had "seen the neatness and economy" of Shaker villages "felt an unwillingness to believe the slanderous representations Mrs. Dyer."[94] Ultimately the Shakers' works spoke louder than Dyer's words.

Mary Dyer did not argue for greater rights for women or even for equal rights with men; she argued for restoration of "those just rights which belong to [her] sex."[95] Her extraordinarily public and complex apostasy was unconventional, but she sought a very conventional goal: to mother her children. Dyer's high visibility provides a good case study for reassessing the sociocultural tensions that undergirded apostate conflict. The strong Shaker response illuminated points of tension and concern within Shakerism as leaders grappled with issues of gender inequality, family, and community structure. That the Dyer-Shaker dispute appeared largely in print culture attests to the participants' keen awareness of the potential of print to persuade the public. In addition, the Shakers' decisive and extensive rebuttal testifies to their mature experience and adept skill in a medium they had only begun to exploit just a few years before Mary Dyer joined the Enfield Shakers.

A Portraiture of Shakerism was an active voice in the social construction of American society in the 1820s. Dyer's text stimulated a public discussion and Shaker response unlike any prior or later anti-Shaker work. Opponents and proponents denounced or supported a particular sectarian faith, but imbedded within the discourse were beliefs about the proper role for women, mothers, husbands, and fathers and the limits of religious belief and practice. Dyer's experience among and after the Shakers taught her, and her readers, not only the consequences of joining a sectarian group, but the consequences of straying from the narrowly defined gender path presented to women in the early nineteenth century.

5

In Deep Affliction

In the 1830s, Mary Dyer dropped from public view. She published nothing, and Shaker letters failed to mention her, a vast difference from the 1820s when Dyer was at the center of controversy and a frequent topic of Shaker correspondence. Ensconced in her little cottage on Mount Calm just a few miles from the Enfield Shaker village, Dyer watched her surviving children mature. She would not return to anti-Shaker activity until the next decade, prompted by the 1840 death of her son Joseph, Jr. In that decade Dyer would once again use her well-honed skills to gain public attention to the cause of mistreated women and children who suffered as a result of Shaker practice. In the 1830s, though, Dyer was quiet.

But in the years between 1830 and 1840, the public's view of Shakerism had changed, and apostate accounts faced increasing competition from other print sources of information on the Shakers. Shaker works had begun to outweigh their accusers' words. Shaker industry and order were a model for emulation in a time period of economic fluctuations and uncertainty. The Shakers' temperate life and respectable habits represented a moral core that many feared would be extinguished by the increasingly urban, capitalist culture. And their unique, if not old-fashioned, dress clearly identified the Shaker membership and what they stood for, a task not easily accomplished with an increasingly diverse American population. "Shaker" had come to represent a nostalgic image of an agricultural, American past, one that many Americans worried had vanished in the wake of rapid growth in the name of progress.

James Fenimore Cooper, writing in 1828, captured the public praise for Shaker order and industry in his *Notions of Americans:*

> They are an orderly, industrious sect, and models of decency, cleanliness, and of morality, too, so far as the human eye can penetrate. I have never seen, in any country, villages so neat, and so perfectly beautiful, as to order and arrangement, without, however, being picturesque and ornamented, as those of the Shakers. . . . They are renowned retailers of garden seeds, brushes, farming utensils, &c., &c.[1]

Cooper was one of many men and women of his era who visited the Shakers as a leisurely excursion. A glut of written works, both fiction and nonfiction, addressed the public's continued fascination with the Shakers. Central in written works was a focus on the physical form of Shakers. Caroline Lee Hentz's "Shaker Girl," a short story published in *Godey's Lady's Book* (1839), provided a typical description. Shaker women wore "garments as peculiar and unbecoming" as the men's garments were "ancient." The author described in sickly terms the physical features of Shaker women who wore "a mob cap of linen fastened close around the face, from which every tress of hair was combed carefully back, [this] constituted their chill and ghost-like attire. [A] . . . phantasmagoria of a dream, so pale and unearthly did they seem."[2] "Shaker Girl" featured a frequently considered plot—love within a Shaker village. In story after story, authors used near-death images to suggest that without love, there was no life. Ghostly, tubercular Shaker women, lacking roles of wife and mother, simply wasted away and died. The tension between the Shakers as models of efficiency and the Shakers as arcane, religiously misguided individuals played itself out in stories that inevitably portrayed the Shaker experiment as destined to disappear.

In addition to fiction, nonfiction visitor's accounts appeared in newspapers and magazines. As in fiction, the appearance of the Shaker body provided information. Just as phrenologists read bumps on the head, the clothing and physical form of Shakers revealed their cloistered life. Nathaniel Hawthorne, who visited the Harvard (Massachusetts) Shakers several times in the 1840s and 1850s, found the women "pale" and "none of the men had a jolly aspect."[3] Hawthorne's visits provided inspiration for two short stories with Shaker themes, "The Canterbury Pilgrims" (1833) and "The Shaker Bridal" (1837). Charles Dickens, who visited the New Lebanon community in 1842, described a "grim old Shaker, with eyes as hard, and dull, and cold, as the great round metal buttons on his coat and waistcoat: a sort of calm goblin."[4]

Humorist Artemus Ward visited a New York Shaker community and described in 1861 a Shaker woman as "a solum female, lookin sumwhat like last year's beanpole stuck into a long meal bag."[5]

In addition to the well-known visitors who published their experiences (Ralph Waldo Emerson and Herman Melville were also among the notable visitors to Shaker societies), many visitors recorded their impressions in private journals and letters. These visitors, Americans drawn to Shaker services by curiosity, combined a favorable impression of Shaker villages with commentary on the Shakers' physical form. Susan Yandell wrote to her parents following an 1825 visit to the Pleasant Hill, Kentucky, community where her "curiosity was completely gratified." Yandell's husband wrote to his father of the same visit and remarked on how useful the visit had been for his daughters. "The girls were much amused by the religious ceremonies of the Shaking Quakers. They are observant of everything, & wile [sic] improve greatly their stock of practical & curious information."[6] Henry Waller, an 1833 graduate of the U. S. Military Academy, also visited Pleasant Hill where he observed that "[t]he appearance of the females was generally very course, and they all seemed to be of the lower class." Waller had a more favorable impression of some of the male members "whose countenances struck me as highly intelligent."[7] Miner Kilbourne Kellogg, during an 1833 visit, found the girls at Shakerville, Ohio, unattractive and reasoned that apostasy had had an effect as "*All* the *pretty* girls, and I can't say how many *ugly* ones, have left them." The remaining sisters "with their little, plain white caps, with tabs to come under their chin, their long faces with sunken eyes & cheeks," reminded Kellogg "of ghosts more than anything else."[8] Nonetheless, the Yandells, Waller, Kellogg, and numerous other visitors found much to praise in the Shaker villages, and although their private musings were not published, their favorable comments, passed along in letters and conversation, helped build acceptance of Shakerism.

Despite the perceived physical appearance of Shakers, public attitude had largely shifted from scorn of their religious beliefs to admiration for their agricultural and industrial practice and products.[9] Newspaper articles at mid-century continued the praise and offered advice. A *New York Weekly Tribune* article urged the Shakers to vote and stated that "there is no portion of the community who better conform to the requirements of morality, industry and society." In their refusal to vote, the *Tribune* argued, the Shakers "expose themselves to assaults by neighbors" such as the continual petitions to the legislature.[10] Even apostate authors at mid-century accepted aspects of Shaker life. The Shakers were no longer evil, simply misguided, and within the various public critiques of the movement lay a core belief in the value of the continuance of at least certain parts of Shakerism, rather than letting the entire movement fade away. As an anonymous apostate recorded: "My impression has long been that when any considerable number of persons accept a certain idea and act upon it for a lengthened period, it must be because such [an] idea comprises more or less of truth and practical worth."[11] In fact, by the mid-nineteenth century, the Shakers were looked upon not as a threat to society, but were seen by some as a model for society. The anonymous author's language of praise was typical:

> I said the Shakers had characteristics which might advantageously be copied by the world at large. They present to that world a spectacle of order, sobriety, and untiring, successful industry, which were not easily matched, and certainly not transcended, were you to circumnavigate our globe in the search.[12]

Authors seemed to suggest a compromise: If the Shakers would not abandon celibacy and adopt the world's procreative practice, then let the world adopt the best of Shaker habits and prosper.

In addition to the competition from fiction and nonfiction accounts about the Shakers, apostate authors faced competition from seceders from a number of other curious groups. As Shaker apostate author Benjamin Green had indicated, by 1830 concern about the Masons was rampant, especially in the wake of the kidnapping and murder of William Morgan, whose book *Illustrations of Masonry* had revealed Masonic secrets. When the crime was discovered, the public was aghast at the Masonic society's ability to break the law, hide their crime, and escape punishment, a challenge to the republican ideal of equality before the law. Investigatory committees, anti-Masonic societies, and a "convention of seceding masons" published numerous pamphlets and books revealing even more detail of the latest challenge to American society.[13] Shaker apostate author William Haskett touched on the popular interest in Masons when he alleged that Mother Ann knew freemasonry by revelation.[14] Catholics were also under intense attack and a flurry of convent narratives purported to reveal the secret rituals and heinous crimes hidden by convent walls. As mobs had stormed Shaker communities in the previous decades, anti-Catholic mobs attacked and burned Catholic convents attempting to remove the Catholic threat from their Protestant midst.[15] Apostate author John McBride took the oft-cited comparison between Shakers and Catholics and moved it to the eye-catching title page of his 1834 *An Account of the Doctrines,*

Government, Manners and Customs of the Shakers, in which he announced the work included "Remarks on Confession to Catholic Priests and Shaker Elders."[16] By the end of the decade, Mormons would become the group to be feared, and, shortly thereafter, accounts of women escaping Mormon polygamy would become the popular read. The Shaker apostates' timeworn accusations paled in comparison to the threat presented by these new dangers to American society.

Apostates also faced competition from the Shakers themselves, who in addition to works rebutting the apostates' accusations, published numerous texts, pamphlets, essays, and guides, explaining their beliefs and practices in increasingly straightforward speech. A third edition of *The Testimony of Christ's Second Appearing* was offered in 1823, and a fourth in 1856. Shakers Seth Youngs Wells and Calvin Green compiled *Testimonies Concerning the Character and Ministry of Mother Ann Lee and the First Witnesses . . .* in 1827 and offered the reader an opportunity to hear the words and deeds of the Shaker founder from the individuals who had witnessed the events. Shaker works published for internal community use, including juvenile guides and hymn books, found their way to worldly readers, further disseminating information, and lessening the mystery. The Shakers, by 1840 more than six decades on the American landscape, had moved from a "strange, new religion" to a more moderate, mature, more mainstream communal group. Their economic success, the visual order of the villages, the patterned marches of worship (replacing the ecstatic chaos of the previous century), and their longevity as a group, when weighed against the newer (and revived) threats to the nation—Masons, Mormons, Catholics—Shakerism failed to raise the public's concern as it had in decades past.

Nonetheless, Shaker seceders continued to pen accounts of their experiences and offer them to the public for their consumption.[17] And although Dyer herself was apparently quiet during the 1830s, her name and association with anti-Shakerism remained before the public. New Hampshire apostate C. C. Hodgdon's 1838 account of his *Life and Manner of Living among the Shakers* strategically featured Dyer, although his motivation for her prominence is unclear. Hodgdon began his narrative with his youth in 1820s Portsmouth, New Hampshire, where he first learned of the Dyer situation from his coworkers. Although he had not read *Portraiture,* Hodgdon was aware at the time that Dyer claimed the Shakers abused children, and he recalled how her accusations of Shaker crimes filled people with "dismay." He wrote that "all this, and such like stories filled my ear and my soul, with raging surprise and hatred."[18] He feared there "would be an insurrection" that would be fatal to the Shakers.[19] Despite this hatred and fear,

Hodgdon moved to the Canterbury Shakers with two of his sisters shortly thereafter, when he was roughly seventeen years old. He remained for two-and-a-half years.[20]

Hodgdon's work, published nearly a decade after his apostasy, praised the Shakers and discounted Dyer's allegations of abuse. He explained that his reason for apostasy was the difficult personal sacrifices Shakerism required, an up-front explanation that marked apostate accounts of the 1830s and later. For Hodgdon, celibacy "seemed rather too tough a cud for me to chew."[21] In fact, the young Hodgdon had fallen in love with a Shakeress with whom he undertook a secret correspondence and clandestine meetings. His account of secret love read very much like the fictionalized accounts of Shaker romance Nathaniel Hawthorne and other writers of the day had penned. In an attempt to procure sales for his narrative, Hodgdon may have cited Dyer's name to cash in on her fame and borrowed the romance story format in a similar opportunistic vein. At any rate, Hodgdon and his beloved apostatized, married, and had two children before her 1828 death from "mortification of the bowels."[22]

Hodgdon wrote to counter the slanderous texts published by those who "have left them, or who have been sent away for some misdemeanor and then lay their own blame to the Shakers."[23] One of those authors may have been Benjamin Green, yet another Enfield apostate who put complaints against the Shakers in writing. Green, who had lived in the North Family with Mary Dyer, published his account, *The True Believer's Vademecum, or Shakerism Exposed,* in 1831. Like Dyer, Green insisted on his own interpretation of scripture and of the teachings of Ann Lee. Green, believing he had a clearer vision of the faith than the Shaker elders, attempted to spread his version of Shakerism first orally within the Enfield community, then in a printed format to the non-Shaker world following his apostasy.

But Hodgdon's appraisal of Shakerism was considerably more moderate than that of the self-praising Green. Hodgdon commended the Shakers for the fair treatment, clothing, and transportation his wife received upon her departure. His only criticism concerned the lack of wages paid to seceders, and he couched his critique in comparatively mild terms.[24] Of his positive assessment of Shaker life he wrote how he had "no interest in giving this little work to the world, as applauding and upholding the Shakers in every transaction. They are as liable to be wrong sometimes as any other society. But in regard to such punishments as those [Mary Dyer] mentioned, they have no connection with the truth."[25] Hodgdon wrote little of theology and scripture and saw his experience as simple and straightforward. He went to the

Shakers for training in a craft, and when he found he "could not believe in all their religious creeds, or practice with them in every thing," he departed.[26]

Hodgdon had not read *Portraiture,* but the public discussion of Dyer's allegations had formed a strong memory. He concluded his narrative with a two-page attack on Dyer and argued that for the best proof of the Shaker lifestyle readers should "go and stay among them . . . and then judge for yourselves."[27] He offered to meet Dyer in debate and believed "she can not be satisfied when she retires to repose her head against the pillow, so long as the devil and she keeps company in abusing an innocent class of people."[28] His final attack took the form of a poem that was printed both on the last page of his text and on the exterior of the back cover, a place of maximum visibility. The poem read:

To Mary Dyer as a Slanderer

Avaunt! Thou fiend! nor hither bend
   Thy dark, mischievous way;
Dark as the infernal gulf thy mind,
   Where damned spirits are confined
And never for mercy pray.
   To the most dear pain'd virtue's tear,
All evil glads thine eyes;
   Thy sweetest music is the groan
Of some poor wretch by thee undone,
   Who sinks beneath thy lies!
Thou canst not sleep till others weep
   O'er virtues name destroyed!
This, to thy soul is mad'ning bliss
   The food of all thy happiness;
Than life more priz'd—enjoyed!
   Avaunt! Thou fiend! nor hither bend
Thy dark mischievous way!
   Destruction tips thy slanderous tongue,
And poisons from thy heart are wrung;
   O, Mary! have your way![29]

Hodgdon's attack on a fellow apostate reflected the shift in apostate literature that had begun in the 1820s. With the exception of Mary Dyer, in the 1830s and 1840s apostate authors mixed praise with accusation. In 1824, western apostate Absolem Blackburn praised the organized work habits and neat appearance of Shaker women and suggested to his readers, "ladies of Kentucky," that the Shaker sisters serve as a model for the world's women. Consistent with many visitor's reports, Blackburn also praised the structures in Shaker villages. He wrote how even the gardens were "worthy of remark that the vegetables, flowers, &c. opposite each other on the right and left of the main walk, are exactly alike, or of the same kind, size, position, &c. and thus by examining one side of the gardens you can see what is the regotation of the other."[30] John Whitbey, whom the elders forced out of the Pleasant Hill, Kentucky community, nonetheless praised the Shakers as "a people of excellent morals, very industrious, and in cleanliness, decency, temperance, and good order, unequaled: and as a body, remarkably kind and benevolent."[31]

Yet Mary Dyer found little to praise in the group that had separated her family and led her to a lonely life. Dyer's 1847 account, *Rise and Progress of the Serpent,* and her anti-Shaker activities of the late 1840s were out of step with both public perceptions of the Shakers and with the genre of anti-Shaker writing. Although quiet in the 1830s, Dyer regained public attention when she framed her renewed anti-Shaker campaign as a social reform movement, the seeds of which Dyer had planted twenty years earlier and in the 1840s, in a period of widespread social reform, had come to fruition. Dyer's anti-Shaker campaign in the 1840s no longer centered on retrieving her children. Although it was too late to save the lives of her dead children, son Joseph and daughter Betsey, and her three surviving children were, by 1840, grown men, it was not too late to fight for other mothers and their Shaker-held children.

In 1848, thirty-one years after her first legislative appearance, Dyer once again petitioned the New Hampshire legislature for a bill against the Shakers. Dyer's petition, signed by an additional fourteen people, was one of four petitions representing a total of 498 petitioners from across New Hampshire. Collectively, the petitioners sought to establish a law that would prevent the Shakers from indenturing minor children and would provide for the protection of women and children whose husbands or fathers joined the Shakers. In addition, the petitioners requested the development of a system of notification of relatives and friends when Shaker members became ill. Handwritten phrases scattered in the margins and among the signatures on the petitions revealed the signers' sentiments and goals: "Hillsborough County—Save Your Children from the Shakers."[32] Arguing that the Shakers posed a threat to society, the petitions stated that the Shakers practiced "many gross and inconsistent practices, subversive of the public good."[33] The petitions were filed on November 30 and December 4, 1848, and were assigned to a ten-member judiciary committee.

Dyer also filed a second, individual petition. To gain public support, Dyer requested permission to present a free lecture in Concord in the Hall of the House of Representatives. One representative called Mary a "proper" person and supported the notion but others disagreed and felt a lecture would be inappropriate. One legislator deemed "it extremely improper that this woman should come in here and make *ex parte* statements in relation to subjects under consideration by the legislature or its committees."[34] After considerable debate on whether to permit a precedent-setting public lecture in the House, a vote was taken, and the resolution was defeated. One legislator expressed his disapproval of the idea and hinted at the mixed feelings Mary Dyer's public reappearance generated, especially since, "[t]he complaints of this woman had been heard by the legislature twenty years ago and decided to be unfounded."[35] Mary Dyer would have her day before the legislature, but that was the only venue in which some were willing to listen.

While some legislators were expressing dismay at another round of anti-Shaker hearings, Dyer's renewed efforts were facilitated by an extensive network of supporters. Although records of this apostate group are scarce, it is clear that apostates from across New Hampshire, Massachusetts, Maine, and Vermont, corresponded, met, and planned large-scale anti-Shaker activities. The Shakers were well aware of Dyer's active role in this group and expressed shock that at age sixty-eight "*that* old false and currupt [sic] engine should be resuscitated and set in motion after so many years of comparative silence."[36] A New Lebanon Shaker commented on this revived anti-Shakerism and how, once again, Shakers were "in deep affliction in consequence of the seceders stirring up to do them all the harm they can by working on the minds of the Legislators and Mary Dyer at the bottom of it."[37] Members of this group circulated copies of the petition and gathered signatures. Others appeared as witnesses during the legislative hearing. A large, organized group of apostates provided legislative testimony on Shaker child abuse.[38] Anti-Shakers from the Lowell, Massachusetts, area were particularly prominent in this massive legislative action, perhaps even instigating the entire campaign. Regardless, whether as instigator, associate, or emeritus anti-Shaker figurehead, Mary Dyer was once again center stage.

The judiciary committee began its hearings in early December. The committee subpoenaed the New Hampshire Shaker trustees: David Parker from the Canterbury community and, to represent Enfield,

Mary's son Caleb. In addition, the committee interviewed sixteen
Shakers from Canterbury and nine from Enfield. Nine additional witnesses, mostly physicians, testified for the Shakers. Thomas Chadbourne,
a physician involved with the independent investigation of Dyer's medical claims in 1818, was among those supporting the Shakers. Parker
and Caleb Dyer presented copies of covenants and Shaker publications
to support their oral testimony. The Shakers were represented by a team
of lawyers led by future United States president Franklin Pierce.

A single attorney, John S. Wells, represented the 498 petitioners.
Seventeen witnesses, twelve of whom were apostates, appeared on behalf
of the petitioners. The witnesses testified on the Shaker mistreatment
of children, how the Shaker gospel broke apart families, and how the
elders deceived new members out of their property. The sessions were
lengthy and ran from 6:30 P.M. to nearly 11 P.M. After three weeks of
testimony, the entire House and Senate convened to hear closing statements from the attorneys. The room was filled to capacity with legislators, the governor and his council, Shakers, petitioners, and
interested parties. Franklin Pierce spoke first. His lengthy defense of
the Shaker right to religious freedom began at 3:30 P.M., broke once
for a forty-minute recess, then continued until 7:50 P.M. Pierce, at the
height of his career as a Concord lawyer, "addressed the House in a
speech seldom equaled in its ability and eloquence."[39] The court scribe
could not keep pace with Pierce's energetic presentation and stopped
writing mid-speech. At the conclusion of Pierce's defense, the petitioners'
attorney began his three-hour reply in which he dismissed Shakerism
and its spirit-filled rituals.

The rituals of Shaker practice, including the recent phenomenon of
"Mother's Work," were very much at issue during the testimony.
Mother's Work began in August 1837, when Shakers at Watervliet,
New York, witnessed a mystifying event. Several young girls whirled
around uncontrollably, sang previously unknown songs, and fell to the
ground. They told their amazed brethren that founder Ann Lee had
guided them around Heaven. The phenomena quickly spread to Shaker
communities throughout the northeast and out to the west. During this
period (roughly 1837–1850), spiritual visitations from Ann Lee, other
founders, and deceased Shakers reestablished a personal connection
between the present Shakers and those of the past. Under inspiration
Shakers created hundreds of songs and visual art in the form of spirit
drawings, detailed colorful glimpses of the world beyond communi-
cated to Shakers via special messengers called instruments, often young
girls. In addition, verbal and written messages were offered from past
to present Shakers. Some messages contained uplifting personal mes-

sages, others contained more general admonitions for behavior, instructions for daily Shaker life, or physical directives such as spinning, laughing, or stomping.[40]

The various gifts and messages invigorated Shaker meetings that, with the inspired singing, dancing, and instrument's messages, became tourist destinations for curious non-Believers intrigued by the apparent contradiction between the neat and ordered Shaker villages, and the disorder and bodily chaos of the Shakers in worship. Increasing numbers of worldly visitors crowded Shakers services, but with little respect for the religious proceedings. Hooting, jeering, and other disruptions mocked Mother's Work and placed the Shakers under increasing stress. In the 1840s, the Shakers closed their worship services to the world. The Canterbury Shakers, plagued by "apostates and wicked neighbors," placed a notice in the newspaper to alert the public to the changes in policy.[41] Although the Shakers shielded their meetings from prying public eyes, their spiritual activities were not unknown. Apostates published descriptions of the ecstatic services in a new spurt of anti-Shakers accounts, feeding a growing public curiosity exacerbated by the Shakers' closed-door policy.

At the heart of public inquiry regarding Mother's Work was the question of whether these various gifts and inspirations were from God or created and edited by the elders. During the 1848 legislative hearings, one Canterbury sister was cross-examined at length regarding her inspired writings and participation in the whirling gift. When asked who created the gifts, the Shaker Holy Orders, one witness explained that "All good comes from God. The orders are good, and we'll conclude they came from God." She added the obvious, that "[w]ithout order and regulation no Society could hold together."[42] While none disagreed that Shaker order and regulation made for a prosperous society, it was the source of inspiration that was difficult to accept.

The Shakers believed that God worked through the body of the instrument. The apostates argued that the elders directed the members. The human body was the locus on which Shakerism, as controlled by the elders, had its effect. The petitioners' complaints of corporeal punishment of children, the unusual illness of adults, the mesmeric power of the elders, and the strange actions of those under inspiration were elements in the larger argument that Shakerism destroyed individual physical autonomy. Theresa Willard described how her sister whirled and whirled during inspiration and when she failed to stop at the elder's command was thrown down a flight of stairs. Willard's sister, Mira Bean, rebutted that testimony and explained that she was thrown down the stairs by the power of God, not injured, and had always been treated kindly by the Shakers with whom she still lived. In another incident, a member was roughly treated by the assembled community. Shaker John Whitcher described the incident as controlled by "supernatural power" that inspired the Shakers to mimic the actions of savages. He admitted that one man received rough treatment, but that it ceased as soon as the elders appeared.

Former Shakers revealed in legislative testimony the physical details and dangers of the Shaker experience. Many apostates described an evening ritual known as "retiring," in which members were to sit upright on a chair without leaning against the back and without movement for up to an hour. The complaints regarding this disciplined action were brought largely by those who experienced the difficult act of body control and silent contemplation as children. More graphic testimony came from witnesses who reported how children had been whipped and beaten for minor infractions, hung from trees, force fed, or left kneeling or standing for hours. Apostates painted a portrait of cruelty and bodily assault. Their oral testimony, as well as written accounts in Dyer's *Rise and Progress* and other apostate accounts, drew listeners/reader into the physical experience of Shakerism, a visceral pull to a sensationalistic story.[43]

A particularly sensational aspect of the legislative hearings concerned the 1840 death of George Emery, a five-year-old boy who was said to have fallen and hit his head on a rock while living with the Canterbury Shakers. One witness claimed that the children's overseer, James Bracket, had been known to beat Emery's head upon the floor prior to his death and to discipline all the children harshly. Cross-examination exposed much of the apostate testimony as hearsay. For example, although Theresa Willard had testified that children were whipped and beaten, she admitted under cross-examination that she was "always treated well *myself*."[44] Another witness for the petitioners revealed under cross-examination that, in fact, the Shakers recognized a problem with James Brackett's treatment of children and immediately removed him from the caretaker position and that further, "the elders always inculcated mild punishment" for children.[45] Many witnesses were present at Emery's funeral, and they described his black and blue face viewed in his coffin. None, however, witnessed the accident, his medical treatment, or his subsequent death.

The Shaker's attorneys called several physicians to the stand.[46] Two physicians were involved with Emery's treatment, and testimony centered on whether the drug laudanum and the amount given had been the best course of treatment for the injured boy. The discussion during the testimony strongly suggested that it was not Emery's injury that led to his unfortunate death, but inappropriate medical treatment from a young and inexperienced physician. Physicians also testified that the Shakers were as healthy as other rural farmers. Shakers suffered no higher rates of cancer, insanity, or other diseases than the general population. The body of Shakers worked hard, ate simply, and lived strictly, yet Shaker bodies suffered no unusual physical effects as a result of their religious choice.

Testimony also concerned how the Shakers educated children. As with the allegations of abuse, under cross-examination much of the deponents' testimony regarding education fell apart. Townspeople and members of town school communities from Enfield and Canterbury remarked on the solid education the Shakers offered and how orderly and well disciplined the scholars appeared. Former Shakers admitted they had received schooling, boys in the winter and girls in the summer, a pattern consistent with many agricultural communities. Although some deponents declared that the elders prohibited members from speaking against the Shakers (or they would go to Hell), all admitted that they had never been expressly told to lie about Shaker practice and belief. Likewise, although the Bible was not used in school or religious education, several individuals admitted that they had not been forbidden to read it, and that Bibles were available in Shaker communities. Franklin Pierce and his legal team drew out specific responses from the apostates' generalizations, and often those responses weakened the petitioners' case.

After hearing all the testimony, the Committee on the Judiciary created a bill entitled "An Act for the Better Protection of Married Women and Children." The bill was passed by the House and sent to the Senate. The bill extremely restricted the Shakers in their conversion attempts. If the bill passed, all rights to property and assets of incoming male members would be terminated and distributed to wife and children, or an appointed guardian should the wife join the Shakers as well. New members would be unable to make deeds with the Shakers, and minor children would not be permitted to join without approval from the local probate judge. In addition, any children currently among the Shakers could be released to any parent or relative who petitioned the superior court for a writ of habeas corpus.

The majority of the investigating committee had favored the bill, but the minority members issued their contrasting conclusions in a published report that argues that the allegation of abuse and neglect were simply unproven and that most of the statements regarded alleged events twenty years in the past.[47] Those Shakers involved in such incidents were long dead or had been removed by the Shakers from positions of authority. To the minority of the committee the proposed bill represented a gross violation of the right to religious freedom guaranteed by the New Hampshire State constitution.

From the House, the bill moved to the Senate where it was met with less success. After discussion, a unanimous vote decided to postpone indefinitely the bill. Although attempts to resuscitate the bill were made in the House, the bill died and failed to become law. An alternative bill to aid women and children was proposed and passed both by the House and Senate. This bill, far less restrictive, changed the waiting period for divorce from three years to six months should one partner join the Shakers. This amended the divorce law that had resulted from Mary Dyer's petitions thirty years earlier and gave women whose husbands had joined the Shakers a faster recourse to freedom than Mary Dyer had endured.[48] Interestingly, in the next case to use the Dyer-inspired divorce clause (in 1865), Canterbury seceder Edward Fitts sued his wife Eliza Fitts for divorce when she refused to leave the Shakers with him.

The 1848 bills recognized that joining the Shakers was a voluntary act but that when a husband joined, his wife and children were forced to follow or find themselves, as did Mary Dyer, without property of protection. The legislators sought to affirm the right of the individual to determine one's own living situation. The first bill was designed to protect women and children by making, for men, the cost of joining the Shakers too high. Although the bill provided property for women and children, it severely restricted the autonomy of new members and the Shakers. The revised bill recognized the autonomy of wives and children without impinging on the practices of the Shakers. It provided a means for women to distance themselves from a Shaker husband and to act on their own behalf by law. Changes in the perception of divorce also aided passage of the bill. A later decision explained the purpose of the revision: "It [was] the policy of the law to encourage the marital relation, not only because it tends to promote the welfare of the parties, but because it also promotes the public good." Thus in cases where one spouse decided not to join (or remain with) the Shakers "and desires to have those [marital] relations restored, [the court saw] no reason why a refusal to return to them should not have the same effect as if the applicant had never joined the Society." In other words, divorce in this case did not destroy society by encouraging spouses to abandon marital bonds, a fear expressed by opponents of both Eunice Chapman's and Mary Dyer's divorce petitions, but rather the law supported society by allowing the continuation of the practice of marriage by allowing new families to form.[49]

The apostate group continued their work against the Shakers. In early 1849, the report of the legislative committee was published. In at least some copies, Mary Dyer slipped in her own printed statement, a small printed sheet tipped into the report following Caleb Dyer's testimony. Mary's subversive statement asserted that Caleb's testimony was "not true." She again put into print how Joseph and the Shakers had first tried to force her to sign an indenture, then deceived her into signing by promising her signature "would restore [Mary] to her children." Mary also denied "seeking to rule," instead she "was willing to be in any humble condition, if they would let [her] have the care of [her] dear babes." As in her written will, Dyer separated Caleb the Shaker, from Caleb her son, and wrote how he "with others, while they are Shakers, must and do state falsehoods to screen the Society from blame."[50] Dyer's phrase, "My son, . . . while [a] Shaker," indicated her belief in the temporary nature of Shaker behavior and placed blame for such behavior squarely on the elders. When out of the mesmeric control of the elders, the lying and deceitful behavior of individuals, her sons included, would change. The phrase, so similar to that in her will ("Caleb and Orville while with Shakers . . ."), reflected Dyer's still present hope that her sons' dalliance with Shakerism was temporary.

The apostate group gathered together to witness the release of the official report of the Shaker examination. The Shakers commented:

> The day the report was finished and made ready for the public eye, quite a number of the most influential among the apostates assembled at Concord, from different parts of this state and Lowell, Mass., it appears, to see the effect and lend a helping hand. But discovering the tide flowing back into the sea, they rushed back with it and sank into their hold. What will be done next, time will disclose.[51]

Although the apostates had hoped to agitate the public, "the Report [had] not met with so favorable reception as was doubtless anticipated."[52] Public favor leaned toward the Shakers.

Nevertheless, Mary Dyer continued her campaign against the Shakers, lecturing in New England and promoting her latest book. Dyer had published *The Rise and Progress of the Serpent From the Garden of Eden to Present Day* (Concord, 1847), her fourth anti-Shaker work, just prior to the legislative hearings in anticipation of the petitions about to be placed before the New Hampshire legislature. Dyer enlarged her audience for her writings and included Shaker youth, to whom she would reveal the "truth" of Shakerism. To the public Dyer repeated her warning to be "on its guard against the dangerous practices and designs of the Shakers."[53] From her earlier experience with *A Brief Statement* and later with *Portraiture,* Dyer had learned the power of print to sway public opinion. Prior to the legislative hearings and long after, *Rise and Progress* continued Dyer's anti-Shaker campaign.

Rise and Progress was a more reader-friendly text than the complex, multivocalic 446-page *Portraiture.* Dyer edited and reformatted *Portraiture* into a much smaller work, 268 pages of text, the majority drawn directly from *Portraiture.* The lengthy, two-part work was rearranged into several smaller discrete chapters. Dyer added a table of contents, providing a quick overview of the work. Legislators and the public had read Dyer's pamphlet during her 1818 hearing; in 1848 Dyer's book was available as an introduction to Shakerism, its history, and its sad effects on women and children. Dyer provided an index to the affidavits facilitating the reader's quest for the information they sought. The lengthy, two-column list of seventy-four names, placed opposite the first page of chapter one, reiterated that Mary Dyer was not alone in her complaints against the Shakers. Dyer also included her portrait on the frontispiece opposite the title page. Dyer's eyes looked directly at the reader, and with quill pen in raised hand she appeared as if momentarily interrupted in her writing. The portrait reflected a much younger Mary Dyer. Engraved in mid-1820 by David Watson of Concord, New Hampshire, for the never-realized second edition of *Portraiture,* Dyer was captured in her early forties.[54] With dark hair, smooth, unwrinkled skin, and a solemn, steadfast gaze, the portrait reflected a determined woman, saddened but not beaten by her experience. Her neat appearance spoke of a capable, rational woman, not the crazed fury her opponents made her out to be. With pen in hand, Dyer asserted that she herself had written the text to follow, and that she would continue to record Shaker abuses. In 1847, the portrait no longer reflected an accurate rendering of the near seventy-year-old Dyer. Yet the image reflected the continuing role Dyer wished her readers to see: a mother, a role that knows no age boundaries. With the already-crafted image at Dyer's disposal it made financial sense to make use of it. Nonetheless, the portrait of the younger, vital woman reflected her timeless mother's love. As Shaker Frederick Evans remarked, "Dyer's perseverance . . . is somewhat remarkable. . . ."[55] Below the oval framed portrait was her typescript signature. Devices of an author's authenticity, portraits and an autograph allowed the readers to assess Dyer's character.[56]

Rise and Progress reflected Dyer's change in name and marital status, raising marketing questions for her work. Dyer included both her married and her maiden name on the title page, alerting readers that the work contained information on "The Life and Sufferings of the Author, who was Mary M. Dyer, but is now Mary Marshall," her savvy recognition of the selling power of the name Mary Dyer and a hint to her readers of the personal transformation she would reveal in her work. Three versions of Dyer's printed autograph exist. Two versions (one in a formal italic type, and one resembling handwriting) use "Mary M. Dyer." A third version, in italic type, identifies "Mary Marshall." Most copies of *Rise and Progress* were bound in leather-covered boards. A few copies were bound in green or purple embossed cloth, a style more prevalent in the 1850s. The variety of bindings and signatures suggests that the text was printed and then bound over time as needed, or as Dyer's funds allowed. Regardless of the intricacies of the various forms of signature and binding, any profits from the sale of the book went to Dyer: Mary Marshall held the copyright to *Rise and Progress,* a reflection of her hard-won independent state.

Chapters one and two of *Rise and Progress* concerned the religious predecessors to Shakerism beginning in eighteenth-century Europe through Ann Lee's history in England and 1774 arrival in the American colonies. Such a historical retelling, laced with terms such as "impostors," "deceivers," and "delusions," emphasized the Shakers' foreign (non-American) roots and alignment with short-lived or obscure sectarian groups. Affidavits revealed Lee's alleged activities as a Revolutionary-era Tory spy, camp prostitute, and fortune-teller. Chapters three through six described the rise of the Shakers in New Lebanon, in several places in Massachusetts, in Enfield, and in Canterbury. Each chapter included text drawn from *Portraiture* and affidavits both previously published and newly gathered. In her chapter on New Lebanon (chapter three), Dyer printed affidavits gathered in 1825 and 1826 in response to Shaker James Farnham's broadside attack on Dyer. Chapter five was composed entirely of affidavits gathered in 1825 and 1826. A lengthy passage concerned a lawsuit on behalf of Seth Babbitt from the Harvard, Massachusetts, community. Babbitt was mentally ill, and for his own protection, the Shakers placed Babbitt in a locked house. Babbitt's alleged mistreatment—interpreted as being held captive against his will—incited a mob and galvanized area townspeople to suppress the Shakers.[57] The chapters on Shakerism in New Hampshire contained both previously published affidavits and statements from several individuals who reconfirmed their previous assertions. These updated statements (recorded in 1824) had been made in response to Shaker complaints about the veracity of the initial statements.

Dyer included previously published anti-Shaker material in *Rise and Progress*. Apostate Daniel Rathbun's 1785 account was incorporated in the third chapter. His decades-old statement was introduced by an 1826 "recommendation" from eight individuals, including several apostates and anti-Shaker activists, who swore that his eighteenth-century pamphlet contained the truth.[58] Eunice Chapman's story formed chapter seven, and chapter eight discussed the rise of Shakerism in Kentucky and Ohio with text drawn from anti-Shaker author James Smith. Chapter nine introduced Joanna Halloway who had lived with the Whitewater, Ohio, Shakers as a child. Halloway had published her account of growing up Shaker in the Rochester, New York, *Voice of Truth* in March and April of 1847. Copies of Halloway's lengthy descriptions of Shaker corruption and abuse were sent to Mary Dyer who included them in *Rise and Progress*. Halloway's reprinted texts both preceded and followed affidavits concerning abuse of children at Canterbury and Enfield, setting the New Hampshire allegations of abuse into a Shaker society-wide context. The final 110 pages of *Rise and Progress* were dedicated to the "Life and Sufferings of the Author," a reworked and elaborated version of Dyer's *A Brief Statement*.

Dyer continued to make extensive use of affidavits to support her assertions and to craft this volume as a work of history. In *Rise and Progress* affidavits represented three time periods. The first group consisted of statements previously printed in *Portraiture* and initially gathered from 1817-1822. A second group included those statements gathered in 1825 and 1826, following the initial publication of *Portraiture* and gathered in anticipation of a never-realized second edition of that book. The third collection of affidavits were those gathered between 1844 and 1847. Unlike the multiple, overlapping voices of *Portraiture*, in *Rise and Progress* one voice spoke at a time. Affidavits were generally placed within the body of the text as they related to the narrated story. Dyer served as the narrator of the entire history of Shakerism and used short sentences to introduce pertinent affidavits. Footnoted commentary was minimal. When used, the footnotes provided updated information or explanation on affidavits from an earlier period. In *Rise and Progress*, the flowing narrative, the chronological chapter by chapter structure of the book, and the consistent authorial voice produced a work of history. Dyer wanted her readers to see the Shakers as having had predecessors in "ancient and modern impostors," drawing on a historical framework and rhetoric to help justify her argument of the danger Shakers presented. As literary scholar Nina

Baym has argued, women writing history participated in "forging and publicizing national identity."[59] In the history Dyer presented, the Shakers were dangerous outsiders—in their European origins and in their practices—and therefore threatened American identity.

Dyer reformatted her life story for *Rise and Progress,* tapping into current social concerns, a reduced public fear of the Shakers, and changes in attitudes towards family and gender roles. In the 1847 version of the Dyers' pre-Shaker marital difficulties, Joseph became a more vivid and less sympathetic character. Mary detailed several incidents of his drunken behavior and the dire consequences his actions brought upon his wife and young children. Similar to novels and tract literature with temperance themes popular in this period, Mary's story focused on how she was forced to pay Joseph's debts and settle his business affairs—to step into the more masculine public sphere—in order to maintain her family. In *A Brief Statement* and *Portraiture,* the Shakers caused her unhappiness. In *Rise and Progress,* alcohol precipitated her family's sufferings. Mary portrayed herself as the model wife, and despite the rum all around her she took no part, a pillar of temperate behavior for her husband and sons to emulate, the very role American mothers were expected to play. When Joseph took her to a party that featured rum and a fiddler, Mary "retired to an adjoining room with some aged people, for which they called me proud and scornful."[60] Although Joseph drank to excess, Mary pointed out that when not drunk Joseph was a kind husband. Joseph's eventual religious conversion during the Freewill Baptist revival and his abstinence from alcohol at Mary's behest was the quintessential temperance reformation story. The strong moral woman guided and provided strength for the weak husband. Dyer's earlier works had painted a picture of a dutiful, obedient wife, who followed her husband to the Shakers, (and following her departure twice returned to live there with him) because it was her role (despite her fears). In 1847, Dyer reflected the enhanced (and critical) importance of wives as the moral guideposts for their family, and by extension, for the American nation. In this version of the story, Dyer did all she could to change her husband's immoral and dangerous behavior, rather than accede to it. But in the Dyers' story, there was no happy ending. Joseph's seduction by alcohol was replaced by his seduction into Shakerism, like alcohol a means of depriving the individual of his self-control. And similarly, as Dyer had tried to reform her husband and protect her family from the evils of alcohol, in *Rise and Progress* she would continue her reform campaign, protecting the nation by warning her readers of the dangers of Shakerism.

Temperance provided one theme for *Rise and Progress* and in apostate accounts from the period in general, although not everyone agreed with Dyer's timeworn accusations of inebriated elders, another indication of how Dyer's work had drifted away from apostate literature norms. Apostate Hervey Elkins, writing in 1853, fervently rejected accusations of excessive drinking among the Shakers, and David Lamson cited in 1848 the Shaker affirmation of temperance as one reason for his initial attraction to Shakerism. As temperance rhetoric argued, drinking led a family to ruin but temperance led to prosperity. Where intemperance had led to disorder and abuse, temperate self-control promoted order and stability. Elkins, Lamson, and others reasoned that since the Shaker villages were models of efficiency and order, it was unlikely that the Shaker communities were maintained by inebriated leaders.[61] As in the legislative hearings, the visual evidence of Shaker success outweighed hearsay and old accusations.

Dyer's children were grown and although portions of the public sympathized with her hard life, little could be done for Mary in terms of releasing her grown children (Caleb age forty-eight, Orville forty-four, and Jerrub forty-two) and reuniting her family. Realizing this herself, in *Rise and Progress* Dyer's presentation shifted from a focus on her immediate needs for assistance (as she had emphasized in *A Brief Statement* and *Portraiture*), to a detailed retelling of her past so that others might learn from—and avoid—her sad experiences. Dyer added details to the story she had previously published, often cleverly mixing the chronology of events for better dramatic effect and to highlight her claim that Shaker membership often meant death for the deceived Believer. The death of her son Joseph, Jr., presents an example of her savvy manipulation of facts. She described the day in 1815 when her husband and James Chapman forcibly removed her from the Enfield Shakers and settled her in Orford. Before her departure, Mary spent a few final moments with her youngest son Joseph whom she described as sickly and "so lean of flesh." Dyer described her son's condition: "He was never well from the time the Shakers stole him, when I went for those children Mr. Dyer left there. They now took him away forever. He is since dead! Oh, the sorrow I feel when I consider the contrast between his health when with me, and when with the Shakers!"[62] In a similar manner, Mary described her winter flight from the Shakers with young Joseph tucked into her cloak. When Mary's husband arrived in Hanover he "came staving in" to Mr. Towle's home and dragged the screaming child from Mary's arms: "My husband was raving; he held the child with one hand, and with the other thrust me from the door, and went out. It was so cold, the horse was white with frost; yet he took this child back [to the Shakers], without any covering for his head or body. Poor boy! he is since dead."[63]

Dyer's descriptions implied that Joseph died in childhood as a result of Shaker mistreatment. In fact, Joseph died in 1840 at age thirty. Later in *Rise and Progress,* Mary revealed Joseph lived "until he proved himself to possess superior talents," but blamed his death on Mother's Work. Dyer wrote: "His death was at a time when the Shakers exercised much of their magic influence and I was informed by the neighbors, that on the Sabbath before his death, he was in their meeting, when the leaders fastened their mesmeric power on him and others to that degree, that they were wrenched backward and forward and yerked [*sic*] around, until he was as pale as a corpse!"[64] The following day, a visitor to the village saw Joseph, Jr., and another young man ill on the floor of a shop. "Those infatuated subjects, not understanding this magic influence, believed they were suffering under the mighty power of God. [Joseph] died in a few days after, in the most excruciating misery."[65] In *Rise and Progress,* Dyer highlighted the danger of the Shakers' magic power and its effect of the loss of bodily self-control. Dyer continued from her earlier works the assertion that the Shaker elders possessed a mind-controlling power but she changed the nature of that power. In previous publications Mary claimed that Shaker power deluded susceptible individuals such as Mary's husband Joseph. The power was contained in the words of the elder who used it during meetings to control the Shaker congregation. In the 1840s, Dyer argued, Shaker power had a magical and more sinister effect. Shaker elders were mesmerists and controlled the members of their congregation in body and spirit. Not unlike the power of alcohol, the elders' power would destroy individuals, families, and eventually, the productivity and stability of society itself.

Testimony to the legislature and apostate accounts described the effects of Shaker mesmeric power. From the preface of *Rise and Progress,* Dyer asserted "that the Shaker spirit is magnetism, mingled with sexual passion, and absolutely opposed to the pure spirit of Christ."[66] Her footnoted commentary reinterpreted statements from earlier affidavits as evidence of the long-standing use of this power by disreputable religious leaders. For example, in the first chapters of *Rise and Progress* Dyer described the eighteenth-century French Prophets, a sectarian ecstatic religious group then identified as a European antecedent to the Shakers. She asked in a footnote of the French Prophets' ability to gain numerous converts, "Was not this magnetism, Shakerism, or devilism?" neatly tying together mesmeric power, sectarian religion, and evil.[67] On the following page, Dyer, again in a footnote, described James and Jane

Wardley, leaders of an English sectarian Quaker group of which Ann Lee was a member, as having received "magic influence." Dyer interpreted and copied into *Rise and Progress* an unidentified magazine description of early Shaker worship. When an early Shaker leader was described as "filled with a zeal of this fanaticism," Dyer defined fanaticism as "magic influence."[68] Dyer emphasize the effect of mesmeric power in the hands of unscrupulous leaders: "that persons can be operated upon by mesmeric influence so as to distract them, or even to take their lives," as had happened to her youngest child Joseph.[69]

Dyer used the language of electricity when she elaborated on the theme of magic power and magnetism in relation to her own experience.[70] Used in discussions of spiritualism, mesmerism and phrenology, electricity was a new and mysterious power that could be transferred to human beings. In spiritualism for example, women were said to be "negative" while men were "positive," and balancing these charges was required for a successful spiritualist event. Mary described male and female Shakers tapping into electricity to increase "their Holy Ghost power, (as they called it,) or truth would call it, increasing the sexual passion," a potentially threatening situation of uncontrolled passion.[71] Dyer, who stated she refused to be "electrized" while living among the Shakers, described familiarity between the sexes that "must . . . have been caused by the passion being inflamed by electric fluid, mingled with animal magnetism."[72] Here was yet another way elders deluded their followers and abused their power. Animal magnetism, Dyer claimed, deceived the common Shakers who had been led to believe it was the "power of the gospel."[73] Even her children such as young Joseph, wrote Mary, were "deceived by this magic power, believing it is the Holy Ghost power."[74] Author Catherine Sedgwick described the arrival of "animal magnetism" among the Shakers in an 1849 magazine article and explained how this power was used clandestinely by certain Shakers who would manipulate unsuspecting followers into believing in heavenly gifts.[75] In *Rise and Progress,* Mary warned her readers of the mesmerist's power to channel electrical energy that would deceive innocent people into thinking they were experiencing God, when in fact they were the dupes of a Shaker elder.

In addition to Joseph's death by mesmeric power, Mary blamed Betsey Dyer's 1824 death on Shaker practice. In *Rise and Progress,* Dyer described the January 1824 death of her daughter that happened while Mary was selling books in Massachusetts. Mary described Betsey's illness, actually consumption, as having occurred "in consequence of an imposition by Shakerism," blaming Shaker religious practice and daily life for her daughter's illness.[76] Dyer's grief was twofold. As she wrote of her children's deaths she wept and still mourned their passing, yet she also struck out in pain and anger that she learned of their illnesses and deaths secondhand. The prominence of the deaths of Betsey and Joseph, Jr., in *Rise and Progress* highlighted two demands of the 1848 petitions to the New Hampshire legislature: to investigate the alleged Shaker abuse of children and to rectify the failure of the Shakers to notify non-Shaker relatives upon the illness or death of a friend or family member.

When Eunice Chapman's books and Mary Dyer's *A Brief Statement* were first published the captivity/slavery imagery was used as a literary convention, a device that permitted Chapman and Dyer to tell their tales in an acceptable format. When those same texts were republished as part of *Rise and Progress,* the slavery motif tapped into a specific social issue, abolition. Apostate author David Lamson also portrayed the Shaker Elders as slaveholders and in his 1848 text concluded, "Shakerism is therefore nothing more nor less than a system of slavery carried on by cunning and fraud. A game perpetrated upon the innocent and unsuspecting by the crafty."[77] Lamson argued that it was only the "counteracting influences" from society that kept the Shaker system in check and prevented the total degradation of its subjects into a life similar to that of southern slaves.

Similar to the structure of *A Brief Statement,* in *Rise and Progress* Mary concluded her book with affidavits attesting to her respectable and truthful character. Eight of the ten affidavits were dated from May and June 1845 and two additional statements dated May 1847 from Concord were gathered immediately prior to the publication of *Rise and Progress.*[78] Dyer, in the mid-1840s nearly seventy years of age, had not traveled far to obtain these statements—Enfield, Lebanon, and Hanover—documenting her character since the time of her divorce. Dyer did not appear to be active in anti-Shakerism in the 1830s. The affidavits revealed a quiet life: Mary was a teacher and a member of the Congregational Church. These affidavits described Dyer as possessing "superior abilities" and a "strong mind." In 1818, Mary's unruly tongue and desire for self-rule were seen as liabilities. In 1847 Dyer's associates could praise these capabilities and independence as assets. Several statements noted Dyer's industry in having provided and maintained her own home, a point of pride for Mary who had complained bitterly of being moved from boardinghouse to boardinghouse prior to her divorce.

The failure of the petitions to the legislature did not end Dyer's attempts to restrict Shaker access to property and children, although her ability to command sustained attention from those in power diminished quickly. In November of 1849, she petitioned the Vermont House of Representatives for permission to make a public speech about the Shakers in the legislative hall, a request similar to one she had made to the New Hampshire legislature the previous year. Similarly, her request was denied.[79] In 1850 the Shakers reported that Dyer, "alive yet and . . . smart," lectured in Vermont, Massachusetts, and New Hampshire, advertising her free lectures on single sheet broadsides that encouraged the reader's attendance "with the ladies of the household."[80] She continued to make use of her support network. While in Charlestown, Massachusetts, presenting a lecture on the "Foundation and Effects of Shakerism" (December 25, 1850), Dyer stayed with the Shedd family, with whom she had stayed in 1825 while promoting *Portraiture*. Although her children were grown, Dyer fought vociferously for the children of other mothers, a social reform issue of her own design. As her broadside indicated, Dyer felt "it to be her duty to expose by all practicable means, the cruel and unnatural practices of the secluded and cunning sect."[81]

The Shakers did not think much of her unceasing effort and concluded "it will not amount to much. Most of the respictible [*sic*] part of the state are growing tired of the old crazy woman."[82] The following year (1851) Shaker correspondents again reported that Dyer planned to "create another Shaker excitement" in the legislature. Dyer, the letter's author continued, was "always busy in her master's service, and for all she is so crazy brained she has many friends who sympathize with her life of misfortunes, her distressed and lonely condition, isolated as it were, from her husband and family of babes."[83] But despite Dyer's continued activity and her continued association with a network of anti-Shaker activists, shortly after the 1848 legislative hearings, the Shakers concluded, "that sort of business is sinking rather low in the feelings of the better part of the people of this state. . . . Mary Marshall, *who still lives*, and others have been active, and rumor has been afloat for a purpose; but with all the efforts made, and with all the excitement raised, it has effected but little."[84] Shakers could speak with confidence of their apparent triumph over Dyer. In the 1840s, many communities (including Enfield and Canterbury, N. H.) had reached new heights in population, the Enfield community (as with many other Shaker enclaves) was economically productive, and with the waning of Mother's Work, Shakers were receiving little notice other than praise for their products. While the Shakers had numerous internal problems to handle, many the legacy of Mother's Work, Dyer's long-repeated accusations had ceased to rile up people as they had in the 1820s. Dyer was old news.

Despite fading public interest, Dyer published one more anti-Shaker text, *Shakerism Exposed* (ca. 1852). To enhance public recognition of its author, *Shakerism Exposed* was published under the name of Mary Dyer, to which she had legally returned in 1852, perhaps prompted by her fading anti-Shaker campaign.[85] *Shakerism Exposed* took the form of a pamphlet, thirty-two pages long, and paperbound. Published in nearby Hanover, New Hampshire, *Shakerism Exposed* was a mixture of old and new affidavits, comments on spiritual marriage, a selection from late eighteenth-century apostate author Reuben Rathbun, and still another version of Mary's life story. Testimony from the 1848 legislative hearings was included, but it was neither a focal point of the work nor directly addressed. This work lacked the organization, clarity, and thematic development of her earlier works. There is no indication the work was actively promoted by Dyer or any remaining associates. Unlike the Shaker response to Dyer's previous publications, *Shakerism Exposed* received scant notice in Shaker correspondence and journals. Age, isolation, and frustration may have finally taken its toll. *Shakerism Exposed* remains a difficult and confusing work to read, especially in the manner in which Dyer related her personal story.

The preface introduced *Shakerism Exposed* as an abridgement of *Rise and Progress* and as a response to Joseph Dyer's *Narrative*.[86] The latter purpose is curious. *A Compendious Narrative* was last published in 1826, and although copies were occasionally distributed to counteract Mary's activities, a new edition had not been published and, further, Mary had responded to Joseph's accusations in *Portraiture* thirty years before. Although no record exists, perhaps the Shakers redistributed copies of *A Compendious Narrative* to counter the bad press generated during the 1848 hearings, an old but effective strategy to rebut apostate claims.

Dyer began this version of her story with the 1817 legislative session that she described as a "solemn scene."[87] This was followed by a brief description of composing *A Brief Statement* from her testimony "to prevent the necessity of my going in person to the court [in 1818]," another curious statement as Dyer did attend both legislative sessions.[88] Joseph was the focus of both these very brief paragraphs. In reference to the 1817 legislative hearing Mary described how Joseph in public stated that Mary had told the truth of their going to the Shakers. She also remarked that the Speaker of the House forced Joseph to take his seat when he attempted to elaborate upon his answer, a brief moment of triumph for Mary in gaining the (last) word. The 1818 legislative session was remarkable to Mary in that the Shakers obtained a copy of her *Brief Statement* and "found means to contradict all parts of it with absolute falsehoods, striving for my ruin."[89] Her difficulty with the Shakers increased when she first read Joseph's *Narrative* in 1819, a work that Mary found "distressingly unjust."[90] She described how she could "find no rest until I wrote the following letter [to Joseph]," a letter that Mary had previously printed in *Rise and Progress*.

Dyer then turned to affidavits. Statements attested to her good character. Several affidavits came from individuals with whom she boarded, a substitute family for a woman displaced. By page eight of *Shakerism Exposed*, Dyer had returned to relating her life story with brief accounts of her 1813 arrival and 1815 departure from the Shakers, the desperate sleigh ride to Hanover with young Joseph, and then her divorce. From her long life, these were the crucial events that defined her: She joined and left the Shakers, she attempted to retrieve her children, and she received her autonomy only through a legal divorce. Perhaps a bit obsessively, Dyer continued to relay these life-changing experiences to any who would listen, an almost ritualistic recounting of who Mary Dyer was and in telling others, telling herself.

Very little of Dyer's voice is heard in this work; when she does speak, her comments highlighted the Shaker treatment of children. Her comments were often bracketed within the text and directly addressed to the reader, a conscious personal plea to her reading audience. For example, she followed Gardner and Theresa Willard's statements to the 1848 legislature (regarding corporal punishment) with a direct statement to her readers, restating and then answering a question on the public's mind and challenging her readers to think about Shaker truthfulness in court. "Why don't all their children die? That All-seeing eye knows that there have been scores who have died at the Shakers by cruel abuse. Any person can see that the foundation of Shakerism is, to state, or testify favoring the Shakers, or they must lose their souls, or go to hell. What dependence can be put on their testimony? Reader, Consider!"[91] Her voice was also heard near the end of the work in a vitriolic paragraph in which she called the Shakers a "mongrel set of papists or Catholics, of aristocrats and slaves."[92] She continued her attack and argued, with a hint of anti-industrialist rhetoric, that "children [were] not being taught that which is beneficial to body or soul, they are blindly taught that obedience to the leaders is the will of God. Thus cruelly made to do, as machines, that which is most profitable to that society."[93] Dyer concluded that the Shakers should "replenish their society with their own children, or become extinct. They would then have parental affections, not cruel hate. They would be fathers and mothers, sons and daughters, instead of task-masters, task-mistresses, servants and slaves."[94] Many commentators of the day assessed that Shaker celibacy would ultimately doom Shaker society. The belief that the Shakers would surely cause their own extinction had lessened public fear of the sect. For Dyer, the absence of biologically related parents and children doomed Shaker society not only to extinction but also to immorality.

Dyer was not alone among apostates in suggesting the Shakers eliminate celibacy as a religious tenet. Several apostate authors of this period had urged a Shaker reform, a remarkable shift from earlier apostate demands for the total suppression of the faith. Apostate David Lamson, for example, was genuinely disappointed that his experience with Shakerism was not spiritually and intellectually satisfying. He advocated a unique course of action for those who were equally dissatisfied. Instead of promoting apostasy, as other apostates had so strongly urged, Lamson argued that current disenfranchised Shakers should remain within the community and initiate a correspondence and conversation with similarly minded Shakers. Given enough time, Shakerism reform would emerge from within, and the autocratic elders would be overthrown.[95]

One of the last apostate accounts, Hervey Elkins's *Fifteen Years in the Senior Order of the Shakers,* reflected how the public had come to accept Shakerism on the American landscape. *Fifteen Years* was published in August 1853 and in part rebutted *Shakerism Exposed.*[96] Elkins condemned Dyer's accusations against the Shakers and offered his own interpretation of the Shaker experience. His title stated his claim to authority, "Fifteen Years Among the Senior Order," a one-upmanship marketing claim to top David Lamson's 1848 claim of *Two Years Experience Among the Shakers.* Further, Elkins offered that not only had he been a Shaker, but he had been in close contact with the elders that Dyer had so scurrilously accused. Compared to Dyer's *Shakerism Exposed,* Elkins's text was considerably larger (136 pages), more durable, and probably had a much larger press run as numerous copies survive today; Dyer's final work is rare. *Fifteen Years* was certainly a much easier and more entertaining read. As the Shakers responded strongly to its publication and distribution, *Fifteen Years* was likely a popular read, at least in the vicinity of the New Hampshire Shaker villages.

Elkins's sympathetic account of Shakerism mirrored the transition in public feeling about the Shakers and in apostate writing. Comparing Dyer's last two works with those of Elkins (1853) and of David Lamson (1848) shows how much Dyer's works had drifted away from what we might call mainstream apostate writing of the day. Where Dyer reiterated her decades-old accusations, both Elkins and Lamson offer a balanced appraisal of Shakerism. Particularly in the disjointed *Shakerism Exposed,* Dyer's anger and frustration obscures her formerly well-articulated complaints. Both Elkins and Lamson found some aspects of Shakerism disagreeable, both admitted they left—not escaped—to find personal satisfaction elsewhere. Both were converts, not captives, to Shakerism. While apostate texts were never uniform in their appraisal (or in their critiques) of Shakerism, by 1850 Dyer's texts had moved far away from others in that genre. To put it another way, Dyer's texts remained highly critical of all aspects of Shakerism, while other apostate writers, along with the general public, moved to a moderate and accepting position of Shaker society.

Elkins organized *Fifteen Years* in three parts. Like Dyer's *Rise and Progress,* Elkins considered Shaker history first and then his personal experience. In the first part he summarized Shaker history and, consistent with the practice of other apostate authors of his generation, referred the reader to Shaker publications for further information, allowing the Shakers to speak for themselves on matters of faith. In Part Two Elkins discussed his personal experience with the Shakers. He joined at age fourteen in November 1837 and worked in a variety of positions including as a tailor, a farmer (at one time supervised by Jerrub Dyer), and a schoolteacher, a position that provided both satisfaction and uneasiness. Elkins craved knowledge, and in the end, it was his desire for further learning and the departure of several of his friends that prompted his 1852 apostasy.

Elkins launched his complaints against the Shakers in the third and final part of *Fifteen Years.* Elkins focused on the absence of romantic love, the suppression of which, he argued, led women's health to wither. With a nod to the fictionalized accounts of Shaker love so prevalent in his day, Elkins described the sad case of failed love between Urbino and Ellina, pseudonyms for two Enfield Shakers. When love and purity clashed, tragedy inevitably resulted. In Elkins's poignant example, Ellina died of a broken heart. Here Elkins's speaks from sad experience. His romantic tale was autobiographical.

Despite Elkins's concern for women without love, his comments that the trustees were less righteous than other Shakers, and his revelation that several of the leading Shakers were unhappy in their confinement, Elkins's account was largely sympathetic to the Shakers. He concluded his work with praise for Shaker products and industry and noted the strong health of the brethren. Elkins conceded that after having been in the world he realized that there was more sin, cheating, and lying in the world than among the Shakers, and thus he felt he could not speak out against his former communal home. He concluded as he stressed throughout his work that any fault with the Shakers lay within the individual member, not within the doctrine itself, the very same argument the Shakers had been making in their own defense for so long.

The desire for knowledge weakened Elkins's faith. Once in the world, Elkins planned to share the knowledge he gained with his former brethren with the reading public. Elkins made use of the apostate network to promote his books as well as to gain favor with the Shakers. He met with Edward Cummings, a seceder from Canterbury, in Boston. Cummings told Elkins that Elder Lorenzo Grosvenor and a few Shaker sisters at the Harvard community had read his book and praised it. This knowledge, true or not, encouraged Elkins and he wrote to Grosvenor for his suggestions with plans to incorporate them in a proposed second edition. Elkins also contacted his still-Shaker brother Samuel evidently to inquire about distributing his books within Shaker communities. Books were sent to New Lebanon as well. In a response similar to the Dyer situation of decades past, the Shaker leaders reported on Elkins's activity in a flurry of letters in 1853, condemning Elkins's portrayal of their faith for "altho he has published and talked some things favorable to our cause and show a strong faith in our principles, he is an apostate, he is a hypocrite and clandestinely contriving to undermine souls yet within the fold of Zion. . . ."[97]

Elkins had left the Enfield Shakers during an increased period of apostasy, in part a reaction to the increasingly strict proscriptions placed on behavior at the height of Mother's Work, an attempt to regain the purity of a Shaker past. Disillusioned by the overwhelming number of visions, inspirations, and strange gifts, the rate of apostasy rose dramatically.[98] Apostate David Lamson, writing in 1848, argued that Shakerism had drifted away from its roots in simplicity. What remained was simply silly and "silliness is folly, an approach to foolishness."[99] Leaving the Shakers was especially prevalent among the younger men who saw more freedom and economic opportunities beyond the Shaker enclave's walls. In October 1852, Jerrub Dyer left the Enfield Shakers, and Mary, in small part, finally achieved the liberation of one of her beloved children. Jerrub had been with the Shakers since the age of five. As an adult he had held the position of community physician and was described in Shaker journals throughout the years as a solid Believer.[100] At age forty-seven, Jerrub was slightly older than the typical seceder, but as a physician he had marketable skills enabling him to provide easily for himself in the world. But in addition to economic possibilities, Jerrub likely left for a more emotional reason. He had fallen in love. Shaker records made no commentary on Jerrub's departure although a letter written shortly after he left discussed the wave of apostasy in New Hampshire and reported how " . . . the male youth whom Satan it seems, takes occasion to sift as wheat; and although the substance remain in the garners there is much chaff blown away and those subjects . . . drop off one by one like withered blossoms and fall to decay but go to nourish and build up the elements of the old creation which are so fascinating to the young mind."[101] Jerrub, suddenly independent at age forty-seven, settled in nearby Lebanon, New Hampshire, and for several months in 1853, Mary lived with her son in Lebanon. But for Mary, Jerrub's defection was bittersweet. In June 1854, Jerrub married twenty-four-year-old Lucy Ann Colburn, a former Shaker, and migrated west settling first in Wisconsin and then Minnesota. Mary returned to her home in Enfield. Jerrub and his family, including his daughters, Mary's grandchildren, Hattie (born 1856 in Wisconsin) and Rose (born 1860, Minnesota), would not return to the East for several years.

Following the 1848 legislative hearings, anti-Shaker attitudes did not disappear entirely but their public visibility changed. The Shakers had ceased to be an object of fear. Shakers by mid-century had become both an American curiosity for their "peculiar" belief in celibacy and the objects of respect for their self-sufficiency and material products. By the Civil War, the Shakers were relegated to a part of the American agrarian past, an icon of a simpler time. The Shakers themselves were changing, too, much to the dismay of some of the older members who bemoaned the increasing interaction between Believers and non-Believers, and the growing infiltration of worldly items and ideas within the Shaker communities.[102] Following Dyer's 1852 *Shakerism Exposed* and Elkins's 1853 *Fifteen Years,* apostates ceased to use the book as a vehicle of attack. Authors on Shaker topics, with few exceptions, favored periodical articles that could be distributed to an even larger number of readers than a limited press run of a book. Articles were shorter, could be written more quickly, and could be drawn out over time in serialization. As the technology of publishing continued to advance, illustrations of Shaker life, worship, and products were added, providing yet another source of information on the sect, from both Shaker and non-Shaker authors.

Dyer remained quiet for the remainder of her life. Her hard-fought campaign had led to changes in New Hampshire divorce law and a better appreciation of the problematic standing of wives of Shaker husbands. Although her cleverly organized texts, especially *Portraiture,* attracted the public's attention, by 1850 her style of aggressive, bitter apostasy had failed to stimulate widespread support. Dyer's personal charisma and pathos-filled presentation of her personal experiences could move individuals, but her larger arguments—that the Shakers were slaveholders and intemperate mesmerists—failed to have an effect. Many of her arguments, like eighteenth-century Shaker apostate Amos Taylor's Revolutionary rhetoric, became quickly dated. The rest of Dyer's apostate presentation was intimately connected to her gender and thus presented a form unusable by later male authors. No apostate author abstracted portions of any of Dyer's texts to include in their own.

For the most part, apostates' accusations ceased to worry the public. Although apostate texts included valuable insight into the inner workings and tensions readily apparent within the growing and maturing faith, readers focused on a more general appraisal of the faith and practices. Even here there was little to fear: Shakerism had several commendable aspects but because of the faith's central tenet, celibacy, most people believed that Shakerism was on the wane.

6

Notorious Against Them

As the Shakers would have phrased it, Mary Marshall Dyer presented a considerable weapon against Zion. Although her gender precluded certain actions, especially when she commenced her anti-Shaker campaign, it did not prevent her from undertaking a lifelong battle against the Shakers. Indeed, as many historians, and Shakers, have noted, it was the longevity of her campaign that made it most striking. But it was not simply a long campaign; it was a highly complex one. Dyer displayed her apostasy in a very public theater, a wide assortment of venues that included personal presentations, legislative appearances, newspapers, court battles, books, and pamphlets. Dyer crafted and made exceptional use of a network of apostasy that was both literary and literal. Through republishing earlier anti-Shaker works, she connected two generations of apostates; in reprinting extracts from authors in Ohio Dyer connected eastern and western anti-Shaker communities. These literary connections created community on the pages of her works, an imagined community of the sort Benedict Anderson defines in which the shared experience of reading unites authors and readers across space, and even across time.[1] From her literal community of fellow apostates Dyer learned strategies, gained affidavits and allies, and traveled across New England. Dyer influenced other apostates as well. Her presence in person or by way of her texts inspired additional anti-Shaker actions such as the New Hampshire legislative petitions of 1828 and 1848 and an extensive legal suit in Maine (1826). She was not a woman deranged, beset by her emotions. In fact, Dyer's writings and public successes indicate she was intelligent, strong-minded, and independent. She turned her anguish into action and made apostasy her life-long role in a lengthy and fascinating life.

Dyer sought the just rights that belonged to her sex but the vivid response her campaign prompted tells us of a society troubled by women like her. None disagreed that a mother should raise her own children, yet Dyer's public, aggressive means of reaching that goal was antithetical to the domestic image she tried to portray. Further, although Dyer condemned the Shaker faith, she herself represented one of the most troubling aspects of the faith for many mainstream Protestants: women's leadership. As Dyer turned her preaching aspirations into preaching against the Shakers, she evoked not only Ann Lee's New England journey and Lucy Wright's strong leadership, but the troubling image of women taking an ever increasing role in mainstream religious practice in antebellum America.[2]

More than any other anti-Shaker writer, Dyer's texts forced a Shaker response. Joseph Dyer's *A Compendious Narrative* (in two editions), McNemar's *The Other Side of the Question, Review of Portraiture,* a handbill, multiple remonstrances to the New Hampshire legislature, and numerous newspaper statements brought the Shaker perspective into this public discussion. Dyer's works were not universally accepted among anti-Shakers. Her account of the Enfield Shakers inflamed other apostates including William Haskett, Hervey Elkins, and C. C. Hodgdon, who challenged her experiences when they wrote of their own. The fact that Dyer's, and Eunice Chapman's, accusations came from women, the moral bearers of society, heightened interest in their cause and helped them attract a public audience. It also left them vulnerable to greater attack and at risk for a greater personal loss than male apostates faced. Dyer was keenly aware of her gendered position in society and argued simply to be a mother. She framed her life story first as a captivity narrative and a test of Christian progress. Later, Dyer reframed her story to show that life among the Shakers was the moral and physical equivalent of slavery and that the autocratic Shaker leaders were guilty of a wide range of hypocritical sins including intemperate, lustful behavior and the use of delusion, mesmerism, and magic influence to dupe unsuspecting converts. Yet, although Dyer kept her texts culturally current when she tapped into prevalent social causes, by the late 1840s her last two texts had drifted away from a more sympathetic trend in apostate literature. While other apostates mixed moderate praise with constructive critique as Shakerism came of age, Dyer's texts did not and became out of step not only with Shaker apostate literature but also with public perception of the Shakers that saw the sect through curious yet sympathetic eyes.

Dyer was a highly visible, and unpredictable, player in apostate-Shaker confrontation and the Shakers kept careful reconnaissance of her movements and activities. For example, in 1818, following Dyer's second unsuccessful legislative petition, the New Hampshire Ministry reported to the Ministry at Watervliet that "Mary Dyer was around [Canterbury, N. H.] calling meetings and preaching. She is after all the carrion that she can find to prepare the minds of the public against next session. She expects to have another pull."[3] And in 1826, in a passage reminiscent of the one above with its raptorial imagery of Dyer, the Shakers at Hancock told the Harvard community that "Mary Dyer the *Abominable,* is in these parts, she has crept over into Lebanon hollow and like a sitting goose or turkey-buzzard is brooding over her nest of lies, and generating them into life by her lasivious [sic] pen. She is still now, and probably will be during her incubation."[4] Twenty-five years later, the Enfield Shakers still took notice of Dyer's actions. But in the following passage, instead of describing the fecund possibilities of a young and active woman, the Shakers dismissed Dyer:

Old Mary Marshall [Dyer] is alive yet and is smart, having spent the past winter in her master's service, lecturing in Vermont and New Hampshire about her poor little childrens being torn from their mother, and procuring sales for her books. She has also been getting signers to a petition similar to her former ones to be presented to the New Hampshire legislature the coming June session but we think it will not amount to much. Most of the respectible [sic] part of state are growing tired of the old crazy woman.[5]

The Shakers concluded that her advanced age, decreased sanity, and gender had rendered her weak and harmless. Nonetheless, they remained cautiously aware of the potential of their long time adversary writing in 1854 that Dyer was still "quite smart and lively, . . . an uncomfortable personage [who] still retains her persecuting spirit against Believers."[6] Shaker commentary on Dyer's lifelong anti-Shaker campaign empowered Shaker communities by dismissing her potential and enhancing their own.

Dyer spent the remaining years of her life in her small house in Enfield. In the 1820s, town residents and selectmen had feared that husbandless women like Dyer would demand the town's financial support and drain the town of resources. Later in her life, Dyer would herself assist the Enfield poor. From 1857 through 1859, the Town of Enfield paid Dyer rent for rooming George Fisher, a poor man who may have lived in the second of her two properties and who likely provided labor to the aging Dyer.[7] Dyer never did become a drain on Enfield. She paid her town taxes in full each April. Tax records indicate her ambiguous social role, as she is variously identified as Mary Marshall, Mrs. Mary Marshall, Mrs. Mary M. Dyer, and in one entry, to cover all possibilities, "Mary M. Dyer or Marshall."[8] The Shakers saw Dyer as "somewhat deranged" and according to one brief oral history, as remarkable as it sounds, in later years the Shakers supplied Dyer with wood and provisions whenever they passed by her home.[9] Massachusetts resident William Shedd visited Mary Dyer in October 1856 and found her in "good health and even vigorous."[10] Shedd had visited on behalf of his parents who had "ever esteemed her for her intelligence and moral worth," and with whom Dyer had stayed for several weeks in 1825 in their Brighton, Massachusetts, home.[11] During his visit, Shedd convinced Dyer to present a copy of *Rise and Progress* to the Massachusetts Historical Society. Along with Dyer's gift, Shedd presented *A Review of Portraiture of Shakerism* and *A Reply to a Review,* writing to the secretary of the historical society that "after much investigation of the matter I consider her book entitled to the highest confidence and herself entitled to the highest respect."[12] Shedd also reported that in 1856, near eighty years old, Dyer was still attempting to have a bill passed by the legislature to restrict Shaker access to children. But despite her continued attempts to change Shakerism, Dyer had moved from an active apostate to a living legacy. Libraries across New England held copies of Dyer's books, but Shedd's donation to the Massachusetts Historical Society suggested that Dyer's life work had moved from apostasy to history. Her works would not be read for information on the current state of Shakerism, but in a historical society, would be read to reveal an understanding of the past.

Shedd was not the only individual to take interest in Dyer's story. In 1861, Reverend H. P. Andrews of Enfield drew material from *A Portraiture of Shakerism* to present "A Picture of Shakerism: Mrs. Mary M. Dyer."[13] Published in *The Ladies' Repository,* a monthly periodical of religion and literature, Andrews focused on the effect of Shaker practices on mothers, an alternative, darker picture of Shakerism than what was commonly printed at the time. The article, sympathetic to Dyer's "bitter experience," repeated the stories of her three captivities at the Shakers, roughly her life from 1813–1819. Andrews asserted he had much more data to expose "all the windings and subtleties of Shaker barbarism, deception, and wickedness" but was forced to end his article lest the evidence "swelled this sketch into a volume."[14] Reflecting the mixed public assessment of Dyer's decades-old claims, Andrews asserted that he had "entire confidence" in Dyer's story and cited her affidavits, many of whom were his "townsmen and numbered among the warmest friends of [his] parents."[15] It is clear Andrews's article represented a second-generation anti-Shakerism. Like Shedd acting as an emissary from his parents, Andrews had learned of Dyer's story from his parents and parents' friends, had then read *Portraiture* and like Enfield townspeople four decades earlier, became incensed at the cruel treatment Dyer described. The body of his article, and even the title, was borrowed liberally from Dyer's text. Although he had met Caleb Dyer and considered him "one of the most talented men in their society,"[16] Andrews did not indicate that he personally had ever had trouble (or witnessed any) with the Shakers. In addition, several factual errors and the limited current information presented on Mary indicated he did not know Mary Dyer well, if at all other than by sight. Of the "present condition of the mother," Andrews reported that Dyer, "a humble, earnest, trusting Christian woman," lived alone in her "little cottage" on Mount Calm.[17] Although Dyer was near the end of her life, *Portraiture* and her other texts continued to live and spread her message.

Anti-Shaker sentiment and fascination with Dyer's experience did not fade with the death of Mary Dyer. In 1869, two years after Dyer's death, an anonymous author published *Shakerism Unveiled*.[18] Just under fifty pages long, this pamphlet claimed to contain extracts from the Shaker *Holy Roll* and "Mary Dyer's work who was eighteen years among them."[19] In fact, with the exception of the brief paragraph-long preface, *Shakerism Unveiled* was drawn exclusively and verbatim from the first forty-five pages of *Rise and Progress*. Despite the presence of a copy of *Rise and Progress*, the author made errors in the text, not the least of which was the assertion that Dyer lived eighteen years among the Shakers. Most of the text, in fact, dealt with the Shaker's theological background and early behavior and very little with Dyer's story. The potential power of apostate texts was illustrated in the use the author of *Shakerism Unveiled* put to his text. A man named Munger printed the pamphlet in 1869 in cooperation with a man named Hamilton, who may have written (or compiled) the work. During a legal action against the Enfield, Connecticut, Shakers, Hamilton, who had purchased 1,000 copies of the pamphlet, gave a copy of *Shakerism Unveiled* to a member of the jury, thus prejudicing the outcome. Years after her death, Dyer's words and accusations continued to be heard.[20]

Considering Dyer's prominence on the title page of *Shakerism Unveiled*, it appeared that even posthumously Dyer's name was still a draw for book sales. Her name had been inextricably linked with anti-Shakerism. In 1871, apostate Enoch Cummings chided his Shaker brother John, claiming the Shakers valued John only for his labor. He informed John, "You have become notorious among them and a laughing stock. The same as Mary Dyer & myself became notorious against them."[21] Dyer's notoriety, at least for Enoch Cummings, was a source of apostate pride. For the Shakers, there was no pride in the virulent battles of the antebellum period. Historian William Cathcart approached Shakers in the early twentieth century, looking for early books for his study of the Shaker movement. He inquired about Dyer's writings but was informed in 1912 that " . . . the book called M. Dyer's has been destroyed as no one supposed it could be of use. . . ." Shaker Rosetta Cummings continued her letter and revealed how 100 years after Dyer had joined the Enfield Shakers, her words still had power: " . . . but on the contrary [Dyer's book] might be a means of lessening the respect of future members. . . ."[22] William Shedd preserved Dyer's history, the Shakers erased it.

⁂

Over the long course of Shaker history, those who eventually left the Shakers outnumbered lifelong converts. The Shakers were resigned but hopeful that they would survive as they faced a continual parade of turnoffs, apostates, and seceders. For the Shakers, the initial cost of apostasy was evident: the loss of a potential member.[23] In a celibate community whose only source of new members was conversion, each seceder was one less Shaker. Apostasy affected not only the future of Shakerism but also the present. When members chose to abandon the faith, Shakers provided seceders with money, clothing, and sometimes material goods, such as, for example, a horse and saddle, tools or sewing implements.[24] Departing members signed a disclaimer that listed items received from the Shakers and agreed not to make any further claims. Despite the signed agreement, numerous defectors returned to their former communal homes and demanded more money or goods. Several seceders brought their dissatisfaction to a legal level and sued the Shakers for the value of goods and property owned when they had joined, or, more commonly, for back wages. These legal battles cost the Shakers time and money, regardless of the success or failure of the suit.

One Shaker leader informed the New Lebanon Ministry in 1827: "since the general troubles have taken place, in this society we have given much to apostates, and to lawyers &c in our general defence[.] Within the last two years, our account for money and property given for such purposes, mostly in cash, amount to nearly $5,000; and there has yet to be paid, agreeably to understanding, at least, $2,700 more."[25]

David Parker described the physical cost of participation in the 1848 legislative hearings brought about by Mary Dyer and others: "I would write more but time forbids for I have been detained at Concord about 4 weeks to the exclusion of everything else, and deprived of any real rest, and much of my sleep."[26] While lengthy court proceedings detained Shaker leaders, other Shaker business languished. Calvin Green explained why Shaker books ready at the printer's office could not be retrieved: "The books will not be taken from the printer's office until paid for, and it would be desirable that, they should all be paid for, when the work is done, but we have had to bear heavy expenses in vexatious lawsuits bro't on by apostates in the most unjust manner . . . these things have cost us much and are not yet ended."[27] Theft, embezzlement, destruction of property, and community disruption were also a part of the total cost of apostasy. While the Shaker community no doubt benefited from the loss of troublesome and unfaithful individuals, they paid dearly for it.

Seceders paid a price as well. Unhappy with their Shaker lives, they chose to go to the world. Anna Bennet, who left the Shakers in 1796, found herself disowned by her parents, who sent her a heartbreaking letter the following year. They wrote that as they had chosen to remain Shakers "we cannot recollect you without feeling an abhorrence."[28] A great number of seceders traveled from one Shaker community to another seeking one more "privilege," or opportunity to try the Shaker life again. Many found their plan for warm meals and a bed foiled by the ministry leaders' constant correspondence that alerted distant brethren to potential pilgrims. For example, a letter from the Whitewater, Ohio, Shakers warned the Hancock community of Nathan Burlingame, a man with a "vain spirit" and a "corrupter of female virtues." Forced from Whitewater, Burlingame settled in at Union Village and it was only with great difficulty that the elders there prompted him to begin his proposed trip to the east. The Ohio Shakers stated clearly their opinion of Burlingame in a letter to the eastern leaders:

> But if he should make it out to git [sic] among the believers in the east and git any hold of gospel union thare [sic] it is our desire that he may abide thare and not return to this country any more to live again. We think he never will be able to do any more good here but most likely would make us a great deal of trouble unless he should become a very altered man.[29]

Reputation followed former Shakers both in intercommunity correspondence and, occasionally, between Shakers and the world.

Some seceders feared their apostasy was folly. One former Believer wrote to his still-Shaker sister and explained that he had made a terrible error, realizing too late that he should have truly confessed all his sins while with the Shaker community. A true and complete confession would have prevented his present condition—"suspended over the brink of hell with nothing but a strand, & when that breaks, I certainly must perish."[30] The act of apostasy had a cost for both Shakers and the apostates, financial, physical, and emotional.

Shaker apostates contributed to oppressive legislation, frenzied mobs, costly lawsuits, and, of course, the sheer numerical loss of members. But these acts and effects of forgoing Shakerism, although devastating, were not entirely harmful to the Shaker movement. Apostasy winnowed out the unfaithful, the troublemakers, and those unwilling to commit fully to the demands of communal life. Apostate actions, although negative, destructive, and at times violent, at least in part formed a source of continuity and strength for the Shakers. The Shakers interpreted the fate of apostates and other persecutors and made it part of their own drama of life in the millennium. In short, the Shakers used persecution as a source of strength. In correspondence, in worship meetings, and in print, Shaker leaders told tales of woe, stories of the dismal fate of those who dared deny Shakerism's truths. In these stories, opponents of Shakerism bragged of their worldly successes, only to have it all erased by financial ruin, family tragedies, and lonely deaths. For the faithful Shakers, these stories provided resilience for their remaining numbers, reaffirmed their beliefs, and offered a confidence in their future.[31] Roger Launius and Linda Thatcher, writing about dissenters in Mormon history, also noted how such conflicts helped generate solidarity among members as they rallied "together to either punish deviants or to save them from unorthodoxy."[32] The Shakers, the Mormons, and other groups like them, thus turned a community draining force into a community empowering one.

Apostate allegations forced the Shakers to articulate their faith and practices. In responding to allegations, in courts, in print, and in front of mobs and legislators, the Shakers defined the ideological boundaries of Shakerism—what was included in, and what was excluded from, the faith. The construction of boundaries between sect and mainstream community was a dynamic enterprise; the boundaries of Shaker belief were not dictated by one leader, but rather were built (and rebuilt) in conjunction with one's opponents. Apostate narratives were actors in this process and played a key role in enhancing the legitimacy of both the Shakers and the anti-Shakers who opposed them. The very aggressive accounts, like those of Mary Dyer, helped pull public opinion toward the view that the Shakers were not a legitimate religious group; the more neutral accounts, such as those of Hervey Elkins or David Lamson, pulled opinion in the other direction, legitimizing Shakerism as a viable religious alternative. Likewise, the apostate narratives legitimized anti-Shaker activity by providing experiential and historical evidence of the alleged danger the Shakers presented.[33] For both the Shakers and the members of anti-Shaker groups, by repeatedly defining the Shaker self, and by extension the non-Shaker other, each community gained an empowering cohesiveness.

We can not underestimate the importance of print in this story. As the Dyers' experience illustrated, Shaker books proselytized, bringing the faith to families near and far. Print commodified the Shakers. As historian R. Laurence Moore argued, if a religious group does not commodify themselves, someone else will do it for them.[34] In tracts, pamphlets, and books, anti-Shaker authors commodified Shakerism and sold it to a curious reading public. Until the Shakers responded in kind, the anti-Shaker authors controlled the Shaker image. But once the Shakers did respond, entering print culture in earnest with the 1808 publication of *The Testimony of Christ's Second Appearing*, they learned quickly the advantages of print. In subsequent editions of the *Testimony*, Shaker editors debated language use, length, and accessibility as they were keenly aware of how the so-called Shaker Bible had come to represent—to market—their faith. Other publications followed. As Mary Richmond's 1972 bibliography of Shaker literature indicates, the Shakers published more than 1,700 books, articles, broadsides, advertising tracts, and other forms of printed material from 1790 to 1972. In the same period, Richmond records more than 3,800 pieces published about the Shakers, a trend that continues well into today with scholarly monographs, Shaker autobiographies, coffee table books, cookbooks, and Shaker murder mysteries all offered for public consumption.[35]

For the Shakers, print culture brought more than converts and a convenient format for defending the faith. As it did for members of the anti-Shaker community, print culture strengthened ties between Shaker communities by providing a unified (and unifying) set of doctrines and rules to which individual members could turn. Print provided the Shakers, although separate from the world, a means by which to participate in the important discussions of the day as Shaker authors Philemon Stewart, Frederick Evans, Anna White, and Leila Taylor (to name a few) used the power of the pen to keep Shaker voices heard. By the late nineteenth century, the Shakers printed their own periodical, providing a site for sharing information and for creativity, as brothers and sisters shared poetry, testimonials, and other writings. Print documented the faith for internal use and for external eyes. Advertising brochures, broadsides, and pamphlets enhanced the reputation and economic success of Shaker industries. The accumulated printed matter provided material evidence that the struggles of Ann Lee and the original Shakers were not in vain; that, as Ann Lee foresaw in her vision, Shakerism had indeed taken root and grown in the New World.

Along with success came challenges associated with print. Literary scholar Etta Madden argues that literacy brought a tension between strengthening the Shaker community and weakening it as more diverse reading (especially after 1850) enhanced individualism and fragmented communities.[36] Thomas Brown was told that to be a good Shaker he needed to put away his books. Those who did not, like Hervey Elkins who as a teacher had access to more reading material, found themselves wanting still more and apostatized. Print also provided a venue for airing complaints and points of tension. On the one hand, the seceders' critiques offered valuable feedback for Shaker leaders on potential problems. On the other hand, such complaints can exacerbate such tensions when shared communitywide.

By mid-century, anti-Shaker writers competed not only with other forms of print culture such as visitors' accounts, fiction, and apostate narratives from newer (and allegedly more dangerous) sects, but they competed with public opinion that found Shakerism far less threatening than it had once been perceived. The Shakers, too, faced the same competition in marketing their texts. In addition, Shakers faced competition from their own former members, seceders who continued to practice Shaker dances, songs, and worship not as a sacred ritual, but as paid, public entertainment. In a striking and quite literal performance of apostasy, former members offered eager consumers an opportunity to witness Shakerism. These seceders repackaged Shakerism, abandoning the image of a dangerous deviant religion in favor of that of an odd curiosity.

During the 1840s, several groups of male and female Shaker apostates traveled around the country and performed Shaker dances, marches, and gifts in Shaker dress in public settings. As part of the entertainment, Shaker belief, worship, and history was explained. Six to eight members comprised each group, and at least two groups had managers who oversaw travel, performance details, and lodging arrangements and collected admission money. Newspaper advertisements and handbills beckoned the curious public to come see the woman who would "whirl round like a top, fifteen hundred times."[37] A Maine newspaper advertised "The Tall Shakers' Concert" and informed the public that this entertainment would be "entirely new, musical, instructive, and refined."[38] A New York newspaper (1846) described an upcoming concert as attracting those with "an inherent curiosity . . . who want to know something more than the accredited members of the community are willing to disclose."[39] The apostate dancers did not profess to believe in the tenets of Shakerism; newspaper reviews of the performances reported the underlying sarcasm and mocking disbelief present in the apostate dancers' commentary. The apostates dance groups literally performed as entertainment what they had once participated in as a religious faith. Like the apostate authors before them, the dancers became spokespersons for a faith they no longer espoused. The concerts offered a prurient view into the hidden world of Shakerism, revealing the bodily chaos that formed their religious worship while also implicitly suggesting that Shaker gifts, such as the whirling gift or speaking in unknown tongues, could be called up on demand and thus were not necessarily of divine origin.

The Shakers were appalled at such a bold public display of their sacred worship. The New Hampshire ministry described an apostate group from Canterbury who had recently performed in Boston with the shocked review of "What audacity! What blasphemy! and what Heaven daring rebels!"[40] These performers claimed an authenticity of behavior but not of belief. The Shakers described this audacious behavior as "heaven-daring," a phrase that described both the apostates' attitude and action. Having made Shaker worship a marketable commodity, the apostate performers mocked the Shakers. What was sacred had become secular as the apostate dancers exchanged the support of the utopian Shaker community for the financial support of an unbelieving worldly public. The public, curious still about Shaker life, paid for a source of knowledge that both amused and informed.[41]

•••••• •••••• ••••••

When Mary Dyer revised her will in 1852, two of her children were dead. Betsey died of tuberculosis in 1824 at the Shaker village in Enfield. Mary's youngest child, Joseph, died a Shaker in 1840 of a cause unrecorded. In the early summer of 1848, Mary's former husband, Joseph, accompanied by his son and Shaker physician Jerrub, spent six weeks in Boston seeking a cure to an unspecified illness.[42] In late February 1858, the ministry reported that Joseph was "in quite a feeble state and does not leave his room."[43] A few weeks later Joseph died at the age of eighty-five of an unrecorded cause. His obituary in the *New Hampshire Patriot and State Gazette* described him as "universally respected for his honesty, frankness, and sincerity of purpose, wherever he was known." Perhaps somewhat against his desire for a quiet life, Mary had goaded Joseph onto the public stage, giving Joseph the reputation of "a remarkably active supporter of the principles and interests of the Society."[44]

Mary's second son, Orville (1804–1882), lived out his life as a Shaker. As a young man he worked as a cooper. Like his older brother Caleb, Orville became a leader in the Enfield Shaker village, serving twenty-eight years as the elder of the Church family. Orville was a much respected and much beloved leader and his obituary praised his "strong mental powers," and honesty. He was described as " . . . a plain 'matter of fact' man, with a spirit akin to angels. Although human and subject to human frailties, few men had less faults."[45] During the 100th anniversary celebration of the founding of the Enfield Shaker community, his portrait was hung ceremoniously in the hallway of the Church Family dwelling house.

Jerrub Dyer (1806–1886) and his family returned to New Hampshire in 1861. He settled in Lebanon where Jerrub continued to work as a physician and farmer until his death of "old age" in 1886. Jerrub's daughter, Mary's granddaughter, Hattie, an unmarried schoolteacher, died from consumption in 1888. Her sister Rose married twice but had no children. She was killed in a train accident in the early years of the twentieth century.[46]

Mary's stepson, Mancer (born 1798), had also joined the Enfield Shakers with his father Joseph and his stepbrothers and stepsister in 1813. Two years older than Caleb, Mancer was never mentioned by either Mary or Joseph in the course of their debates, perhaps because he was so close to adulthood. Mancer served as a trustee for the North Family in the 1820s, paying the Shakers' taxes and undertaking various business relationships. By the end of the decade, Mancer had left the Enfield Shakers, and the Shakers posted a notice to prevent him from charging goods to their account. He lived in Enfield during 1830, and then moved on, to where is unknown.[47]

The fate of Mary's firstborn, Caleb Marshall Dyer, was imbued with an irony the Enfield Shakers could not have overlooked. As a young man, Caleb rose quickly through the ranks of the Enfield Shaker community and by 1821 was the assistant trustee. In 1838, Caleb accepted the position of Senior Trustee, a position he would hold for life. During his career, Caleb oversaw many important projects including the building of the Church Family Great Stone Dwelling (1837–1841), a stone bridge across Mascoma Lake (1849), and the development of the very profitable Shaker mill industry. As trustee, Caleb was the link between the internal Shaker community and the external world, and his business acumen helped the town of Enfield and the Shakers prosper. During the Civil War, Enfield resident and one-time short-term Shaker Thomas Weir asked the Shakers, represented by Caleb, to care for his two youngest daughters while he served in the army. Weir signed an indenture and left for the war. Troubled by chronic diarrhea, Weir was discharged in 1862 and returned to retrieve his children. Caleb Dyer refused to release the girls who, he claimed, wanted to stay with the Shakers. After several attempts, including an attempted mob, a planned kidnapping, and intervention by friends and attorneys, Weir turned to violence proclaiming that if Weir could not have the children, then neither would Caleb Dyer. Late in the afternoon of July 18, 1863, Weir confronted Dyer, determined to retrieve his Shaker-held children. Once again Caleb refused and Weir shot him with a colt revolver, a fairly new weapon praised for its portability and ease of hiding.

On July 18, the New Hampshire ministry at Canterbury learned of the assault by telegram and passed it along to another Shaker community in a letter:

> A sad item of news has reached Canterbury by telegram thus: "Caleb M. Dyer shot by Thomas Wiers [sic]. Doctor thinks not fatal but uncertain." . . . Presume we shall have further intelligence soon, and shall be better able to communicate the facts. We sincerely hope beloved Elder Caleb will recover. It would be a serious loss to Enfield people to have him die.[48]

In the early morning hours of July 21, Caleb Marshall Dyer, whose apostate mother fifty years earlier had made similar attempts to retrieve him and his siblings, died. Where Mary Dyer, constrained by gender, used the power of the pen to gain vindication over the Shakers, Weir used the power of the gun in a futile attempt to retrieve his children.[49]

Caleb's death left an immeasurable gap in the Enfield Shaker community. Not only was Caleb a guiding force, he also managed all of the community financial dealings. Unfortunately for the Enfield Shakers, Caleb left no written business records, and his death led to fiscal chaos and numerous lawsuits as his brother, Orville, appointed September 26 to take Caleb's place, struggled to replicate the missing records.[50] A local company turned money owed to the Shakers into money owed to them, suing the Shakers to make good on the alleged debt. The case dragged on for twenty years; the Shakers lost and were forced to pay nearly $20,000 in claims and legal costs. The shock of the violent murder, the loss of their talented leader, the endless legal battles, and the financial cost all took a toll on the Enfield community. Looking back at Enfield Shaker history, Caleb Dyer's death can be seen as a pivotal event that precipitated a slow slide into quiescence that would end when the Enfield Shakers closed their community in 1923. On the last day, before they moved to Canterbury, the few remaining Enfield Shakers had a tea party on the porch of the Great Stone Dwelling, the magnificent structure built under Caleb Dyer's leadership.

*   *   *

The possibility of preaching, an escape from the labor of frontier life, the desire to keep her family together, and curiosity all drew Mary Dyer to the Shakers. Shaker life and doctrines had stimulated Dyer much in the same way she was stimulated by the religious revivals that had swept across the Coös, her brief experience with the Quakers, Methodists, Freewill Baptists, and with Congregationalists. Dyer portrayed herself as a sufferer at the hands of the Shakers, but her texts bore testimony between the lines of a resilient, strong-minded, ambitious woman who clearly understood the social dilemma in which she found herself and clearly saw the way in which she could achieve extrication.

But for all her success, the pain of losing her children and her social dislocation remained with Mary her entire life. Her lonely existence above Mascoma Lake was a testament to the desire to be near her children. She fought aggressively, vociferously, tenaciously, and towards the end of her career, perhaps, obsessively, to prevent what had happened to her family from happening to others. But while she carried her grudge against the Shakers to her grave, Dyer never counted her children among her enemies. As her last will and testament so clearly stated, even after four decades, to Mary Dyer her children were simply located "with" the Shakers, they were not Shakers themselves.

In January 1867, Mary Marshall Dyer died alone in her home in Enfield of an apoplectic fit, what today we would call a stroke. Her obituary in the *Granite State Free Press* described her "vigorous intellect." The editor wrote that Mary was "of a masculine cast of mind— what may be called a 'strong-minded woman'—and thought and acted with great independence."[51] Her obituary noted that she was an author, citing *Rise and Progress*. She was remembered as the mother of the murdered Caleb and for the length of her life, spanning the years between the American Revolution and the Civil War. Jerrub lived up to the conditions of Mary's will, settled his mother's estate and buried her in a small, tree-lined cemetery not far from her home. Alone for most of her life, Mary would be alone in death—the only Dyer buried in the small cemetery. Jerrub and his family were buried in Lebanon; Joseph,

Sr., and the remaining Dyer children—Caleb, Orville, Joseph, Jr., and Betsey—were buried at the Enfield Shakers. As Mary had required, Jerrub erected an appropriate gravestone. The inscription offered her birth and death dates and this standard nineteenth-century epithet: "Mary M. Dyer, wife of Joseph Dyer," an awkward phrase considering Mary carried her former husband's name, but had not been his wife for several decades. One wonders why Jerrub chose this phrase. "Mother," an equally common nineteenth-century epithet, was equally inappropriate. Mary Dyer's children were raised by the Shakers and as such learned to disavow any special feelings between offspring and parent. Mary's role as a mother provided the motivation for her campaign, her status as Joseph's wife provided the obstacles that blocked her way to independence. Her lonely grave and her problematic epithet reflected her life as a childless mother and a husbandless wife, a woman out of place in her marriage, at the Shakers, and later in her life as an apostate.

The fear Dyer and others expressed has not dissipated. While the Shakers no longer inspire such terror, other groups do. Recent media focus on the Branch Davidians and Heaven's Gate renews attention to many of the hundreds of communal groups and alternative religions extant today in the United States. As political scientist Richard Hofstadter and others have argued, fear of difference and the belief that such difference is dangerous would seem to be a pervasive facet of American society.[52]

Likewise, the role of seceders and networks of apostates and other opponents has also remained strong. Print media produce numerous accounts from former members of various contemporary groups who found themselves tricked, captured, or imprisoned, escaping only by the intervention of God, fate, or sympathetic outsiders, and then publish their experiences as a warning to others. Formal organizations, such as the American Family Foundation and the new Cult Awareness Network, promise to provide information, newsletters, and a means to connect with other former members, scholars, or various professionals. The internet plays a vital role in facilitating these networks. The website of the Peregrine Foundation serves as a virtual meeting point for "families and individuals living in or exiting from experimental social groups." Former members of the Bruderhof are particularly well organized and remain in contact for mutual support through an organization called KIT (Keep in Touch).[53]

Mary Dyer's legacy, like her life, remains ambiguous. Beyond Shaker studies and a few nineteenth-century town histories, Dyer and her story are unknown.[54] Her books sit quietly on the shelves of historical societies and archives, for the most part overlooked. The last time the Boston Atheneum's copy of *Portraiture* was read was in 1886. But when her books are carefully read and closely examined, her legacy is one of many lessons. Her long campaign brought attention to the tension between the rhetoric of individually endowed rights and the sociocultural and legal reality of women's dependence on their husbands. In demonstrating her social and legal liminality as a Shaker husband's wife, Dyer prompted debate on the rights and obligations of spouses to one another, and to the relationship between marriage and the stability, and future prosperity, of society. The amendment to New Hampshire divorce law her situation inspired was one small step toward increasing the ability of women to regain autonomy. That her same complaints were politely dismissed in her latter years is in part a testament to a slow but steady accumulation of other just rights for women, including further facilitation of divorce and the creation of married women's property acts. Mary's legacy is thus seen in part in economics; public discussion of family, husbands, wives, and marriage hovered around the critical necessity of productive and reproductive labor to further the new nation's success.

Dyer's legacy is also in part a commercial one. Through the visibility of her texts, Dyer participated in the commodification of Shakerism. Things Shaker and things anti-Shaker sold. The Shakers would use this to their great advantage in the nineteenth century as they created, and responded to, a booming market for their products, practices, and ideas. Print played an early and important role in this process. Mary Dyer's texts demonstrated the efficacy of print culture to wage a battle, a lesson not lost on apostates who followed her, as well as any number of readers, authors, reformers, and social protestors who took pen in hand to market an idea in a culture where knowledge equaled power and reading became a necessity of life.[55] Dyer's texts were on the one hand commodities, but on the other were means to give the underrepresented, the voiceless, and the powerless an opportunity to participate in crafting American identity. On the cusp of the rise of the modern world, Dyer's life story encapsulated and reflected back to her readers the new world of print, industry, and the market that precipitated, necessitated, and facilitated changes in gender roles, family dynamics, and social organization.

When Mary Dyer shook the faith, she unsettled more than ideas about a particular religious sect. Throwing into sharp relief tensions and concerns of her day, Dyer's campaign stirred up people's minds and led them to question what they had once believed as irresolute truth. Dyer's campaign, though, also provided a means to cope with the difficult issues she raised. Mary Dyer fostered and strengthened two communities. Dyer created and used a network of apostates that found in each other a replacement for the communal family they had abandoned, and a safe haven from the mainstream world that looked upon them with suspicion. Membership in the apostate community solidified around, at its best, simply being decidedly "not Shaker," and at its worst, in an all-out attack on the faith. The actions of Dyer and her colleagues strengthened the Shaker community as Shakers were forced to articulate their faith in print, in the courtroom, and in their own hearts. Both communities invited the mainstream public to join them in spirit, offering an opportunity to construct an identity based on what one was, or what one was not. In this dynamic interaction, in the midst of building a nation, Mary Marshall Dyer and the anti-Shaker movement of the antebellum period illustrated that community is built both from within and from without.

Notes

Notes to Introduction

1. Mary Marshall Dyer, Last Will and Testament, May 17, 1853. Papers of the History of Enfield, New Hampshire. Dartmouth College Library.
2. Detailed descriptions of Shaker theology are found in the Shakers' seminal nineteenth-century work on which all later theological works were based, Benjamin Seth Youngs's *The Testimony of Christ's Second Appearing*, which appeared in four editions (Lebanon, Ohio: John M'Clean,1808; Albany, N. Y.: E. and E. Hosford, 1810; Union Village, Ohio: B. Fisher and A. Burnett, 1823; [Albany, N. Y.]: United Society Called Shakers, 1856). See also Theodore E. Johnson, *Life in the Christ Spirit* (Sabbathday Lake, Maine: United Society of Shakers, 1969).
3. Jean M. Humez, "'Weary of Petticoat Government': The Specter of Female Rule in Early Nineteenth-Century Shaker Politics," *Communal Societies* 11 (1991): 1-17. See also her edited collection of Shaker thought on this theme: *Mother's First-Born Daughters: Early Shaker Writings on Women and Religion* (Bloomington: Indiana University Press, 1993).

   On the role of women in Shaker communities see also, Lawrence Foster, *Women, Family, and Utopia* (Syracuse: Syracuse University Press, 1991); Louis Kern, *An Ordered Love* (Chapel Hill: The University of North Carolina Press, 1981); Marjorie Procter-Smith, *Women in Shaker Community and Worship* (Lewiston, N. Y.: Edwin Mellen Press, 1985); and Catherine Wessinger, ed., *Women's Leadership in Marginal Religions: Explorations Outside the Mainstream* (Urbana: University of Illinois Press, 1993).

   Note that the description of Shaker community organization offered here reflects an ideal community. In reality, especially after the Civil War when the Shakers began their numerical decline, there were often situations when there was an absence of qualified individuals to fill these important posts. Some positions were eliminated and some individuals filled more than one post simultaneously.

4. The formal name of the Shaker faith is The United Society of Believers in Christ's Second Appearing. The terms *Shaker(s)* and *Believer(s)* are used synonymously in this research to refer to the members of the communal group. The Shaker origin story found in contemporary popular works derives more from a nineteenth-century Shaker reinterpretation than eighteenth-century primary documents. Stephen Stein discussed the paucity of sources for the English and early-American period in *The Shaker Experience in America* (New Haven: Yale University Press, 1992), 3-10. The best treatment of the religious context from which Shakerism emerged is found in Clark Garrett, *Spirit Possession and Popular Religion: From the Camisards to the Shakers* (Baltimore: The Johns Hopkins University Press, 1987). On the American emergence of Shakerism, Stephen Marini, *Radical Sects in Revolutionary New England* (Cambridge: Harvard University Press, 1982) described the development of American Shakerism as part of a New England sectarian impulse that also prompted the development of the Freewill Baptists and the Universalists. On Americans' early attraction to Shakerism, see Priscilla J. Brewer, *Shaker Communities, Shaker Lives* (Hanover, N. H.: University Press of New England, 1986), 1-12.

5. On the "porous boundaries" between Shakers and the world, and the ease with which some converts moved across them see Stephen J. Stein, "The "Not-So-Faithful" Believers: Conversion, Deconversion, and Reconversion Among the Shakers," *American Studies* 38 (Fall 1997): 5-20.

6. The exception is a richly informative source of information on the post-Shaker life of Angell Matthewson. In decades of correspondence to his brother Jeffrey, Angell, who left the New Lebanon, New York, Shaker community in 1799, described his varied experiences as he traveled and settled in New York State. Though Angell led no anti-Shaker mobs or published any anti-Shaker material, his Shaker experience made an indelible mark on the way he saw the world. Over the years, Angell related to his brother numerous stories of individuals who had been duped or tricked by one means or another. His summary comment on these incidents was often that these people "were as ignorant as if [one] had been educated by the [Shaking] Quakers." See, for example, Letter XXXII, "Reminiscences in the Form of a Series of Thirty-nine Letters to His Brother Jeffrey," Shaker Collection, New York Public Library (microfilm, Winterthur Museum and Library).

7. See the discussion in Stein, "The 'Not-So-Faithful' Believers," 8-11.

8. Bryant is described in a letter from Lucy Smith, Pleasant Hill, to Lucy Wright, New Lebanon, August 12, 1825. Edward Deming Andrews Memorial Shaker Collection, The Winterthur Library, Winterthur, Delaware (hereafter cited as Andrews Collection, Winterthur).

9. On print culture in America see Ronald Zboray, *A Fictive People: Antebellum Economic Development and the American Reading Public* (New York: Oxford University Press, 1993). On the act of reading, Cathy N. Davidson, ed., *Reading in America: Literature and Social History* (Baltimore, Maryland: The Johns Hopkins University Press, 1989). On the cultural work fiction performed, Jane Tompkins, *Sensational Designs: The Cultural Work of American Fiction, 1790–1860* (New York: Oxford University Press, 1985), and Cathy N. Davidson, *Revolution and the Word: The Rise of the Novel in America* (New York: Oxford University Press, 1986).

10. Richard H. Brodhead, *Cultures of Letters: Scenes of Reading and Writing in America* (Chicago: University of Chicago Press, 1993), ix, 5.

11. Ann Fabian, *The Unvarnished Truth: Personal Narratives in Nineteenth-Century History* (Berkeley: University of California Press, 2000), 4.

12. See, for example, John Bailey, *Fanaticism Exposed: or the Schemes of Shakerism Compared with Scripture, Reason, and Religion and Found to be Contrary to Them All* (Lexington, Kentucky: Printed at the Reporter Office by W. W. Worsley, 1811). From 1810 to 1869, twelve non-apostate authors penned fourteen anti-Shaker accounts.

13. See, for example, Christopher Clark, *A Shock to Shakerism: or, a Serious Refutation of the Idolatrous Divinity of Ann Lee of Manchester* (Richmond, Kentucky: Printed for T. W. Ruble, 1812).

14. On representations of the Shakers in popular print see Flo Morse, *The Shakers and the World's People* (Hanover, N.H.: University Press of New England, 1980). On Shakers in fiction, see Ruth McAdams, "The Shakers in American Fiction," (Ph.D. diss., Texas Christian University, 1985) and Michael Pugh, "A Thorn in the Text: Shakerism and the Marriage Narrative," (Ph.D. diss., University of New Hampshire, 1994).

15. Valentine Rathbun, *An Account of the Matter, Form and Manner of a New and Strange Religion. . . .* (Providence, RI: Printed and Sold by Bennett Wheeler, 1781), 3.

16. David G. Bromley makes the point that the apostate's " . . . former status is the basis for their current status" in "The Social Construction of Contested Exit Roles: Defectors, Whistleblowers, and Apostates," in David G. Bromley, ed., *The Politics of Religious Apostasy: The Role of Apostates in the Transformation of Religious Movements* (Westport, Conn.: Praeger, 1998), 38.

17. Daniel Carson Johnson discusses the claims and counter-claims made in apostate narratives with a particular focus on "apostates who never were." His discussion of the narrative anchors of biographical history and contextual history are relevant to apostates who were, as well. Daniel Carson Johnson, "Apostates Who Never Were: The Social Construction of *Absque Facto* Apostate Narratives," in David G. Bromley, ed., *The Politics of Religious Apostasy: The Role of Apostates in the Transformation of Religious Movements* (Westport, Conn.: Praeger, 1998), 117.

18. Ministry New Lebanon to Ministry Union Village, March 27, 1819, Shaker Manuscripts, Western Reserve Historical Society, Cleveland, Ohio (hereafter cited WRHS) IV:A-33.

19. A social science perspective on apostasy is offered in Bromley, *The Politics of Religious Apostasy,* and David G. Bromley, ed., *Falling From the Faith: Causes and Consequences of Religious Apostasy* (Newbury Park, Calif.: Sage Publications, 1988).

20. On the interaction between the published captivity narrative and its reader, see Gary L. Ebersole, *Captured by Texts: Puritan to Postmodern Images of Indian Captivity* (Charlottesville: University Press of Virginia, 1995).

21. V. Rathbun, *An Account,* 9.

22. The Shaker apostate narrative shares these features with apostate accounts of alternative religions from the nineteenth century through present day. On the literary analysis of such accounts see John D. Barbour, *Versions of Deconversion: Autobiography and the Loss of Faith* (Charlottesville: University Press of Virginia, 1994); on the publications and activities of former Mormons see Lawrence Foster, "Career Apostates: Reflections on the Life and Work of Jerald and Sandra Tanner," *Dialogue: A Journal of Mormon Thought* 17 (1984): 35-60; Terryl L. Givens, *The Viper on the Hearth: Mormons, Myths, and the Construction of Heresy* (New York: Oxford University Press, 1997); and Roger Launius and Linda Thatcher, eds., *Differing Visions: Dissenters in Mormon History* (Urbana: University of Illinois Press, 1994); on defections from contemporary groups see the essays in Bromley,

Falling From The Faith, and David G. Bromley and Anson Shupe, *Strange Gods: The Great American Cult Scare* (Boston: Beacon Press, 1981).

23. Aquila Bolton, *Some Lines in Verse About the Shakers, Not Published By the Authority of the Society So Called* (New York: William Taylor & Co., 1846).

24. For a discussion of the evolution of the Shaker threat see Elizabeth A. De Wolfe, "'A Very Deep Design at the Bottom': The Shaker Threat, 1780–1860," in Nancy Lusignan Schultz, ed., *Fear Itself: Enemies Real & Imagined in American Culture* (West Lafayette, Ind.: Purdue University Press, 1999), 105-118. Schultz's collection of essays documents a long American history of fearing difference, suggesting that anti-Shakerism was part of a larger social process than an isolated series of incidents.

25. For a contemporary example see David G. Bromley, Anson Shupe, and J. C. Ventimiglia, "Atrocity Tales, the Unification Church, and the Social Construction of Evil," *Journal of Communication* 29 (Summer 1979): 42-53.

26. Fabian, *The Unvarnished Truth,* considers the personal narratives of beggars, convicts, slaves, and prisoners of war. Narratives of cross-dressing are illuminated in Daniel A. Cohen, ed., *The Female Marine and Related Works: Narratives of Cross-Dressing and Urban Vice in America's Early Republic* (Amherst: University of Massachusetts Press, 1997). See also Patricia Cline Cohen's analysis of the competing print narratives regarding the murder of Helen Jewett. Patricia Cline Cohen, *The Murder of Helen Jewett: The Life and Death of a Prostitute in Nineteenth-Century New York* (New York: Knopf, 1998).

27. See Barbara Welter, "The Cult of True Womanhood, 1820–1860," *American Quarterly* 18 (Summer 1966): 131-175, and Nancy F. Cott, *The Bonds of Womanhood: "Woman's Sphere" in New England, 1780–1835* (New Haven, Conn.: Yale University Press, 1977).

28. Susan M. Griffin, "Awful Disclosures: Women's Evidence in the Escaped Nun's Tale," *Publications of the Modern Language Association* 3 (January 1996): 94.

29. The use of sentimentality in captivity narratives is discussed in Ebersole, *Captured By Texts,* 98-143.

30. Mary M. Dyer, *A Brief Statement of the Sufferings of Mary Dyer Occasioned by the Society Called Shakers* (Concord, N. H.: Printed by Joseph C. Spear, 1818), 13.

31. Ebersole, *Captured By Texts,* 111.

32. Thomas W. Laqueur, "Bodies, Details, and the Humanitarian Narrative," in Lynn Hunt, ed., *The New Cultural History* (Berkeley: University of California Press, 1989), 177.

33. Dyer, *A Brief Statement,* 13.

34. Absolem H. Blackburn, *A Brief Account of the Rise, Progress, Doctrines, and Practices of the People Usually Denominated Shakers* (Flemingsburg, Ky.: Printed by A. Crookshanks, 1824),18.

35. Eunice Chapman in Mary Marshall Dyer, *A Portraiture of Shakerism, Exhibiting a General View of Their Character and Conduct, From the First Appearance of Ann Lee in New-England, Down to Present Time* ([Haverhill, N. H.]: Printed for the Author [by Sylvester Goss], 1822), 238.

36. Ann Taves, ed., *Religion and Domestic Violence in Early New England: The Memoirs of Abigail Abbott Bailey* (Bloomington: Indiana University Press, 1989).

37. Ebersole, *Captured by Texts,* 2.

38. Daniel Rathbun in Dyer, *Portraiture,* 85.

39. Erik R. Seeman, "It is Better to Marry Than to Burn: Anglo-American Attitudes Toward Celibacy, 1600-1800," *Journal of Family History* 24 (1999): 412.

40. Benjamin West, *Scriptural Cautions Against Embracing a Religious Scheme*. . . . (Hartford, Conn.: Printed and Sold by Bavil Webster, 1783), 7.

41. Carol Weisbrod, *The Boundaries of Utopia* (New York: Pantheon Books, 1980).

42. Lawrence Foster, *Religion and Sexuality: The Shakers, the Mormons, and the Oneida Community* (Urbana: University of Illinois Press, 1984), 51-53; Jean M. Humez, "'A Woman Mighty to Pull You Down': Married Women's Rights and Female Anger in the Anti-Shaker Narratives of Eunice Chapman and Mary Marshall Dyer," *Journal of Women's History* 6 (1994): 105.

43. On microhistory versus biography see Jill Lepore, "Historians Who Love Too Much: Reflections on Microhistory and Biography," *The Journal of American History* 88 (June 2001): 129-144.

44. Rosabeth Moss Kanter, *Commitment and Community* (Cambridge, Mass.: Harvard University Press, 1972),102-103.

45. See David B. Davis, "Themes of Counter-Subversion: An Analysis of Anti-Masonic, Anti-Catholic, and Anti-Mormon Literature," *The Mississippi Valley Historical Review* 47 (1960): 205-224. A broad overview of persistent anti-Catholicism is offered in Barbara Welter, "From Maria Monk to Paul Blanshard: A Century of Protestant Anti-Catholicism," in Robert Bellah and Frederick Greenspahn, eds., *Uncivil Religion: Interreligious Hostility in America* (New York: Crossroad Publishing Company, 1987),43-71. Nancy Lusignan Schultz considers the anti-Catholic narratives of former nuns in *Veil of Fear: Nineteenth-Century Convent Tales* (West Lafayette, Ind.: Purdue University Press,1999) and the burning of the Ursuline Convent in *Fire and Roses: The Burning of the Charlestown Convent, 1834* (New York: The Free Press, 2000). A cross-cultural perspective on contemporary anti-cult activities is offered in Anson Shupe and David G. Bromley, eds., *Anti-Cult Movements in Cross-cultural Perspective* (New York: Garland Publishing, Inc., 1994).

46. See the essays in Schultz, *Fear Itself*, and Richard Hofstadter, *The Paranoid Style in American Politics and Other Essays* (New York: Vintage Books, 1965).

47. Dyer, *Portraiture*, v.

Notes to Chapter One

1. Mary Marshall [Dyer], *The Rise and Progress of the Serpent from the Garden of Eden, to the Present Day* (Concord, N. H.: Printed for the Author, 1847), 162. In *A Portraiture of Shakerism* (Haverhill, N. H.: Sylvester Goss, 1822), Mary reported the date as 1804 but the earlier date is consistent with Stratford area history.

2. Dyer, *Portraiture*, 334-35. Humez also notes the conversion in the pesthouse in "'A Woman Mighty to Pull You Down': Married Women's Rights and Female Anger in the Anti-Shaker Narratives of Eunice Chapman and Mary Dyer," *Journal of Women's History* 6 (Summer 1994): 108-109, note 42.

3. For as much information as we can tease out of Mary Dyer's publications, there is still a great deal of mystery about her life, not the least of which is her birth date. She provided the date of 1780 in *Portraiture*, 333. Her obituary (*The Free Press*, Lebanon, N. H., January 19, 1867) stated she was born in 1777. A manuscript note from William Shedd, initially tipped into a copy of *Portraiture*, stated that according to Mary's Bible, she was 89 at the time of her death and that this information was provided to Shedd in a letter from Jerrub Dyer, February 6, 1871.

Mary's gravestone records her age at death as 89 years, indicating the 1777 birth date. Northumberland town records for the eighteenth century have not been located.

4. Jeannette Thompson, *History of the Town of Stratford, N. H., 1773–1925* (Concord, N. H.: The Rumford Press, 1925), 420. Mary's niece, Maria Marshall Johnson (d. 1883), described the early days of northern New Hampshire in the *Coös County Democrat* (extracts reprinted in Thompson, *History of Stratford,* 112-114.) "Dorothea," a serialized biography of her maternal grandmother, featured Indian captivity on the New England frontier. Dorothea Gamsby Imeson was a young mother when she settled in Northumberland in the 1780s, roughly the same age as Mary's mother, Zeruiah Marshall. Caleb Marshall's name appeared on a petition to the New Hampshire legislature seeking protection from Indian raids that were a constant threat for settlers in the Upper Connecticut region during the American Revolution. On June 24, 1779, a group of fifteen Indians led by a Frenchmen took two prisoners and plundered two families. See Thompson, *History of Stratford,* 112-114, 473. See also Colin G. Calloway, "An Uncertain Destiny: Indian Captivities on the Upper Connecticut River," *Journal of American Studies* 17 (1983): 189-210. Calloway found that unlike captivities on the later western frontier, the fate of New England captives was uncertain and variable and thus the psychological fear of Indian raids and "an uncertain destiny" kept settlers wary.

5. Although most of Mary's siblings remained in New England, the youngest two, Fanny and Silas, settled in the west. On the genealogy of the Marshall family see Thompson, *History of Stratford,* 419-421, which was drawn from L. W. Prescott, "History of Stratford," a photocopied compilation of articles from *The Berlin Independent,* 1897, in the collection of the New Hampshire Historical Society.

6. *History of Coös County* (Syracuse: W. A. Ferguson, Co., 1888; facsimile of the original, Somersworth, NH: NH Publishing Co., 1972), 550-554.

7. Dyer, *Rise and Progress,* 157. Her grandfather was a robust man with large features and was known for wearing gray, homespun clothes. He was a farmer, businessman, and early proponent of the Revolution.

8. In 1801, Joseph sold his portion of his mother's "widow's third" property to his stepbrother (?) Jedidiah Johnson. He received $190.45. In 1807, Joseph sold a smaller parcel of land to his brother Elijah for $20. Elijah Dyar, Estate papers, File #733, Connecticut State Library. See also Canterbury (Connecticut) Town Records, vol. 13, pp. 9, 257; vol. 15, p.218, Connecticut State Library.

9. Joseph's participation in the out-migration had its basis in the shortage of available farmland for young men. With his inheritance, Joseph could purchase land in a new locale. Stratford was originally incorporated as the town of Woodbury and forty-four of sixty-three of the original grantees were from Woodbury, Connecticut. When the town was reincorporated as Stratford, thirty-two of seventy-two new grantees were from Stratford, Connecticut, thus illustrating the kin and neighborhood groups of settlers moving to northern New Hampshire. Another large block of settlers of the Coös region came from coastal New Hampshire, among them Mary's parents, and Antipas Marshall, her father's cousin and the first Methodist preacher in the area. On the settlement of northern New Hampshire see Charles E. Clark, *The Eastern Frontier: The Settlement of Northern New England, 1610–1763* (Hanover: University Press of New England, 1970; reprint, New York: Alfred Knopf, 1983). Clark argues that settlement of the far interior differed from earlier settlement strategies. In this period (1760–1775) settlement was a quick, massive movement of groups of families to one area. This settlement

process produced a new entity, a "country town" created out of a blend of New England social values and the needs and responses to distinct physical and economic circumstances. In these new towns, the focus was on the family farm, rather than on the village, a departure from the settled life left behind in southern New England and the coastal areas. See also James A. Henretta, "Families and Farms: Mentalité in Pre-Industrial America," *William and Mary Quarterly,* Third series, 35 (January 1978): 3-28. Henretta argues that the lineal family and the concern for distribution of property was a key factor in the mentalité of northern agricultural society in the preindustrial era.

10. Wilson B. Roberts reported the marriage and death of Elizabeth Peverly in his unpublished treatise on the Dyer family, but I have found no primary source evidence of these events. See Roberts, "A Sketch of Joseph and Mary Dyer, Shakers, of Enfield, New Hampshire. Their Children and their Ancestors." Typescript, 1957, in Papers of the History of Enfield, New Hampshire, Dartmouth College Library. The Peverly Family genealogy provides detailed information on Joseph Peverly (her father) and his four children, but does not include any mention of an Elizabeth. There is a nine-year gap between the births of the first (1770) and second child (1779) during which more children could have been born. This would be the time period in which a schoolmate of Mary's would have been born. The last three Peverly children were born within a three-year period making it unlikely that another child was born within that grouping. On the Peverly family see Henry Winthrop Hardon, *Peverly Family: Thomas Peverly of Portsmouth, N. H., 1623–1670,* (Boston: Privately Printed, 1927); and, Hardon, *Peverly Collaterals . . . ,* typescript in the collection of the New Hampshire Historical Society, 1930. Stratford vital statistics and town records from 1785–1800 do not survive.

11. *History of Coös,* "Stratford," 759.

12. Wilson Roberts reported in his history of the Dyer family that Orville was named after the hero in Fanny Burney's 1778 novel *Evelina,* which was very popular at the time of his birth. If true, it is an interesting indication that Mary read fiction and that that particular book made an impact on her. *Evelina* was published in numerous British and American editions. A current edition is found in Fanny Burney, *Evelina, or, The History of a Young Lady's Entrance into the World* (New York: W. W. Norton & Co., 1965).

13. Joseph remained active with the Masons until 1805, when the Dyers moved further north. *One Hundredth Anniversary: North Star Lodge No. 8 A. F. and A. M. . . . 1797–1897* (Lancaster, N. H.: Amos F. Rowell, Printer, 1897). Joseph is listed incorrectly as Joseph Dwyer of Northumberland. His name also appears (correctly) on a register of lodge members 1798-1801. "Register of Lodge Members," photocopy in Roberts, *A Sketch.* See also, *History of Coös,* 139-141; and, Melvin W. Chase to Robert Meader, September 14, 1971, Item #17,325, Emma B. King Library, Shaker Museum, Old Chatham, N. Y.

14. Joseph Dyer, *A Compendious Narrative* (Concord, [N. H.]: Printed by Isaac Hill, for the author, 1818), 36.

15. Thompson, *History of Stratford,* 481, 484; Stratford Town Records, 20, (microfilm, New England Genealogical Historic Society). At the Stratford town meeting on March 4, 1800, Joseph was named one of the town selectmen and also appointed constable and collector. But by summer, July 12, the town had "voted to reconsider the vote of Joseph Dyer being selectman and made choice of William Johnson in his stead." Joseph does not hold a public position again until 1804, when he was appointed one of four highway surveyors.

16. Possibly his cousin Elisha Dyer.

17. "The Geography of Stewartstown, New Hampshire," ca. 1840, Manuscript in the collection of De Wolfe & Wood Books, Alfred, Maine.

18. *History of Coös,* 654, 659

19. Ibid., 656.

20. Ibid., 668-669.

21. See Seena B. Kohl, "The Making of a Community: The Role of Women in an Agricultural Setting," in Allan J. Lichtman and Joan R. Challinor, eds., *Kin and Communities: Families in America* (Washington, D. C.: Smithsonian Institution Press, 1979), 175-186. Kohl argues that women's tasks are the "hidden aspects of production." A similar argument is offered by Gayle Rubin, "The Traffic in Women: Notes on the Political Economy of Sex," in Rayna R. Reiter, ed., *Toward An Anthropology of Women* (New York: Monthly Review Press, 1975), 157-210. Rubin asserts that gender systems are a culturally constructed set of arrangements that "transforms biological sexuality into products of human activity," and that the concepts of gender, sexuality, politics, and economics are interdependent.

22. Dyer, *Rise and Progress,* 162

23. On the lives of farm women, see also Joan M. Jensen, *Loosening the Bonds: Mid-Atlantic Farm Women, 1750–1850* (New Haven: Yale University Press, 1986); Nancy Grey Osterud, *Bonds of Community: The Lives of Farm Women in Nineteenth-Century New York* (Ithaca: Cornell University Press, 1991); and essays in Wava G. Haney and Jane B. Knowles, eds., *Women and Farming: Changing Roles, Changing Structures* (Boulder, Colorado: Westview Press, 1988). On building community in the social sphere, see Karen V. Hansen, *A Very Social Time: Crafting Community in Antebellum New England* (Berkeley: University of California Press, 1994).

24. Dyer, *Portraiture,* 335.

25. Ibid.

26. Marini, *Radical Sects,* 142.

27. On Freewill Baptist theology see Ibid., 139-144.

28. Dyer, *Portraiture,* 335.

29. Ibid.

30. Ibid.; date provided in Dyer, *Rise and Progress,* 165. N. F. Carter, *The Native Ministry of New Hampshire* (Concord, New Hampshire: n.p., 1906) identifies three Elder Quimbys, brothers Daniel and Joseph from Weare and Joshua Quimby from Kingston. In a quarterly magazine, *A Religious Magazine: Containing a Short History of the Church of Christ. . . .* (Portland, Maine), John Buzzell detailed the spread of Freewill Baptists in Maine and New Hampshire in 1811 and 1812. Buzzell mentioned the Quimby brothers' role in New Hampshire revivals but did not identify any specific meetings in the Dyers' locale.

31. Cross describes frontier life in New York as interdenominational by default due to poor roads and widely scattered ministers and potential church members. Ministers of various faiths would share the same facilities for preaching, on alternating Sundays for example. A revival might start with one minister and then continue with the next. Once the revival gained momentum, preachers from all over would rush to the locale in an attempt to attract as many individuals as possible in order to form a permanent congregation. Whitney Cross, *The Burned-Over District: The Social and Intellectual History of Enthusiastic Religion in Western New York, 1800–1850* (Ithaca: Cornell University Press, 1950).

32. Putnam, described as "a young man," was ordained February 6, 1809, in Strafford, Vermont. After his ordination, Buzzell reported that Putnam "left this people [at

Strafford?] and at present not considered under their care." Buzzell, *A Religious Magazine,* 1 (October 1812), 277.

33. Dyer, *Portraiture,* 337.

34. Statement of Joseph Dyer, May 11, 1829, Dyer v. Dyer, Records of Grafton County Superior Court, May Term 1829, Box A98092. New Hampshire Department of State, Division of Records Management and Archives, Concord, N. H.

35. J. Dyer, *A Compendious Narrative,* 9.

36. "Proposal and Other Papers Regarding the Publication of the Testimony of Christ's Second Appearing," MS. #1136, Andrews Collection, Winterthur.

37. [Benjamin Seth Youngs], *The Testimony of Christ's Second Appearing . . . , Second Edition, Corrected and Improved* (Albany, N. Y.: Printed by E. and E. Hosford, 1810).

38. Diary of William Plumer, November 18, 1810. Roll LC1, Frames 524-527. The William Plumer Papers, Library of Congress and the New Hampshire Historical Society (microfilm, New Hampshire Historical Society). Hereafter cited as Plumer Papers.

39. Ibid.

40. "The Shakers," *Newburyport Herald,* ca. September 1808.

41. Ibid.

42. J. Dyer, *A Compendious Narrative,* 12.

43. Dyer, *Portraiture,* 339.

44. On the attraction of Shakerism (and other nonmainstream religions) to women see Mary Farrell Bednarowski, "Outside the Mainstream: Women's Religions and Women Religious Leaders in Nineteenth-Century America," *Journal of the American Academy of Religion* 48 (June 1980), 212-213.

45. Mary in *Rise and Progress* gave this date as February 1811.

46. J. Dyer, *A Compendious Narrative,* 16.

47. Dyer, *Portraiture,* 343.

48. Ibid.

49. Little information is available on the Dyer children during this period. Shortly after their arrival, and while Mary was back in Stewartstown, Jerrub and Joseph suffered the measles. Joseph, who slept up in the loft of the Dwelling House, also had a sore on his arm and had a "weak turn" but was otherwise healthy. Like new adult members, the children were also being socialized into Shaker life through a combination of work and instruction. Caleb advanced rapidly. At one time, he taught the younger Shaker children and even supervised his younger brothers. Deacon Nathaniel Draper saw promise in young Caleb and took him under his care.

50. Etta Madden, *Bodies of Life: Shaker Literature and Literacies* (Westport, Connecticut: Greenwood Press, 1998).

51. At this time, the Enfield Shaker community had several out families. These included groups of individuals living in houses on farmland used by the Shakers for whom there was no available housing within the community. See Wendell Hess, *The Enfield (N. H.) Shakers: A Brief History* (Enfield, N. H.: n.p., 1993), 13.

52. She was not the last either. Aquila Bolton espoused Shakerism for many years and published a pro-Shaker piece. Later in life he apostatized when his ideas became too far from the Shaker center. He took his apostasy to a public forum and published *Some Lines in Verse about the Shakers* (New York: William Taylor & Co., 1846), a long, rhyming diatribe against the Shaker leadership. Roxalana Grosvenor promoted spiritual marriage in the mid-nineteenth century and was

barred from the community. She took her dismissal to court, which decided in favor of the Shakers. See Grosvenor v. United Society, 118 Mass. 78 (1875).

53. Henry C. Blinn, "Historical Notes on Believers Having Reference to Believers at Enfield," Typescript (photocopy), Shaker Library, United Society of Shakers, Sabbathday Lake, Maine, 206.

54. In addition to Mary and Joseph's signatures, Mancer Dyer's name also appears, as does Benjamin Green, a future noted apostate author, and James Chapman, a troublesome member whose wife Eunice would wreak havoc on Shaker communities in New York and New Hampshire. *Book of Records,* MS. # 13614, Emma B. King Library, Shaker Museum, Old Chatham, N. Y. This information was generously shared by Mary Ann Haagen who pointed out the troublesome collection of 1814 Enfield North Family members.

55. Madden, *Bodies of Life,* 20.

56. A similar example is seen in Osterud, *Bonds of Community.* Osterud describes the centrality of kinship in the rural society of the Nanticoke Valley. The kinship system identified women as wives and mothers and daughters and sisters, and it was through the kinship system, particularly via husbands and sons, that women gained access to land. Kinship organized society but also had a direct economic impact.

57. See, for example, Merlin B. Brinkerhoff and Marlene Mackie, "Casting Off the Bonds of Organized Religion: A Religious-Careers Approach to the Study of Apostasy," *Review of Religious Research* 34 (March 1993): 235-257.

58. Dyer, *Rise and Progress,* 205. Although in *Rise and Progress* Mary framed William's visit as an act of Providence, it seems she summoned him to the village herself. Joseph's mother was Elizabeth Williams of Plainfield, Connecticut. This may be the source of John Williams's relationship to Joseph.

59. Dyer, *A Brief Statement,* 11; *Portraiture,* 353.

60. Dyer, *Portraiture,* 355.

61. Dyer, *Rise and Progress,* 206.

62. Ibid.

63. Ibid.

64. Ibid., 207.

65. Ibid.

66. See Stuart A. Wright, *Leaving Cults: The Dynamics of Defection* (Washington, D. C.: The Center for the Scientific Study of Religion, 1987); Janet Liebman Jacobs, *Divine Disenchantment: Deconverting from New Religions* (Bloomington: Indiana University Press, 1989); and the essays in David G. Bromley, ed., *Falling From the Faith: Causes and Consequences of Religious Apostasy* (Newbury Park, Calif.: Sage Publications, 1988).

67. The description of alternating threats and compliments is reminiscent of Shaker Valentine Rathbun's eighteenth-century description of Shaker conversion practices.

68. Grove Wright to Ministry Harvard, August 28, 1847, WRHS IV-A:10.

69. In *A Brief Statement,* 11, Dyer wrote that before leaving she asked all the members of the Shaker family if she had offended or done anything wrong while there. She reported that all the Shakers, even the leaders, replied that she had done nothing wrong, that she simply did not share their faith.

70. J. Dyer, *A Compendious Narrative,* 23.

71. Dyer, *Rise and Progress,* 208.

72. Ibid.; In *Portraiture,* 355, Dyer detailed the vision God provided for her to do so.

73. In *A Compendious Narrative,* 24, Joseph reported that the sleigh's occupants were leaving the village after having observed Shaker meeting. This was another example of how Mary framed her narrative as a series of events directed by Providence.

74. Dyer, *Portraiture*, 358.

75. Dyer, *Rise and Progress*, 210.

76. Six weeks after Mary's arrival, three fellow Quakers called on the Williamses. Mary, praying alone in her room "anxious to know what people were the Lord's beloved," overheard the Quaker meeting and was moved by their worship. Soon she felt the spirit of God and "could plainly discern the difference between the spirit of the Shakers and this." Filled with their spirit, Mary felt happy for two weeks following their departure. Though she had just left one religious society, Mary was already drawn to another in her continued search for religious satisfaction. See Dyer, *Portraiture*, 359; *Rise and Progress*, 212.

77. J. Dyer, *A Compendious Narrative*, 24.

78. Mary Beth Sievens, "'The Wicked Agency of Others': Community, Law, and Marital Conflict in Vermont, 1790-1830," *Journal of the Early Republic* 21 (Spring 2001): 19-39.

79. J. Dyer, *A Compendious Narrative*, 24.

80. *Dartmouth Gazetteer and Grafton and Coös Advertiser*, March 22, 1815.

81. J. Dyer, *A Compendious Narrative*, 24.

82. Ibid., 24-25.

83. Dyer, *Portraiture*, 360, and Dyer, *A Brief Statement*, 13.

84. Dyer, *Portraiture*, 360.

85. Dyer, *A Brief Statement*, 14.

86. Dyer, *Portraiture*, 362.

87. Dyer, *Rise and Progress*, 215.

88. J. Dyer, *A Compendious Narrative*, 24.

89. Dyer, *Portraiture*, 362.

90. Ibid.

91. Elizabeth A. De Wolfe, "So Much They Have Got For Their Folly: Shaker Apostates and the Tale of Woe," *Communal Societies* 18 (1998): 21-35.

92. Dyer, *Portraiture*, 363. Franklin P. Rice, "Shaker Records of Enfield, N. H.," *New England Historical and Genealogical Register* (April 1908), 123, does not note any deaths during this time period.

93. Mary turned to a Biblical reference to refer to her receiving food "by similar characters of that which conveyed the food to Elijah at the brook Cherith before Jordan," in *Portraiture*, 363.

94. J. Dyer, *A Compendious Narrative*, 26.

95. Dyer, *A Brief Statement*, 15.

96. Dyer, *Portraiture*, 363.

97. Joseph described Obadiah Tillotson as a "man of good circumstance," *A Compendious Narrative*, 27.

98. Mary did not realize it at the time but James Chapman had joined the Shakers with his children in New York and had recently surreptitiously moved them to the Enfield village to escape Eunice Chapman's attempts to retrieve them. Eunice and Mary would later become great allies in their respective attempts to regain their children.

99. Dyer, *Portraiture*, 364.

100. Ibid., and Dyer, *Rise and Progress*, 217

101. Dyer, *Rise and Progress*, 217-18.

102. Dyer, *Portraiture*, 364. In the early nineteenth century breast-feeding was promoted as beneficial to the child's spiritual health and a pleasurable experience for the mother enhancing the mother-child bond. Ruth Bloch, "American Feminine Ideals in Transition: The Rise of the Moral Mother, 1785-1815," *Feminist Studies* 4 (1978).

103. Dyer, *Portraiture*, 364.

104. Dyer, *A Brief Statement*, 17.

105. Dyer, *Rise and Progress*, 219.

106. J. Dyer, *A Compendious Narrative*, 29.

107. Eliza Page lived with the Dyers in 1799-1801. M. Dyer, *Rise and Progress*, 161-162.

108. Dyer, *Portraiture*, 371-72. Mary reported in *Portraiture*, 371, that Joseph had gone to Orford looking for her "articles," including the bed. Mary stated she had taken everything with her when she went to Northumberland, which would seem to indicate she had no plans to return to Orford. Joseph stated that these events happened in 1816, and he specifically asked Mary via his text to tell him the location of the bed; *A Compendious Narrative*, 30.

109. Dyer, *Portraiture*, 372

110. J. Dyer, *A Compendious Narrative*, 31.

111. Dyer, *Portraiture*, 373

112. Mary suggested in *Portraiture*, 373, that Joseph supported her effort for a bill. She stated that Rich accepted a note from Joseph signed by Barzilla Brainard for $26, the money to be used to assist in her expenses.

113. Joseph, in fact, also noted that Mary was saving money, although he complained that he was nevertheless supporting her and going further into debt to do so at the time. She bought cloth and a bandanna (total $3.47) on March 3, 1817, from Thomas J. Tillotson, a debt Joseph would later refuse to pay.

114. Plumer to Lydia Coombs, June 17, 1782; and February 19 & 23, 1783, Letterbook 1, Plumer Papers.

115. J. Dyer, *A Compendious Narrative*, 20.

Notes to Chapter Two

1. Hendrik Hartog, *Man and Wife in America: A History* (Cambridge, Mass.: Harvard University Press, 2000), 36.

2. Ibid., 86.

3. Ibid., 35.

4. Lawrence M. Friedman, *A History of American Law,* second ed. (New York: Simon and Schuster, 1985), 207; Hartog, *Man and Wife*, 66, 76.

5. Hartog, *Man and Wife*, 84.

6. Joseph Dyer, *A Compendious Narrative* (Concord, N. H.: Printed by Isaac Hill, 1818), 32.

7. James Chapman, *The Memorial of James Chapman, to the Respectable Legislature of the State of New York, Now in Session* ([Albany]: n.p., March 24, 1817). Chapman's *Memorial* responded to Eunice Hawley Chapman, *An Account of the Conduct of the People Called Shakers: In the Case of Eunice Chapman and Her Children, Since Her Husband Became Acquainted with that People, and Joined Their Society* (Albany: Printed for the Authoress, 1817). On Eunice Chapman's campaign against the Shakers see Nelson M. Blake, "Eunice Against the Shakers," *New York History* 41 (October 1960): 359-378.

8. The necessity of corroborating statements was seen in Shaker commentary on James Chapman's *Memorial*. As James wrote his pamphlet in haste he gathered no affidavits, an oversight that left the pamphlet with a "great weakness." Ministry New Lebanon to Ministry Union Village, March 27, 1819, WRHS IV:A-33.

9. *Indoctum Parliamentum: A Farce, in One Act and A Beautiful Variety of Scenes,* ([n.p., ca. 1817]).

10. *To the Legislature of the State of New York* [n.p.], dated March 20, 1817 and signed by Watervliet Shakers Peter Dodge, Seth Y. Wells, and Joseph Hodgson. The Shakers distributed this eight-page pamphlet to members of the New York Legislature in an attempt to halt repressive legislation.

11. [Isaac Hill], "The Shakers," *New Hampshire Patriot,* June 24, 1817.

12. Leon W. Anderson, *To This Day: The First Three Hundred Years of the New Hampshire Legislature* (Canaan, New Hampshire: Phoenix Publishing, 1981), 103-104, 113.

13. *Journal of the House of Representatives of the State of New Hampshire . . . June 1817* (Concord: Printed by Isaac Hill, 1817), 176, 179, 181, 186. *Journal of the Senate of the State of New Hampshire . . . June 1817* (Concord: Printed by Isaac Hill, 1817), 105, 149-150, 156, 158-159.

14. The *Patriot* was published each Tuesday. Dyer's hearing occurred on a Tuesday creating a one-week delay between the event and its published report.

15. "The Shakers," *New Hampshire Patriot,* July 1, 1817.

16. Ibid., Plumer recorded the comment as "capable critter" in William Plumer, "Autobiography," June 24, 1817, Roll LC4, 352-353, Plumer Papers.

17. "The Shakers," *New Hampshire Patriot,* July 1, 1817.

18. Ibid.

19. William Plumer, "Autobiography," June 24, 1817, Roll LC4, 352-353, Plumer Papers.

20. "The Shakers," *New Hampshire Patriot,* July 1, 1817.

21. Ibid.

22. Norma Basch, *Framing American Divorce: From the Revolutionary Generation to the Victorians* (Berkeley: University of California Press, 1999), 51-52. On divorce in New Hampshire: *Laws of New Hampshire, Vol. 5, First Constitutional Period 1784–1792* (Concord, N. H.: Evans Printing Co., 1921), 732-733 (Chapter 94: An Act to Prevent Incestuous Marriages and to Regulate Divorces); *Laws of New Hampshire, Vol. 9, Second Constitutional Period 1821–1828* (Concord, N. H.: Evans Printing Co., 1921), 357 (An Act in Addition to An Act, Entitled An Act To Prevent Incestuous Marriages); and *New Hampshire Revised Statutes Annotated* (Orford, N. H.: Butterworth Legal Publishers, 1992). See also Roderick Phillips, *Putting Asunder: A History of Divorce in Western Society* (New York: Cambridge University Press, 1988); and idem, *Untying the Knot: A Short History of Divorce* (New York: Cambridge University Press, 1991).

23. Plumer, "Autobiography," June 27, 1817, Roll LC4, 352-353, Plumer Papers.

24. "The Shakers," *New Hampshire Patriot,* July 1, 1817.

25. On the Dartmouth case and the religious toleration act see Anderson, *To This Day,* 114, 116. Both cases were resolved in 1819.

26. Isaac Hill served as a United States Senator from 1830-1836. In 1836, Hill was elected governor of New Hampshire and served three terms. See James O. Lyford, ed., *History of Concord, New Hampshire,* vol. 1, (Concord, N. H.: The Rumford Press, 1903), 407 and *passim.*

27. Susan and Julia Chapman were admitted to the Church Family on February 13, 1815. Henry Blinn, "Historical Notes," vol. 1, 107.

28. There were significant differences as well. Eunice Chapman never joined the Shakers nor lived at the community for any significant length of time. She never claimed to have been a member or attracted to the faith. Thus Eunice Chapman is not an apos-

tate author, but rather an anti-Shaker author. James had in fact taken the children without Eunice's knowledge or consent, and when Eunice began her public protest, the children were moved surreptitiously to Enfield. Although the New York Shakers professed they did not know where James had gone with the children, in fact, the remonstrance and letter indicated they knew the Chapman family was at Enfield.

29. The Shakers recorded that on June 25 they settled Mary Dyer's case and "lost $32.00." It is unclear whether this loss reflected expenses incurred at the hearing or some sort of payment to Dyer. "Manuscript Record of Canterbury, N. H., 1792-1848." Copied ca. 1958 by Sister Lillian Phelps, Private Collection.

30. Deposition of Joseph Merrill, May 12, 1819, Willis v. Dyer, Grafton County Superior Court of Judicature, May Term 1819, Box A98062. New Hampshire Department of State, Division of Records Management and State Archives (hereafter cited as Willis v. Dyer).

31. Ibid.

32. Willis v. Dyer, Deposition of Edward Evans, May 8, 1819.

33. Ibid., Deposition of Lucy Fogg, May 12, 1819.

34. Ibid., Deposition of Lavina Johnson, February 1819.

35. Ibid., Deposition of Joseph Merrill, May 12, 1819.

36. The letters between Chapman and Dyer do not survive but part of their correspondence was included in Dyer, A Portraiture of Shakerism ([Haverhill, N. H.]: [Sylvester Goss], 1822), and, Eunice Chapman, No. 2 Being the Additional Account of the Conduct of the Shakers (Albany, N. Y.: Printed by I. W. Clark, 1818). Although edited, the letters revealed the plans both women made to publicize their troubles. The correspondence commenced in the fall of 1817 and continued into the winter of 1818.

37. Diary of William Plumer, vol. 2, May 17, 1818, Roll LC1, Frame 576, Plumer Papers. Plumer routinely noted the books, magazines, and newspapers he read. Plumer, who visited the Shakers in his youth and again in 1816, read The Testimony of Christ's Second Appearing and wrote a lengthy critique of the work. See his Diary, vol. 2, November 18, 1810, Roll LC1, Frames 524-527.

38. Plumer to Clinton, May 18, 1818, Letterbook VIII, Roll LC4, Plumer Papers.

39. Jesse Hawley to William Plumer, June 16,1818, MS. 818366, Dartmouth College Library. The letter is also recorded in Hawley to William Plumer, June 16, 1818, Letterbook IX, Roll LC4, Plumer Papers.

40. William Plumer, Jr., a newly elected representative and the son of the Governor, was one of the members who traveled to Canterbury.

41. Petitioners used this strategy in non-Shaker-related cases as well.

42. A Remonstrance Against the Testimony and Application of Mary Dyer, Requesting Legislative Interference Against the United Society Commonly Called Shakers (Concord, N. H.: Printed by Isaac Hill, 1818).

43. The selection of Joseph Spear as the printer of her work may have evolved from a Hanover connection. Charles and William Spear bought the local Hanover paper, the Dartmouth Gazette, in October 1808. In the fall of 1810, a third brother, Henry, joined them. Henry and William left in April 1811 to publish the Concord Gazette. Charles Spear remained in Hanover and continued to publish the Hanover paper. Charles E. Widmayer, "Printer's Ink," in Francis Lane Childs, ed., Hanover, N. H.: A Bicentennial Book (Hanover, N. H.: The Town of Hanover, 1961), 238-239.

44. "The Shakers," New Hampshire Patriot, June 23, 1818.

45. See, for example, "DYERS," New Hampshire Patriot, September 22, 1818. Contemporary researchers, this author included, fall for the advertising bait as well.

46. Mary M. Dyer, "Petition to the New Hampshire Legislature," in Henry Blinn, "Historical Notes on Believers Having Reference to Believers at Enfield," Typescript (photocopy), Shaker Library, United Society of Shakers, Sabbathday Lake, Maine, 109-111.

47. Dyer denied seeking a divorce. She wrote: "My great object is to have the privilege of living with my children—if with my husband, it is well. But as he refused by word and deed to take care of me, I want my children and as much property as is thought proper restored to me; and then power to govern it." Dyer, *A Brief Statement of the Sufferings of Mary Dyer Occasioned By the Society Called Shakers* (Concord, N. H.: Printed by Joseph C. Spear, 1818), 31.

48. John Whitcher, "A Brief History of Record of the Commencement & Progress of the United Society of Believers at Canterbury, County of Merrimack and State of New Hampshire," vol. 1: 1782-1871, MS. 21, Canterbury Shaker Village, Canterbury, N. H., 175.

49. Children were released from indenture to the Shakers in two cases where the indenture was found to have been improperly executed. In *Curtis v. Curtis* [71 Mass. 535 (1855)] and *In re M'Dowle* [8 Johns. 328 (NY Sup. Ct. 1811)], the children were able to choose for themselves where they wished to live. In a custody dispute of *People ex rel. Barbour v. Gates* [57 Barb. 292 39 How. Prac. 74 (NY Sup. Ct. 1869)], the child, being too young to decide its own residence, was returned to the mother. On Shaker custody suits see Barbara Taback Schneider, "Prayers for Our Protection and Prosperity at Court: Shakers, Children, and the Law," *Yale Journal of Law & the Humanities* 4 (1992):33-78.

50. Henry Blinn, "A Historical Record of the Society of Believers in Canterbury, N. H. From the Time of its Organization in 1792 till the Year One Thousand, Eight Hundred and Forty-Eight," MS.763, Canterbury Shaker Village.

51. "The Society Called Shakers," *New Hampshire Patriot,* June 23, 1818.

52. *Journal of the Senate,* June 1818, 223.

53. Ibid., 230.

54. Ibid., 229. This statement reflected common assumptions about the evolution of religion and society. As Shakerism evolved, it replaced aspects of fanatic behavior with order and discipline. As a society, the Shakers in the early nineteenth century exhibited improvement that, like the surrounding world, was marked by buildings and industry.

55. Ibid., 230.

56. Ibid., 231.

57. Ibid.

58. A strange Shaker-related item was included in the New Hampshire *Patriot* under the heading of "Remarkable Occurrence." A mad dog was killed at an unspecified Shaker village. The dog was buried under a pear tree and three days later, the tree had entirely withered. The Shakers exhumed the dog's corpse and discovered the tree roots had been severed earlier. The author of this article suggested that the poison in the dog had gone into the tree. Since the Dyer debate and examination of the Shakers continued, perhaps Hill was making a metaphorical comment on the effect of outsiders (mad dogs) upon peaceful Shaker communities. Although the Dyer dispute grabbed the headlines, the Shakers also appeared before the legislature in a separate petition to defend their right to a pacifist stance in times of war.

59. Plumer to Hawley, July 11, 1818, Roll LC4, Letterbook IX, pp. 233-34, Plumer Papers. See also William Plumer, Jr., *Life of William Plumer, By His Son, William Plumer, Junior* (Boston: Phillips, Sampson, & Co., 1857), 464-466.

60. Mary Dyer, "Friends of Humanity," *New Hampshire Patriot,* July 14, 1818.
61. [Isaac Hill], "The Shakers," *New Hampshire Patriot,* July 28, 1818.
62. "Shaking Quakers," *Boston Commercial Gazette,* July 23, 1818. The article was also printed in the *Berkshire Star* on August 20, 1818, where a notation indicated the article came from the *Exeter Watchman.* See also a lengthy article in the Boston-based *The Idiot, or Invisible Rambler,* August 29, 1818. The unnamed author of the article, "An Account of the People Called Shakers," sympathized with Mary Dyer and offered his opinions and observations of the New Lebanon Shakers to strengthen Mary's accusations.
63. Ministry New Hampshire to Ministry New Lebanon, December 14, 1818, WHRS IV:A-3.
64. Ibid.
65. Ibid.
66. Blinn, "A Historical Record," 173-174, states that Whitcher helped Joseph. Whitcher, "A Brief History," 112, states that Whitcher compiled the pamphlet.
67. The New Hampshire Ministry sent four copies to New Lebanon, with an explanation for the delay. Ministry at Canterbury to Ministry New Lebanon, February 19, 1819, WRHS IV:A-3.
68. The anonymous manuscript message is found on the *Remonstrance Against . . . Mary Dyer* (Boston: Printed for N. Coverly, 1818) in the collection of the American Antiquarian Society. Robinson's pamphlet is in the collection of the author.
69. Basch, *Framing American Divorce,* 150. On divorce trial pamphlets, 147-185.
70. For example, in *Portraiture,* Mary Dyer reprinted long selections from the anti-Shaker works of Eunice Chapman and Thomas Brown (1812). Chapman (1817) cited Brown and referred to the anti-Shaker activities of James Smith (1810). Thomas Brown discussed the publications of Valentine Rathbun (1780s) and Reuben Rathbun (1800). Reuben Rathbun referred readers to Daniel Rathbun (1785) who in turn had Valentine Rathbun write a preface to his work.
71. Ministry at Hancock to Ministry Harvard, March 27, 1819, WRHS IV:A-19.
72. New Hampshire Ministry at Enfield to Ministry New Lebanon, May 11, 1819, WRHS IV:A-11.
73. Dyer, *A Brief Statement,* 3.
74. Ibid., 3. It also reflected her actual experience, an initial enthusiasm (she tried to like it and joined willingly) and eventual disappointment and rejection of the faith.
75. Ibid.
76. Ibid.
77. The influence of Chapman's *An Account* is seen here in *A Brief Statement.* Dyer framed her dilemma as a struggle to avoid Chapman's well-known situation.
78. Dyer, *A Brief Statement,* 18.
79. J. Dyer, *A Compendious Narrative,* i.
80. Basch, *Framing American Divorce,* 150.
81. J. Dyer, *A Compendious Narrative,* 1.
82. Ibid., 7.
83. Ibid., 3.
84. Hartog, *Man and Wife,* 101.
85. J. Dyer, *A Compendious Narrative,* 5-6.
86. Mary's attempts to show Joseph as unhusbandly and Joseph's attempt to portray Mary as unwomanly was not unique in divorce and separation cases. In a later divorce case, James Gill and Mary Gill both argued that the other had neglected

to act according to standards of proper gender behavior. See the discussion in Norma Basch, *In the Eyes of the Law: Women, Marriage, and Property in Nineteenth-Century New York* (Ithaca: Cornell University Press, 1982), 95-96.

87. On discipline see Philip Greven, *The Protestant Temperament: Patterns of Childrearing, Religious Experience, and the Self in Early America* (New York: Alfred A. Knopf, 1977).

88. J. Dyer, *A Compendious Narrative*, 22.

89. Ibid., 9.

90. Ibid., 9-10.

91. Ibid., 14.

92. Ibid, 22.

93. Ibid.

94. Basch, *Framing American Divorce*, 62.

95. Ibid.

96. Ministry Hancock to Ministry New Hampshire, March 27, 1819, WRHS IV:A-19.

Notes to Chapter Three

1. Neither Eunice nor Mary elaborated on this premob agitation, but it seems likely that Eunice sent the books in advance to Mary in the care of James Willis with whom she stayed, another example of the workings of the apostate network. Abram Van Vleet, *Account of the Conduct of the Shakers* (Lebanon, Ohio: Van Vleet and Camron, 1818), 79-80.

2. George Rudé, *The Crowd in History: A Study of Popular Disturbances in France and England, 1730–1848* (New York: John Wiley and Sons, Inc. 1964; revised London: Lawrence and Wishart, 1981) and Paul A. Gilje, *The Road to Mobocracy: Popular Disorder in New York City, 1763–1834* (Chapel Hill: University of North Carolina Press for the Institute of Early American History and Culture, 1987). Additional works on the actions of American mobs in the early nineteenth century include: Leonard L. Richards, *"Gentlemen of Property and Standing": Anti-Abolition Mobs in Jacksonian America* (New York: Oxford University Press, 1970) and Paul O. Weinbaum, *Mobs and Demagogues: The New York Response to Collective Violence in the Early Nineteenth Century* (Ann Arbor, Mich.: UMI Research Press, 1979). On public disorder in England see R. Quinault and J. Stevenson, eds., *Popular Protest and Public Order: Six Studies in British History, 1790–1920* (New York: St. Martin's Press, 1975).

3. Mobs in that period frequently focused their anger towards a specific goal. For example, in the "Doctor's Riot" in New York City of 1788, rioters, angered by physicians robbing graves to obtain bodies for dissection, destroyed the dissecting instruments but left the hospital building unharmed. In an attempt to enforce public morality, riots against bawdy houses destroyed the bedding and furniture, but did not harm the prostitutes. See Gilje, *The Road to Mobocracy*, 71-92.

4. Ministry, Turtle Creek, Ohio, to Lucy Wright, New Lebanon, December 19, 1805, MS. 107, Andrews Collection, Winterthur. On another evening townspeople returned and broke windows, stole several horses, and gashed the ears and shaved the tails and manes of the horses left behind. Fearing injury, the Shakers remained inside during these attacks.

5. Dyer, *A Portraiture of Shakerism* (Haverhill, N. H.: Sylvester Goss, 1822), 293.

6. "A Statement Concerning the Mob at Enfield," May 25, 1818, The Milton Sherman Collection, Armonk, N. Y.

7. Ibid.

8. Ibid.

9. Ibid.

10. Dyer, *Portraiture,* 299. On James Chapman's activities see New Hampshire Ministry at Canterbury to Ministry New Lebanon, December 14, 1818, Shaker Collection, Western Reserve Historical Society, Cleveland, Ohio, IV:A-3 (hereafter WRHS); and Ministry Enfield to Ministry Watervliet, July 30, 1818, MS. 115, Shaker Collection, Library of Congress. On the release of the Chapman daughters and on James's whereabouts, see Dyer, *Portraiture,* 303-306.

11. Dyer, *Portraiture,* 378-379.

12. Eunice Chapman disappeared from anti-Shaker activities after 1819. Nonetheless, the Shakers recalled her persistence and ability to stir up the public. In 1826, a Shaker correspondent wrote of the anti-Shaker activities of Catherine Kingsly, whose actions had increased "To an alarming degree insomuch that we began to be afraid of another Eunice Chapman." Sodus Bay to New Lebanon, July 4, 1826, MS.1046, Andrews Collection, Winterthur.

13. Union Village to New Lebanon, August 30, 1819, WRHS IV:A-69.

14. Ministry New Lebanon to Ministry Union Village, March 27, 1819, WRHS IV:A-33.

15. Ibid.

16. Ibid.

17. Richard McNemar, *The Other Side of the Question. In Three Parts* (Cincinnati, Ohio: Looker, Reynolds, and Co., Printers, 1819).

18. The New Lebanon Shakers responded to Union Village's request for information on Terry, but doubted he was sincere in his desire to live once again the life of a Shaker. Some believed he was sent west by Chapman or her allies to gather information to use against the Shakers. Ministry New Lebanon to Ministry Union Village, March 27, 1819, WRHS IV:A-33.

19. Blackburn, *A Brief Account of the Rise, Progress, Doctrines, and Practices of the People Usually Denominated Shakers* (Flemingsburg, Ky.: Printed by A. Crookshanks, 1824), 32.

20. "Petition of Joshua Stevens et al to the New Hampshire State Legislature, June 1818," in Dyer, *A Brief Statement,* 34-35.

21. On the ongoing tensions between communal group and host society see Donald E. Janzen, "The Intentional Community-National Community Interface: An Approach to the Study of Communal Societies," *Communal Societies* 1 (1982): 37-42.

22. New Hampshire Ministry at Canterbury to New Lebanon Ministry, December 14, 1818, WRHS IV:A-3.

23. In the meeting between the mob participants and the Shakers, Joseph stated his refusal to support Mary. Judge Blaisdell, who oversaw the meeting, suggested that Willis sue Joseph as a means to force support. See Dyer, *Portraiture,* 398-400.

24. Statement of Polly Clifford, September 5, 1818, Willis v. Dyer, Grafton County Superior Court of Judicature, May Term 1819, Box A98062, New Hampshire Department of State, Division of Records Management and State Archives, Concord, N. H. (hereafter cited as Willis v. Dyer).

25. Dyer, *Portraiture,* 399. Dyer refuted this testimony and explained that the Shaker witness, James Pettingill, had seen only two handkerchiefs and had never actually

touched them. Dyer asserted that she brought only four half square handkerchiefs, two "red and white factory" and two white. She had marked each of the handkerchiefs with the first letters of her sons' names. Mary also brought one of her own handkerchiefs for her daughter Betsey. Dyer, however, did not see her children on this visit and was unable to present her gifts.

26. In the first decades of the nineteenth century the courts increasingly recognized the separate nature of the wife and took steps to enhance her identity, for example in decreasing the amount of time necessary to declare a woman abandoned. This was not a departure from the common law but rather a way to prevent women from becoming drains on the community when trapped within the disabling nature of coverture. In Mary's situation, the court affirmed that Joseph had provided for her. She may not have agreed with his mode of support, but it was his right to decide the form that support would take. See Norma Basch, *In the Eyes of the Law: Women, Marriage, and Property in Nineteenth-Century New York* (Ithaca: Cornell University Press, 1982), 25-26.

27. Dyer, *Portraiture*, 400.

28. Affidavit of Polly Clifford, in Dyer, *Portraiture*, 401-402.

29. Mary Dyer to Mills Olcot, August 1819, MS. 819490.1, Dartmouth College Library. Olcot was one the leading men of Hanover, New Hampshire. In July 1819 Hannah Ames, whose children were at the Enfield Shakers, also wrote Olcot pleading for assistance. See MS. 819431.

30. Isabele Lehuu, *Carnival on the Page: Popular Print Media in Antebellum America* (Chapel Hill: University of North Carolina Press, 2001), 4.

31. Valentine Rathbun is the notable exception.

32. Ministry Canterbury to J. Frost, Harvard, August 14, 1819, WRHS IV:A-11.

33. On Dyer's activities from July 1818 to July 1819 see: Ministry Enfield to Watervliet, July 30, 1818, Shaker Collection, Manuscript 115, Library of Congress; Ministry Canterbury to Ministry New Lebanon, December 14, 1818, WRHS IV:A-3; Ministry Hancock to Ministry Harvard, March 27, 1819, WRHS IV:A-19; Ministry Canterbury to Ministry New Lebanon, August 14, 1819, WRHS IV:A-3; Dyer, *Portraiture*, 391-392, 398, 400.

Notes to Chapter Four

1. Dyer, *A Portraiture of Shakerism* (Haverhill, N. H.: Sylvester Goss, 1822), 410.

2. Stein, *The Shaker Experience in America* (New Haven: Yale University Press, 1992), 95-98.

3. Ministry Canterbury to Ministry New Lebanon, December 14, 1818, Shaker Manuscripts, Western Reserve Historical Society, Cleveland, Ohio, IV:A-3 (hereafter WRHS).

4. Dyer, *The Rise and Progress of the Serpent from the Garden of Eden, to the Present Day* (Concord, N. H.: Printed for the Author, 1847), 233. See also William Little, *The History of Weare, N. H., 1735–1888* (Lowell, Massachusetts: Published by the Town of Weare, printed by S. W. Huse & Co., 1888), 342-343.

5. "History of the Shakers, &c. &c.," *The Grafton and Coös Intelligencer*, April 18, 1821. The advertisement ran through July. The advertisement also appeared in the *Providence Patriot* on May 26, 1821.

6. Ibid.

7. Ministry New Hampshire to Ministry New Lebanon, March 12, 1823, WRHS IV:A-3.

8. "Shaking Quakers," *Boston Commercial Gazette,* July 23, 1818. The same article was reprinted in the *Berkshire Star* (August 20, 1818) in which it was noted as having appeared in the *Exeter Watchman.*

9. I'm grateful to Meredith McGill for her discussion of copyright law and procedure during the 1997 Seminar on the History of The Book at the American Antiquarian Society.

10. Dyer, "To The Public," *New Hampshire Intelligencer and Grafton & Coös Advertiser,* June 11, 1823.

11. Errors seemed to plague Dyer's works. A copy of *Reply to the Shakers Statements* contains the manuscript message: "errors are many. . . ."

12. Ministry Harvard to Ministry New Lebanon, January 17, 1824, WRHS IV:A-22.

13. Mary Clark, Letter to Francis and Eliza Jackson, July 16, 1823, The Papers of Francis Jackson, Massachusetts Historical Society, Boston (hereafter cited as MHS).

14. Mary Clark, Letter to Francis Jackson, July 2, 1821, The Papers of Francis Jackson, MHS.

15. Mary Clark, Letter to Francis and Eliza Jackson, July 16, 1823, The Papers of Francis Jackson, MHS.

16. Mary Clark, Letter to Francis Jackson, August 1, 1823, The Papers of Francis Jackson, MHS.

17. Mary Clark, Letter to Francis Jackson, June 18, 1824, The Papers of Francis Jackson, MHS.

18. Susan Bramley, Alfred, Maine, to Sophia Frost, York, Maine, ca. 1824, private collection.

19. See the discussion of a similar public debate in Daniel A. Cohen, "The Respectability of Rebecca Reed: Genteel Womanhood and Sectarian Conflict in Antebellum America," *Journal of the Early Republic* 16 (Fall 1996): 419-461. In addition to noting respectability, certifying statements frequently noted the religious affiliation of the affiant illustrating the affiant's move towards more mainstream faiths and away from sectarian impulses.

20. Dyer, *Rise and Progress,* 258.

21. Ministry Enfield to Ministry New Lebanon, March 18[?], 1827, WRHS IV:A-11.

22. In the summer of 1818 Dyer collected affidavits in the towns surrounding Canterbury, including four statements from Freewill Baptists. These individuals then introduced Mary to Judge Philbrick of Weare. See the "Canterbury Freewill Baptist Records," typescript in the collection of the New Hampshire Historical Society, Concord, N. H., 91, 94, 95. I am grateful to historian Catherine Brekus for alerting me to Dyer's preaching activities in Weare. See Little, *The History of Weare, N. H. 1735–1888,* 357.

23. See Catherine Brekus, *Strangers and Pilgrims: Female Preaching in America, 1740–1845* (Chapel Hill: University of North Carolina Press, 1998).

24. Shaker descriptions of Mary and her associates are found in manuscript letters dated June 15, 1824, WRHS IV:A-34; July 30, 1825, WRHS IV:A-35; and Dec. 12, 1825, WRHS IV:A-1.

25. On Dyer's activities in Maine see Ministry Alfred to Ministry New Lebanon, September 12, 1825, and December12, 1825, WRHS IV:A-1.

26. Dyer, *Portraiture,* 119.

27. Chapman, *An Account of the People Called Shakers* (Albany, N. Y.: Printed for the Authoress, at 95 State Street, 1817), and, *No. 2 Being the Additional Account of the Conduct of the Shakers* (Albany, N. Y.: Printed by I. W. Clark for the Authoress, 1818); Daniel Rathbun, *A Letter From Daniel Rathbun* (Springfield, Mass.: Printed at the Printing Office Near the Great Ferry, 1785); James Smith, *Remarkable Occurrences Lately Discovered Among the People Called Shakers; Of A Treasonous and Barbarous Nature, of Shakerism Developed* (Carthage, Tenn.: Printed by William Moore, 1810).

28. D. Rathbun in Dyer, *Portraiture*, 85

29. Dyer, *Portraiture*, v.

30. On the use of hymns in nineteenth-century texts see Cheryl Boots, "Earthly Strains: The Cultural Work of Protestant Sacred Music in Three Nineteenth-Century American Popular Novels" (Ph.D. diss., Boston University, 2000).

31. Dyer, *Portraiture*, 446; Humez, "'A Woman Mighty to Pull You Down': Married Women's Rights and Female Anger in the Anti-Shaker Narratives of Eunice Chapman and Mary Marshall Dyer," *Journal of Women's History* 6 (Summer 1994), 105.

32. Rathbun, *An Account*, 9.

33. On Indian captivity narratives see June Namias, *White Captives: Gender and Ethnicity on the American Frontier* (Chapel Hill: University of North Carolina Press, 1993). In his study of deconversion narratives, Barbour identified the captivity narrative as the literary ancestor to the modern day cult deconversion narrative. See Barbour, *Versions of Deconversion*, 174.

    Raised on the northern New Hampshire frontier, Dyer was familiar with captivity accounts through local history that included stories of Indian raids in Mary's father's lifetime. Dyer, a reader, may have read any of a number of captivity narratives including that of Hannah Dustan whose story was included in Cotton Mather's *Magnalia Christii Americana*, a book Dyer cited in her history of Shakerism. Dyer also had access to Eunice Chapman's publications that used the captivity narrative format. Dyer may have been inspired (or taught by Chapman) to present her work in a similar manner. Humez, "A Woman Mighty to Pull You Down," 95-97, also notes the use of the captivity narrative format.

34. Dyer, *Portraiture*, 337.

35. Eunice Chapman in ibid., 238.

36. The Haverhill (N. H.) Circulating Library, located at *Portraiture* publisher Sylvester Goss's office, contained a copy of Dyer's *Portraiture*. In June 1824, Abigail Abbott Bailey's *Memoirs* were added to the collection. The circulating library's holdings were advertised in *The New Hampshire Intelligencer and Grafton & Coös Advertiser*, November 26, 1823, and June 16, 1824.

37. Ministry Canterbury to Ministry Harvard or Shirley, April 19, 1824, WRHS IV:A-3.

38. John Whitcher, "A Brief History or Record of the Commencement & Progress of the United Society of Believers at Canterbury, County of Merrimack and State of New Hampshire," vol. 1: 1782–1871, MS. 21, Canterbury Shaker Village, Canterbury, New Hampshire, 129.

39. Ministry Canterbury to Ministry Harvard or Shirley, April 19, 1824, WRHS IV:A-3.

40. Ibid., Isaac Hill published the countertestimony in the *New Hampshire Patriot*.

41. Ibid.

42. Ministry at Canterbury to Ministry New Lebanon, May 28, 1824, WRHS IV:A-3.

43. Ibid.
44. *A Review of Mary M. Dyer's Publication, Entitled "A Portraiture of Shakerism,"* *Together with Sundry Affidavits, Disproving the Truth of Her Assertions* (Concord, N. H.: Printed by Jacob B. Moore for the United Society, 1824).
45. Inscriptions on title page, both volumes in the collection of the American Antiquarian Society, Worcester, Massachusetts. *Portraiture* was presented on October 7, 1825.
46. Ministry Canterbury to Ministry Harvard, June 7, 1824, WRHS IV:A-3.
47. Seth Wells to New Lebanon [?], June 15, 1824, WRHS IV:A-34.
48. Ibid.
49. *A Review,* 9.
50. Ibid., 26.
51. Dyer, *Portraiture,* 148.
52. The Shakers rewrote other statements as well. Following the appearance of a condemning statement by a William Lee in the *Boston News-Letter and City Record* (April 29, 1826), the Shakers rewrote the "very erroneous" statement and mailed it to him. See W. X.Y. to Major William Lee, June 2, 1826, WRHS IV:A-35.
53. Daniel Carson Johnson, "Apostates Who Never Were: The Social Construction of *Absque Facto* Apostate Narratives," in David G. Bromley, ed., *The Politics of Religious Apostasy: The Role of Apostates in the Transformation of Religious Movements* (Westport, Conn.: Praeger, 1998), 121.
54. *A Review,* 18-19.
55. Ibid., 58-59. The Shakers in later correspondence referred to this statement with humor writing in 1826 that Dyer had come to Enfield "to see her little six feet boys." Joseph Dyer to Seth Wells, June 25, 1826, WRHS IV:A-11. Mary Dyer responded to her son's sarcasm by quipping, "My second son boasts of his stature. Watts measures a man by his mind." Dyer, *Reply,* 84.
56. J. Dyer, *A Compendious Narrative, Elucidating the Character, Disposition, and Conduct of Mary Dyer* (Concord, N. H.: Printed by Isaac Hill, 1818), 22, 54-58.
57. Dyer, *Portraiture,* 421-423.
58. *A Review,* 34-35.
59. Dyer, *A Reply to the Shakers' Statements* (Concord, N. H.: Printed for the Author, 1824), 26-27.
60. See David G. Bromley, ed., *The Politics of Religious Apostasy: The Role of Apostates in the Transformation of Religious Movements* (Westport, Conn.: Praeger, 1998), 4.
61. Mary Dyer, "To the Elders and Principals of the Shaker Societies" (n.p., 1825). It may also indicate that Dyer's earlier claim to knowledge based on a two years' residence may have come back to haunt her as readers questioned her participation with a sect she now assaulted.
62. Ibid.
63. Ibid. Three of the seventeen depositions survive. MS. 825, Edward Deming Andrews Memorial Shaker Collection, Winterthur Museum and Library, Winterthur, Delaware.
64. James Farnham, "To The Public. Having Lately Seen a Scandalous Handbill in Circulation, Published by Mary Dyer, Containing, Among Other Malicious Falsehoods, a Slanderous Charge Against Me" (n.p., 1825).
65. Ministry Canterbury to Ministry New Lebanon, January 18, 1826, WRHS IV:A-3.
66. Ministry New Lebanon to Ministry West Union, July 30, 1825, WRHS IV: A-35.

67. Ministry Harvard to Ministry New Lebanon, ca. 1825, WRHS IV:A-22.

68. "Shakerism," *Boston News-Letter and City Record,* April 29, 1826, Item No. 676, Andrews Collection, Winterthur.

69. Ministry Alfred to Ministry New Lebanon, December 12, 1825 WRHS IV:A-1; see also Ministry Alfred to Ministry New Lebanon, September 12, 1825, WRHS IV:A-1.

70. Ministry Alfred to Ministry New Lebanon, December 12, 1825 WRHS IV:A-1.

71. Advertisement was published May 6, 1828, and recorded in Blinn, "Historical Notes on Believers Having Reference to Believers at Enfield," vol. 1, p. 196, Typescript (photocopy), Shaker Library, United Society of Shakers, Sabbathday Lake, Maine.

72. Richard McNemar, comp., *Investigator, or A Defense of the Order, Government, and Economy of the United Society Called Shakers, Against Sundry Charges and Legislative Proceedings* (Lexington, Ky.: 1828; reprinted New York: Egbert, Hovey, and King, 1846), 12.

73. *Some Account of the Proceedings of the Legislature of New Hampshire, in Relation to the People Called Shakers, in 1828* (n.p.: n.d.), 4.

74. Ministry New Lebanon to Ministry West Union, July 30, 1825, WRHS IV:A-35.

75. Ministry Hancock to Ministry Harvard, March 27, 1826, WRHS IV:A-19.

76. Ministry New Lebanon to Ministry West Union, July 12, 1826, WRHS IV:A-35.

77. See the discussion on alterations in Joseph Dyer to Seth Wells, June 25, 1826, WRHS IV:A-11.

78. Dyer, *Portraiture,* iii-iv.

79. The similarity of countersubversion movements is discussed in David B. Davis, "Themes of Counter-Subversion: An Analysis of Anti-Masonic, Anti-Catholic, and Anti-Mormon Literature," *Mississippi Valley Historical Review* 47 (1960): 205-224.

80. Ministry Enfield to Ministry New Lebanon, March 18[?],1827, WRHS IV:A-11.

81. Benjamin Green, *Short Account of the Life of Benjamin Green: A Man Who Started in Pursuit of The Theory of the Connexion Between God and Man and Found It* (Concord, N. H.: Published by the Author, 1848), 42.

82. "An Act in Addition to an Act, entitled, An Act to Prevent Incestuous Marriages and to Regulate Divorces [December 21, 1824]," in *Laws of New Hampshire, Vol. 9, Second Constitutional Period, 1821–1828* (Concord, N. H.: Evans Printing Co., 1921), 337.

83. Statement of Mary Dyer, n.d., Dyer v. Dyer, Records of Grafton County Superior Court, May Term 1829, Box A98092, New Hampshire Department of State, Division of Records Management and Archives, Concord, N. H. (hereafter cited as Dyer v. Dyer).

84. Statement of Joseph Dyer, May 11, 1829, Dyer v. Dyer.

85. Norma Basch, *Framing American Divorce* (Berkeley: University of California Press, 1999), 3. See also Nancy Cott, *Public Vows: A History of Marriage and the Nation* (Cambridge: Harvard University Press, 2000), 2.

86. Hendrik Hartog, *Man and Wife in America: A History* (Cambridge: Harvard University Press, 2000), 152.

87. Ibid., 53.

88. Dyer v. Dyer, 5 NH 271 (1830).

89. Hartog, *Man and Wife in America,* 27.

90. Dyer, *Rise and Progress,* 260-61.

91. Dyer, *Shakerism Exposed* (Hanover, N. H.: Dartmouth Press, [n.d., ca. 1852]), 11.

92. A copy of the letter, dated July 10, [1845], is found in the Congregational Church Records, Enfield, 1826–1907, vol. 1, in the collection of the New Hampshire Historical Society, Concord.

93. Dyer v. Dyer, 5 N. H. 271 (1830); Dyer's name change is recorded June 1832, "An Act to Alter the Name of Certain Persons," in *Laws of New Hampshire 1830–1842* (Concord: John F. Brown, n.d.), 51-52. In 1852 Mary Marshall changed her name back to Dyer. See *Laws of New Hampshire 1845–1854* (Concord, N. H.: John F. Brown, 1853), 1235-1236. Dyer purchased her home on April 17, 1830. Real estate records, Box 14, Folder 15, Papers of the History of Enfield, Dartmouth College. The next couple to use this divorce law found themselves in the opposite situation—the wife remained a Shaker, and the husband sought a divorce. See Fitts v. Fitts, 46 N. H. 184 (1865).

94. *Newburyport* [Mass.] *Herald,* April 27, 1824.

95. Dyer, *Portraiture,* 371-372.

Notes to Chapter Five

1. James Fenimore Copper, "Notions of Americans: Picked Up by a Travelling Bachelor" (1828), quoted in Flo Morse, *The Shakers and the World's People* (New York: Dodd, Mead, and Company, 1980), 85-86.

2. Caroline Lee Hentz, "Shaker Girl," *Godey's Lady's Book* (1839), 49-58. For a chronological listing of works of fiction with Shaker settings and visitors' accounts of the Shakers, see "A Selected Chronological Bibliography," in Morse, *The Shakers and the World's People,* 360-371. See also Ruth McAdams, "The Shakers in American Fiction," (Ph.D. diss., Texas Christian University, 1985), and Michael Pugh, "A Thorn in the Text: Shakerism and The Marriage Narrative" (Ph.D. diss., University of New Hampshire, 1994).

3. Nathaniel Hawthorne, *American Notebooks* (1832) in Morse, *The Shakers and the World's People,* 193-194.

4. Charles Dickens, "American Notes for General Circulation" (1842), in Morse, *The Shakers and the World's People,* 184-185.

5. Artemus Ward, *Vanity Fair* (February 23, 1861), in Morse, *The Shakers and the World's People,* 202.

6. Letter November 7, 1825, from Susan Yandell to Mr. & Mrs. Wendel; Letter November 7, 1825, Lunsford P. Yandell to Dr. Wilson Yandell, MS A Y21 4 Yandell Family Papers, Correspondence November 1825-December 1825, Filson Historical Society (Louisville, Kentucky).

7. Henry Waller Diary, MS A W198 Diary, October 22–November 14, 1835, Filson Historical Society (Louisville, Kentucky).

8. M .K. [Miner Kilbourne] Kellogg's Journal, June 23, 1833, MS. 9K 29.1 RFM, Cincinnati Historical Society (Cincinnati, Ohio).

9. Paige Lilly, "The Shakers and the Media: An Examination of the Shaker Library," *The Shaker Quarterly* 17 (Fall 1989): 101-112.

10. "The Shakers," *New York Weekly Tribune,* April 17, 1852. See also September 6, 1851 for a similar sentiment regarding the Canterbury Shakers.

11. "Three Months with the Shakers," *Portland Transcript* 17 (November 5, 1853). This "interesting sketch" was reprinted from *Bizarre, for Fireside and Wayside,* vol. IV (October 15, 1853): 17-18, and (October 22, 1853): 36-37.

12. "Three Months with the Shakers," *Bizarre, for Fireside and Wayside,* vol. IV (February 11, 1854): 290.

13. On the rise of antimasonry see Ronald P. Formisano with Kathleen Smith Kutolowski, "Antimasonry and Masonry: The Genesis of Protest, 1826–1827," *American Quarterly* 29 (1977): 139–165. On women's argument against masonry, see Mary Ann Clawson, "Nineteenth-Century Women's Auxiliaries and Fraternal Orders," *Signs: Journal of Women in Culture and Society* 12 (1986): 40–61.

14. William J. Haskett, *Shakerism Unmasked, or A History of the Shakers* (Pittsfield, Mass.: Published by the Author, L. H. Wally, Printer, 1828), 158–159.

15. On convent accounts see Nancy Lusignan Schultz, *Veil of Fear: Nineteenth-Century Convent Tales, Rebecca Reed, and Maria Monk* (West Lafayette, Ind.: NotaBell Books, 1999). On the burning of the Charlestown, Massachusetts, Ursuline Convent see Schultz, *Fire and Roses: The Burning of the Charlestown Convent, 1834* (New York: The Free Press, 2000).

16. John McBride, *An Account of the Doctrines, Government, Manners and Customs of the Shakers* (Cincinnati, Ohio: [For the Author], 1834).

17. Three apostate accounts were published during the 1830s. None cited previous apostate texts to support particular claims, and none of the authors mentioned or offered a critique of a specific Shaker book. Two apostate authors, Benjamin Green and John McBride, left the Shakers because of differences in interpreting the message of Shakerism. Based upon a personal reading of Scripture, both Green and McBride espoused their own interpretation of the teachings of Ann Lee and attempted to spread their message, first orally from within the community and then in a written format as an apostate outside the Shaker village. Each believed he held a clearer vision of Shakerism than that of the presiding Elder. McBride still saw himself as a Shaker despite his departure from the community. In his text he frequently used first person plural pronouns such as "we Shakers" to describe his beliefs and ideas. In challenging the authority of the Elders as sole interpreters of Shakerism, the written works of Green and McBride had more in common with the apostate texts of the late 1820s, particularly John Whitbey's work, than they did with C. C. Hodgdon's 1838 book or the apostate accounts that would follow in the 1840s.

18. C. C. Hodgdon, *Hodgdon's Life and Manner of Living Among the Shakers* (Concord, N. H.: Published by the author, 1838), 6.

19. Ibid., 5.

20. Hodgdon stated he was urged to continue his training at the Shakers. He may have been sent to accompany his sisters who were likely sent to ease the pressure on his parents' large family.

21. Hodgdon, *Hodgdon's Life,* 17.

22. Ibid., 26.

23. Ibid., 27.

24. During the first decades of the nineteenth century, the Shakers were frequently in court to settle wage-related complaints brought by seceders. The success of the Shakers in court legitimated Shaker society and reaffirmed the strength of the Shaker covenant as a "merger of religious and legal forms." Although the covenant was a spiritual document, the Shakers were well aware of its legal ramifications. Carol Weisbrod, *The Boundaries of Utopia* (New York: Pantheon Books, 1980), 71.

25. Hodgdon, *Hodgdon's Life,* 27.

26. Ibid., 28.

27. Ibid.

28. Ibid., 30.

29. Ibid., 31.

30. Absolem Blackburn, *A Brief Account of the Rise, Progress, Doctrines, and Practices of the People Usually Denominated Shakers* (Flemingsburg, Ky.: Printed by A. Crookshanks, 1824), 22-23.

31. John Whitbey, *Beauties of Priestcraft* (New Harmony, Indiana: At the Office of the New Harmony Gazette, 1826), 3.

32. "Petition to the N. H. House of Representatives for Legislation Against the Shakers," Can-L/L, Box 34, Folder 2, Library, Canterbury Shaker Village. I am very grateful to Mary Ann Haagen for alerting me to the reappearance of this long-sought document.

33. *Report of the Examination of the Shakers of Canterbury and Enfield Before the New-Hampshire Legislature at the November Session, 1848* (Concord, N. H.: Ervin B. Tripp, 1849), [5].

34. "Anti-Shakerism," *New Hampshire Patriot and State Gazette,* December 7, 1848, 1.

35. Ibid.

36. David Parker to Ministry Harvard, March 4, 1847, Shaker Manuscripts, Western Reserve Historical Society, Cleveland, Ohio, IV:A-5 (hereafter WRHS). Parker reported that Dyer's books were circulating in the area around Dunstable, Massachusetts, and requested that copies of Joseph Dyer's *Narrative* be sent to counter Mary's accusations.

37. "A Journal of Garden Accounts," Mount Lebanon, January 1, 1849, Hancock Shaker Village Library, Hancock, Massachusetts.

38. Ministry New Hampshire to Ministry New Lebanon, December 18, 1848, and January 8, 1849, WRHS IV:A-5. These detailed letters report on the proceedings at the New Hampshire legislature.

39. Richard Upton, "Franklin Pierce and the Shakers: A Subchapter in the Struggle for Religious Liberty," *Historical New Hampshire* 23 (Summer 1968), 8.

40. An excellent analysis of spirit drawings is provided in Sally Promey, *Spiritual Spectacles: Vision and Image in Mid-Nineteenth Century Shakerism* (Bloomington: Indiana University Press, 1993). Her study of visual images 1839-1859 focused on the mode of communication and transaction between the realm of the divine and that of the earth. In her contextual analysis she sought to understand what this activity and the images as material items meant for the Shakers. The gift drawing collection at the Hancock Shaker Village museum can be seen in Sharon Duane Koomler, *Seen and Received: The Shakers' Private Art* (Pittsfield, Mass.: Hancock Shaker Village, 2000).

41. Ministry Enfield to Watervliet, August 4, 1849, WRHS IV:A-13.

42. Upton, "Franklin Pierce and the Shakers," Appendix C, 18.

43. Elizabeth Clark's analysis of the motif of the suffering slave illustrated how authors utilized eyewitness testimony to put the reader "as close as possible to the slave's pain." Elizabeth Clark, "The Sacred Rights of the Weak: Pain, Sympathy, and the Culture of Individual Rights in Antebellum America," *The Journal of American History* 82 (September 1995):463.

44. *Report of the Examination,* 11.

45. Ibid., 26.

46. Mary's son Jerrub, misidentified as James in the report of the testimony, in 1847 was the physician at Enfield and he appeared for the Shakers.

47. *Report of the Minority of the Judiciary Committee upon the Petition of Franklin Munroe and Others, in Relation to the Society of Christians Called Shakers* (Concord, N. H.: 1849). The minority report, a broadside, was reprinted in the larger *Report of the Examination of the Shakers of Canterbury and Enfield* (Concord, N. H.: 1849).

48. Session Laws, November Session, 1848. See Upton, "Franklin Pierce and the Shakers," 11.

49. Fitts v. Fitts 46 N. H. 184 (1865).

50. Statement of Mary Dyer, in *Report of the Examination*, 73.

51. Ministry Enfield to Watervliet, August 4, 1849, WRHS IV:A-13. Lowell anti-Shakers maintained their campaign. The *Lowell Courier* published (ca. October 1849) testimony from the legislative session emphasizing local connections and the "fanaticism, superstition or delusion" of Shakerism. The article was reprinted in the *Granite State Whig*, October 12, 1849.

52. Ibid.

53. Dyer, *Rise and Progress*, iv.

54. Information recorded on a manuscript note by William Shedd on his copy of *Rise and Progress*, in the collection of the American Antiquarian Society, Worcester, Massachusetts.

55. Frederick Evans, Mount Lebanon, New York, North Family Journal, February 29, 1848, Sabbathday Lake Shaker Library, New Gloucester, Maine. Evans attributed Dyer's continued perseverance to her desire to make a profit.

56. See Tamara Plakins Thornton, *Handwriting in America: A Cultural History* (New Haven: Yale University Press, 1996), and Susan S. Williams, *Confounding Images: Photography and Portraiture in Antebellum American Fiction* (Philadelphia: University of Pennsylvania Press, 1997).

57. Seth Babbitt had been a member of the Harvard, Massachusetts, Shakers for over twenty years when in 1815 he asked to be released from the position of Deacon due to declining health. In 1819 he suffered the first of two "paralytic shocks" that left him mentally impaired. By November 1823, the Shakers found it necessary to restrain Babbitt to prevent damage to himself and to property. This was done with the knowledge and approval of his wife and daughter. Several apostates who had known Babbitt persuaded the "apparently peaceable neighbors that [the Shakers] were a cruel and vindictive people especially towards Seth Babbitt." A town committee was appointed, and after investigation, declared that the Shakers were guilty of negligence. A group of two hundred to three hundred townspeople came to the Shaker village to release Babbitt but during the ensuing mob, Babbitt attacked one of the townspeople. Eight Shakers were brought to trial in Worcester on the accusation of assault on Seth Babbitt. Mary Dyer traveled to Harvard at this time to lend her support to the cause. She later wrote a letter to one of the investigators of the case pleading for Babbitt's removal from the Shakers. In court, the eight Shakers were acquitted. See MS.1186 and 830, Andrews Collection, Winterthur; Dyer, *Rise and Progress*, 67-71. See also Suzanne R. Thurman, *"O Sisters Ain't You Happy?": Gender, Family, and Community Among the Harvard and Shirley Shakers, 1781–1918* (Syracuse, N. Y.: Syracuse University Press, 2002), 85-88.

58. Dyer, *Rise and Progress*, 45.

59. Nina Baym, *American Women Writers and the Work of History, 1790–1860* (New Brunswick New Jersey: Rutgers University Press, 1995),1.

60. Dyer, *Rise and Progress,* 162-163.
61. During the 1830s and 1840s the Shakers experimented with a variety of dietary regulations including water fasts, grahamism, and vegetarianism. Shaker correspondence reveals that these diets varied from community to community and even within individual communities.
62. Dyer, *Rise and Progress,* 221.
63. Ibid., 210.
64. Ibid., 221.
65. Ibid., 222. Shaker records did not indicate the cause of Joseph's death on February 7, 1840.
66. Dyer, *Rise and Progress,* iii.
67. Ibid., 16.
68. Ibid., 25.
69. Ibid., 12.
70. See Ann Braude, *Radical Spirits: Spiritualism and Women's Rights in Nineteenth-Century America* (Boston: Beacon Press, 1989), 23.
71. Dyer, *Rise and Progress,* 184.
72. Ibid., 180.
73. Ibid.
74. Ibid., 185.
75. Catherine Sedgwick, "Magnetism Among the Shakers," *Sartain's Magazine* (May 1849), 337-338. Sedgwick's use of the term is in line with a definition of animal magnetism as a power "that enables a person to induce hypnosis" (*Random House College Dictionary,* s.v. "animal magnetism,") or simply, a mesmerist (Oxford English Dictionary, s.v. "animal magnetism"). Edward Andrews documented the Shaker use of electric current via "static" machines. These machines, at least one of which was invented by the Shakers, were used for medical treatment in the 1820s and 1830s. Edward Andrews, *The Community Industries of the Shakers* (University of the State of New York, 1933; facsimile reprint Charlestown, Mass.: Emporium Publications, 1971), 110, 276.
76. Dyer, *Rise and Progress,* 254. On consumption among the Shakers see John E. Murray, "The White Plague in Utopia: Tuberculosis in Nineteenth-Century Shaker Communes," *Bulletin of the History of Medicine* 68(2) (1994): 278-306.
77. David Lamson, *Two Years Among the Shakers: Being a Description of the Manners and Customs of that People* (West Boylston, Mass.: For the Author, 1848), 171.
78. The 1845 dates suggest that Dyer and her cohorts began preparations for their legislative attack two years before the session.
79. *Journal of the House of Representatives, of the State of Vermont, October Session, 1849* (Montpelier: E. P. Walton & Son, 1850), 149. William S. Hurlburt of Huntington proposed the motion.
80. "Free Lecture to the Ladies," December 25, 1850. Broadside in the collection of the American Antiquarian Society, Worcester, Massachusetts.
81. Ibid.
82. Ministry New Hampshire to Ministry New Lebanon, April 26, 1850, WRHS IV:A-6.
83. Ministry New Hampshire to Ministry New Lebanon, April 7, 1851, WRHS IV:A-6.
84. Ministry New Hampshire, August 4, 1849, WRHS IV:A-13.
85. "An Act to Alter the Names of Certain Persons" in *Laws of New Hampshire 1845–1854* (Concord, New Hampshire: John F. Brown, 1853), 1235-1236.

86. Dyer referred to *Rise and Progress* as "Shakerism Exposed," a reference to the binder's title of *Rise and Progress*.

87. Mary M. Dyer, *Shakerism Exposed* (Hanover, N. H.: Dartmouth Press, ca. 1853), 3.

88. Ibid., 4.

89. Ibid.

90. Ibid.

91. Ibid., 24.

92. Ibid., 27.

93. Ibid.

94. Ibid., 27-28.

95. The impetus for reform from within continued in the post-Civil War period. Roxalana Grosvenor and her sister urged marriage among Shakers. Like the trouble with John Whitbey and Pleasant Hill in the late 1820s, Shaker leaders opposed the Grosvenors' suggestions and barred them from the community. When the Grosvenors sued the Shakers for their dismissal, having been members for several decades, the courts upheld the rights of the Shakers to define their own document and dismiss those who refused to live by it. See Grosvenor v. United Society 118 Mass 78 (1875). Grosvenor material was also made available by Maggie Stiers. See also the discussion of the Grosvenor sisters' activities assisting soon-to-be apostates from within the Harvard community in Suzanne Thurman, "Shaker Women and Sexual Power: Heresy and Orthodoxy in the Shaker Village of Harvard, Massachusetts," *Journal of Women's History* 10 (Spring 1998): 70-87.

96. Richmond noted an additional work published at the Dartmouth Press in 1853 under the title "Eleven Years Among the Shakers at Enfield," by William Elking. Richmond found no other reference to this work and located no copy. See Mary Richmond, *Shaker Literature* (Hancock, Mass.: Shaker Community, Inc., 1977), 80 s.v. "Elking."

97. Canterbury to Holy Mount, December 16, 1853, WRHS IV:A-14. See also letter of September 15, 1853.

98. See Stein, *The Shaker Experience in America* (New Haven: Yale University Press, 1992), 197-200; Brewer, *Shaker Communities, Shaker Lives* (Hanover, N. H.: University Press of New England, 1986), 136-157.

99. Lamson, *Two Years,* 83.

100. Jerrub's obituary in the *Granite State Free Press* (December 3, 1886) stated that Jerrub Dyer attended nearby Dartmouth Medical College but refused the medical degree itself because it was "too worldly." A search of the Dartmouth Alumni Catalogue (that includes nongraduates), and class records from the medical school has not revealed any confirmation that Jerrub Dyer was a matriculated student at Dartmouth. Dartmouth archivists stated that nonstudents could purchase a ticket to medical lectures, so it is possible that Jerrub attended some lectures, but not likely he studied for a medical degree. The Shakers used the title "Physician" as an honorific and identifying label; it did not necessarily indicate a medical degree.

101. Ministry New Hampshire to Ministry New Lebanon, November 2, 1853, WRHS IV:A-6.

102. Stein, *The Shaker Experience in America,* 200-215.

Notes to Chapter Six

1. Benedict Anderson, *Imagined Communities: Reflections on the Origin and Spread of Nationalism*, revised ed. (London: Verso, 1991).

2. Susan Griffin makes a similar argument in her analysis of escaped nun's tales arguing that the escaped nun represented not only fears about women's role in Protestantism, but their incapacity to take on such a role. Griffin, "Awful Disclosures: Women's Evidence in the Escaped Nun's Tale," *Publications of the Modern Language Association* 3 (January 1996): 104-105. On the growing role of women in antebellum religious practice see Nancy Cott, *The Bonds of Womanhood: "Woman's Sphere" in New England, 1750–1850* (New Haven: Yale University Press, 1997); Ann Douglas, *The Feminization of American Culture* (New York: Knopf, 1977); Mary P. Ryan, *Cradle of the Middle Class: The Family in Oneida County, New York, 1790–1865* (Cambridge: Cambridge University Press, 1981); and Kathryn Kish Sklar, *Catherine Beecher: A Study in American Domesticity* (New York: Library of America, 1982.).

3. Ministry Enfield, N. H. to Ministry Watervliet, N. Y., July 30, 1818, MS. 115, Shaker Collection, Library of Congress (microfilm, Winterthur Library).

4. Ministry Hancock to Ministry Harvard, March 27, 1826, Shaker Manuscripts, Western Reserve Historical Society, Cleveland, Ohio, IV:A-19 (hereafter WRHS).

5. Ministry New Hampshire to Ministry New Lebanon, April 26, 1850, WRHS IV:A-6.

6. "Journal of a Visit By the Ministries of Union Village and South Union to Eastern Communities." September 1854, p. 64, WRHS V:B-250.

7. Town of Enfield *Annual Reports,* 1857–1859, 1864, New Hampshire Historical Society, Concord. The location of Dyer's second house in Fish Market is unknown. Dyer received between $6.25 and $12 per year for rent and expenses. In 1863, Dyer received $8 from the town for unspecified property damage. Her house on Mount Calm was demolished in the 1950s to make way for the construction of a highway.

8. Tax Records, Enfield, N. H., 1821–1845, 1846–1862, 1863–1874, Enfield Public Library.

9. Statement of Marguerite Frost quoting Myra Green, Item #14,560, Emma B. King Library, Shaker Museum, Old Chatham, New York.

10. William Barrett Shedd, Letter to the Secretary of the Massachusetts Historical Society, October 27, 1856. Bound into Mary Marshall [Dyer], *Rise and Progress of the Serpent,* Massachusetts Historical Society, Boston.

11. Ibid.

12. Shedd's gift was presented to the Massachusetts Historical Society on November 20, 1856 (presentation label on inside cover of pamphlets). At the same time he also presented a copy of William Haskett's 1827 apostate account. Dyer's gift was presented on October 20, 1856 and noted in the *Proceedings of the Massachusetts Historical Society.*

13. H. P. Andrews, "A Picture of Shakerism: Mrs. Mary M. Dyer," *The Ladies' Repository* 21 (May 1861): 273-277.

14. Ibid.

15. Ibid., 277.

16. Ibid.

17. Ibid.

18. *Shakerism Unveiled* (n.p.: Published for the Author, 1869).

19. Ibid., title page.

20. See Hamilton v. Pease 38 Conn. 115 (1871) in which a motion is made to over-turn the previous action against the Shakers because of Hamilton's jury-tamper-ing.

21. Robert P. Emlen, "The Hard Choices of Brother John Cummings," *Historical New Hampshire* 34 (Spring 1979): 59-60.

22. [Rosetta Cummings] to Eldress Catherine [Allen], October 12, 1912. Copy in the Enfield Membership Data Records, Enfield (N. H.) Shaker Museum.

23. In considering the "cost" of apostasy for the Shakers and their apostates, I was influenced by the work of John Murray who analyzed conversion/deconversion statistics using an economic model of cost analysis. Murray saw joining (or leav-ing) a communal group as a rational choice determined by weighing the oppor-tunity cost of each action. John E. Murray, "Communal Living Standards and Membership Incentives: The Shakers 1780–1880," (Ph.D. diss., Ohio State University, 1992).

24. Collection of Discharges, MS. 736, Andrews Collection, Winterthur.

25. Ministry Pleasant Hill to Ministry New Lebanon, June 28, 1828, MS. 1039, Andrews Collection, Winterthur. See also MS. 1044, Andrews Collection, Winterthur.

26. David Parker to Giles Avery, January 9, 1849, WRHS IV:A-5.

27. Calvin Green to John Lockwood, November 8, 1847, reel 7 #87, Shaker Collection, New York Public Library (microfilm, Winterthur Library).

28. Joseph and Lucy Bennet to Anna Bennet, January 26,1797, MS. 732, Andrews Collection, Winterthur.

29. Ministry Whitewater, Ohio, to Ministry, Pittsfield, Mass., October 28, 1829, MS. 1052, Andrews Collection, Winterthur.

30. Ministry Watervliet to Ministry Groveland, March 6, 1861, reel 7, #87, Shaker Collection, New York Public Library (microfilm, Winterthur Library).

31. See Elizabeth A. De Wolfe, "So Much Have They Got For Their Folly: Shaker Apostates and the Tale of Woe," *Communal Societies* 18 (1998): 21-35.

32. Roger Launius and Linda Thatcher, eds., *Differing Visions: Dissenters in Mormon History* (Urbana: University of Illinois Press, 1994), 14-15.

33. David G. Bromley, ed., *The Politics of Religious Apostasy: The Role of Apostates in the Transformation of Religious Movements* (Westport, Conn.: Praeger, 1998), 4, 13. Bromley describes a legitimate-illegitimate continuum along which sectar-ian groups are placed by the actions of a number of organizational actors.

34. R. Laurence Moore, *Selling God: American Religion in the Marketplace of Culture* (New York.: Oxford University Press, 1994), 11.

35. See Sister Frances A. Carr, *Growing Up Shaker* ([New Gloucester, Maine]: The United Society of Shakers, 1994) for the latest Shaker publication, and, for a con-temporary visitor's account, Suzanne Skees, *God Among the Shakers: A Search for Stillness and Faith at Sabbathday Lake* (New York: Hyperion, 1998).

36. Etta M. Madden, *Bodies of Life: Shaker Literature and Literacies* (Westport, Conn.: Greenwood Press, 1998), 15. For a study of a particular Shaker text, see Stephen Stein "Inspiration, Revelation, and Scripture: The Story of a Shaker Bible," *Proceedings of the American Antiquarian Society,* vol. 105, part 2 (1996), 347-376.

37. See Mary Richmond, *Shaker Literature* (Hancock, Mass.: Shaker Community, Inc., 1977), nos. 728-729.

38. "The Tall Shakers' Concert," *The Age,* June 18, 1846 and June 20, 1846.

39. *Commercial Advertiser,* September 1, 1846, in Morse, *The Shakers and the World's People* (New York: Dodd, Mead & Company, 1980), 208.

40. Ministry Enfield to Ministry New Lebanon, April 14, 1846, WRHS IV:A-13.

41. Richard Brown contrasts a pre-Revolutionary period in which information was scarce with a mid-nineteenth century information glut. By the middle of the century, there was a plethora of knowledge forms from which the consumer could choose. Some forms of knowledge sought to inform, other forms sought to entertain. Some forms of knowledge, such as the apostate dances, combined the two aspects. Richard D. Brown, *Knowledge is Power: The Diffusion of Information in Early America, 1700–1865* (New York: Oxford University Press, 1989), 274-275. Similar to the Shaker dancers was the performance of a play entitled "The Shaker Lovers" by S. D. Johnson, based on an 1848 story by Daniel Pierce Thompson. Morse, *The Shakers and the World's People,* 208, illustrates a broadside advertising an 1860 Philadelphia performance.

42. Diary of Seth Bradford, June 24 and July 8,1848, Papers of the History of Enfield, Dartmouth College Library.

43. Ministry New Hampshire, February 27, 1858, WRHS IV:A-14.

44. "Deaths," *New Hampshire Patriot and State Gazette,* April 7, 1858.

45. "Orville Dyer," *The Manifesto* 12 (August 1882): 181-182.

46. Thus there are no living direct descendants of Mary Dyer.

47. Enfield Tax Records,1821-1845, Enfield Public Library. See also entry for September 29, 1829, Manuscript Record of Canterbury, New Hampshire, 1792-1848 (Private Collection); North Family Membership List, 1819, WRHS III:A-4; North Family Membership List, 1829, WRHS III:B-42; North Family Articles of Agreement, 1814, MS. # 13614, p. 19, Emma B. King Library, Old Chatham; and Membership List of the North Family, 1822, Book of Records, p. 62, Emma B. King Library, Old Chatham.

48. Asenah Stickney to Lydia Dole, July 19, 1863, WRHS IV:A-7.

49. On Caleb Dyer's life and death see, Carl Irving Bell, "The Noble Life and Sad Death of Brother Dyer," *New Hampshire Profiles* 13 (June 1964): 36-37, 47; Henry Cummings, "Caleb Dyer," *The Enfield Advocate,* December 30, 1904; Hess, *The Enfield Shakers,* 32-36; and *A Biography of the Life and Tragical Death of Elder Caleb M. Dyer* (Manchester, N. H.: American Steam Printing Works of Gage, Moore & Co., 1863). On the murder see Elizabeth A. De Wolfe, "Tragical Death: The Murder of Caleb Dyer," Paper presented at the *Conference on Murder in New England,* November 10, 2001, Old Wethersfield, Connecticut.

50. Orville would return to the position of elder on October 27, 1867. Blinn, "Historical Notes," vol.1, 72.

51. "Found Dead," *Granite State Free Press,* January 18, 1867.

52. Richard Hofstadter, *The Paranoid Style in American Politics and Other Essays* (New York: Vintage Books, 1965), 7.

53. The original Cult Awareness Network went bankrupt in 1996. The name and assets were purchased by individuals with connections to the Church of Scientology, a long-time target of the Cult Awareness Network. The reorganized Cult Awareness Network (CAN), now run by the Foundation for Religious Freedom (a division of the Church of Scientology), claims to advance "a number of activities relevant to religious freedom and the protection of religious and civil rights." See the CAN webpage at http://cultawarenessnetwork.org (accessed January 6, 2002). The American Family Foundation's mission is "to study psychological manipulation and cultic groups, to educate the public and professionals, and to assist those who have been adversely affected by a cult-related experience." See www.csj.org/aff/aff_about.htm (accessed January 12, 2002). The Peregrine Foundation is found

at www.perefound.org (accessed January 6, 2002). Recent apostate accounts include Nansook Hong, *In the Shadow of the Moons: My Life in the Reverend Sun Myung Moon's Family* (New York: Little Brown and Company, 1998), and Miriam Williams, *Heaven's Harlots: My Fifteen Years as a Sacred Prostitute in the Children of God Cult* (New York: William Morrow and Company, 1998).

54. In a history of Stratford, New Hampshire, L. W. Prescott draws genealogical information on the Caleb Marshall family (Mary's father) from Dyer's *Rise and Progress*. He notes that the book, that he "had sought for years to obtain" is a "work of great interest" and "a most heart-rending narrative of a woman who began her married life in Stratford and of terrible vileness and cruelty among the Shakers." L. W. Prescott, "History of Stratford," (Berlin, New Hampshire, 1897), New Hampshire Historical Society, 71-72. Jeanette Thompson's Stratford history reprinted Prescott's information. Thompson, *History of the Town of Stratford, N. H., 1773–1925* (Concord, N. H.: The Rumford Press, 1925): 420-421.

55. Richard D. Brown, *Knowledge is Power: The Diffusion of Information in Early America, 1700–1865* (New York: Oxford University Press, 1989); William J. Gilmore, *Reading Becomes a Necessity of Life: Material and Cultural Life in Rural New England, 1780–1835* (Knoxville: University of Tennessee Press, 1989). Dyer's success with print is mirrored by the success of Mary Baker Eddy. Historian Gillian Gill notes that "Mary Baker Eddy would succeed in large part through her brilliant and innovative use of books and magazines." Gill, *Mary Baker Eddy* (Cambridge, Massachusetts: Perseus Books, 1998): 5.

Selected Bibliography

Primary Sources

Adams, Hannah. *An Alphabetical Compendium of the Various Sects which Have Appeared in the World from the Beginning*. Boston: Printed by B. Edes & Sons, 1794.

Andrews, H. P. "A Picture of Shakerism: Mrs. Mary M. Dyer." *The Ladies Repository* 21 (May 1861): 273-277.

A Biography of the Life and Tragical Death of Elder Caleb M. Dyer, Together with the Poem and Eulogies at his Funeral, July 21, 1863. Manchester, New Hampshire: American Steam Printing Works of Gage, Moore, and Co., 1863.

Bishop, Rufus and Seth Y. Wells, eds. *Testimonies of the Life, Character, Revelations, and Doctrines of Our Ever Blessed Mother Ann Lee. . . .* Hancock, Mass.: Printed by J. Tallcott & J. Deming, Junrs., 1816.

Blackburn, Absolem H. *A Brief Account of the Rise, Progress, Doctrines, and Practices of the People Usually Denominated Shakers*. Flemingsburg, Ky.: Printed by A. Crookshanks, 1824.

Bolton, Aquila. *Some Lines in Verse About The Shakers, Not Published by Authority of the Society So Called*. New York: William Taylor & Co., 1846.

Brown, Samuel. *A Countercheck to Shakerism*. Cincinnati, Ohio: Looker and Reynolds, 1824.

Brown, Thomas. *An Account of the People Called Shakers*. Troy, N. Y.: Parker and Bliss, 1810.

[Buzzell, John]. *A Religious Magazine: Containing a Short History of the Church of Christ. . . .* Portland, Maine: John Buzzell, 1811-1812.

Carr, Frances A. *Growing Up Shaker*. [Sabbathday Lake, Maine]: The United Society of Shakers, 1994.

Chapman, Eunice Hawley. *An Account of the People Called Shakers*. Albany, N. Y.: Printed for the Authoress, at 95 State Street, 1817.

———. *No. 2 Being the Additional Account of the Conduct of the Shakers*. Albany, N. Y.: Printed by I. W. Clark for the Authoress, 1818.

Chapman, James. *The Memorial of James Chapman, to the Respectable Legislature of the State of New York, Now in Session.* [Albany, N. Y.: n.p.], 1817.

Clark, Christopher. *A Shock to Shakerism: or, A Serious Refutation of the Idolatrous Divinity of Ann Lee of Manchester.* Richmond, Ky.: Printed for T. W. Ruble, 1812.

[Dodge, Peter, Seth Y. Wells, and Joseph Hodgson.] *To The Legislature of the State of New York.*[n.p., 1817].

Dunlavy, John. *The Manifesto, of A Declaration of the Doctrines and Practice of the Church of Christ.* Pleasant Hill, Ky.: P. Bertrand Printer, 1818.

Dyer, Joseph. *A Compendious Narrative, Elucidating the Character, Disposition, and Conduct of Mary Dyer, from the Time of Her Marriage, in 1799, Till She Left the Society Called Shakers, in 1815.* Concord, [N. H.]: Printed by Isaac Hill, for the Author, 1818.

———. *A Compendious Narrative. . . .* Second Edition. Pittsfield, [Mass.]: Printed by J. M. Beckwith, at the Office of the Berkshire American, 1826.

Dyer, Mary Marshall. *A Brief Statement of the Sufferings of Mary Dyer Occasioned By the Society Called Shakers.* Concord, N. H.: Printed by Joseph C. Spear, 1818.

———. *A Portraiture of Shakerism, Exhibiting A General View of Their Character and Conduct, From the First Appearance of Ann Lee in New-England, Down to Present Time.* [Haverhill, N. H.]: Printed for the Author [by Sylvester T. Goss], 1822.

———. *Reply to the Shakers' Statements, Called a "Review of the Portraiture of Shakerism," with an Account of the Sickness and Death of Betsy Dyer; A Sketch of the Journey of the Author: and Testimonies from Several Persons.* Concord, [N. H.]: Printed for the Author, 1824.

———. "To the Elders and Principals of the Shaker Societies." [New Lebanon, New York, 1825].

———. "To the Public." [New Lebanon, New York, 1826].

———. *The Rise and Progress of the Serpent from the Garden of Eden, to the Present Day.* Concord, N. H.: Printed for the Author, 1847.

———. *Shakerism Exposed: By Mary M. Dyer.* Hanover, [N. H.]: Dartmouth Press, [n.d., ca. 1852].

Dyer v. Dyer, 5 N. H. 271 (1830).

Elkins, Hervey. *Fifteen Years in the Senior Order of the Shakers: A Narration of the Facts, Concerning that Singular People.* Hanover, N. H.: Dartmouth Press, 1853.

Extract From An Unpublished Manuscript on Shaker History, By An Eye Witness, Giving An Accurate Description of their Songs, Dances, Marches, Visions, Visits to the Spirit Land, &c. Boston: E. K. Allen, 1850.

Farnham, James. "To the Public. Having Lately Seen a Scandalous Handbill in Circulation, Published by Mary Dyer, Containing, Among Other Malicious Falsehoods, A Slanderous Charge Against Me." [n.p., 1825].

Green, Benjamin. *The True Believer's Vademecum, or Shakerism Exposed.* Concord, [N. H.]: Printed for the author, 1831.

———. *Biographical Account of the Life of Benjamin Green, in which are set Forth His Pretensions to the Throne. Written by Himself.* Concord, [N. H.]: Published by the Author, 1848.

Green, Calvin and Seth Y. Wells. *A Summary View of the Millenial Church, or United Society of Believers (Commonly Called Shakers).* Albany, New York: Printed by Packard & Van Benthuysen, 1823).

Haskett, William J. *Shakerism Unmasked, or the History of the Shakers; Including a Form Politic of Their Government as Councils, Orders, Gifts, with an Exposition of the Five Orders of Shakerism, Ann Lee's Grand Foundation Vision, in Sealed Pages. With Some Extracts from their Private Hymns which Have Never Appeared*

Before the Public. Pittsfield, [Mass.]: Published by the Author, L. H., Walkley, Printer, 1828.

Hentz, Caroline Lee. "The Shaker Girl." *Godey's Lady's Book* 18 (February 1839): 49-58.

Hodgdon, Charles C. *Just Published, Hodgdon's Life and Manner of Living Among the Shakers*. Concord, N. H.: Published by the Author, 1838.

Indoctum Parliamentum: A Farce, In One Act and a Beautiful Variety of Scenes. [n.p.: 1818].

Journal of the House of Representatives of the State of New Hampshire. June 1817. Concord, N. H.: Isaac Hill, 1817.

Journal of the Senate of the State of New Hampshire. June 1817. Concord, N. H.: Isaac Hill, 1817.

Lamson, David Rich. *Two Years Experience Among the Shakers: Being A Description of the Manners and Customs of that People*. West Boylston, [Mass.]: Published by the Author, 1848.

Laws of New Hampshire 1830–1842. Concord, N. H.: John F. Brown, n.d.

Laws of New Hampshire 1845–1854. Concord, N. H.: John F. Brown, 1853.

McBride, John. *An Account of the Doctrines, Government, Manners and Customs of the Shakers*. Cincinnati: n.p., 1834.

McNemar, Richard. *The Kentucky Revival*. Cincinnati, Ohio: Press of John W. Browne, 1807.

———. *"Shakerism Detected, &c" Examined and Refuted, in Five Propositions*. Lexington, Kentucky: Printed by Thomas Smith, 1811; reprinted Watervliet, Ohio, 1833.

———. *The Other Side of the Question.. . .* Cincinnati: Looker, Reynolds, and Co., 1819.

———, comp. *Investigator, Or a Defense of the Order, Government & Economy of the United Society Called Shakers, Against Sundry Charges & Legislative Proceedings*. Lexington, Ky.: Printed by Smith and Palmer, 1828; reprinted New York: Egbert, Hovey, & King Printers, 1846.

Meacham, Joseph. *A Concise Statement of the Principles of the Only True Church According to the Gospel of the Recent Appearance of Christ*. Bennington, Vt.: Haswell & Russell, 1790; Sabbathday Lake, Maine: United Society of Shakers, 1963.

"Orville Dyer." *The Manifesto* 12 (August 1882): 181-182.

Rathbun, Daniel. *A Letter From Daniel Rathbun*. Springfield, [Mass.]: Printed at the Printing-Office Near the Great Ferry, 1785.

Rathbun, Reuben. *Reasons Offered for Leaving the Shakers*. Pittsfield, Mass.: Printed by Chester Smith, 1800.

Rathbun, Valentine. *An Account of the Matter, Form, and Manner of a New and Strange Religion*. Providence, R.I.: Printed and Sold by Bennett Wheeler, 1781.

———. *Some Brief Hints of a Religious Scheme*. Hartford; reprinted Boston: Benjamin Edes & Sons, 1781.

———. *A Brief Account of a Religious Scheme*. Worcester, Mass., 1782.

A Remonstrance Against the Testimony and Application of Mary Dyer, Requesting Legislative Interference Against the United Society Commonly Called Shakers. Concord, N. H.: Isaac Hill, 1818.

Report of the Examination of the Shakers of Canterbury and Enfield Before the New-Hampshire Legislature at the November Session, 1848. Concord, N. H.: Ervin B. Tripp, 1849.

Report of the Minority of the Judiciary Committee upon the Petition of Franklin Munroe and Others. [Concord, N.H.: 1849].

A Review of Mary Dyer's Publication, Entitled "A Portraiture of Shakerism"; Together With Sundry Affidavits, Disproving the Truth of Her Assertions. Concord, N.H.: Printed by J. B. Moore for the Society, 1824.

Sedgwick, Catherine. "Magnetism Among the Shakers." *Sartain's Magazine* (May 1849): 337-338.

Shakerism Unveiled. n.p.: Published for the Author, 1869.

Smith, James. *Remarkable Occurrences Lately Discovered Among the People Called Shakers; Of a Treasonous and Barbarous Nature, of Shakerism Developed*. Carthage, Tenn.: Printed by William Moore, 1810.

———. *Shakerism Detected, their Erroneous and Treasonous Proceedings, and False Publications*. Paris, Ky.: Printed by Joel R. Lyle, 1810.

"Some Account of the Tenets and Practice of the Religious Society Called Shakers." *The American Museum . . . for February 1787, Second Edition*. Philadelphia: Printed by Mathew Carey, 1788.

Taylor, Amos. *A Narrative of the Strange Principles, Conduct, and Character of the People Known by the Name of Shakers*. Worcester, Mass.: Printed for the Author [by Isaiah Thomas], 1782.

"Three Months With the Shakers." *Bizarre, For Fireside and Wayside* IV (October 15, 1853-April 1, 1854): 17-18, 36-37, 65-66, 82-83, 97-98, 214-216, 241-243, 277-278, 289-291, 306-308, 345-347, 357-359, 369-371, 381-383.

Van Vleet, Abram. *An Account of the Conduct of the Shakers, in the Case of Eunice Chapman & Her Children*. Lebanon, Ohio: Printed by Van Fleet & Camron, 1818.

Wells, Seth Youngs. *Thomas Brown and his Pretended History of Shakers*. [Mt. Lebanon?: 1848?].

West, Benjamin. *Scriptural Cautions Against Embracing a Religious Scheme*. Hartford, Conn.: Printed and Sold by Bavil Webster, 1783.

Whitbey, John. *Beauties of Priestcraft, or, A Short Account of Shakerism*. New Harmony, Ind.: At the Office of the New Harmony Gazette, 1826.

Woods, John. *Shakerism Unmasked, Or, A Narrative Shewing the Entrance of the Shakers into the Western Country, Their Strategems and Devices, Discipline and Economy*. Paris, Ky.: Printed at the Office of the Western Observer, 1826.

[Youngs, Benjamin Seth]. *Testimony of Christ's Second Appearing Containing a General Statement of All Things Pertaining to the Faith and Practice of the Church of God in this Latter-day*. Lebanon, Ohio: From the Press of John M'Clean, 1808.

[———]. *Testimony of Christ's Second Appearing Containing a General Statement of All Things Pertaining to the Faith and Practice of the Church of God in this Latter-day. Second Edition, Corrected and Improved*. Albany: Printed by E. and E. Hosford, 1810.

[———]. *Testimony of Christ's Second Appearing Containing a General Statement of All Things Pertaining to the Faith and Practice of the Church of God in this Latter-day. Third Edition, Corrected and Improved*. Union Village, Ohio: B. Fisher and A. Burnett Printers, 1823.

[———]. *Testimony of Christ's Second Appearing, Exemplified by the Principles and Practice of the True Church of Christ . . . Fourth Edition*. [Albany, New York]: Published by the United Society Called Shakers, 1856.

Secondary Sources

Andrews, Edward D. *The Community Industries of the Shakers*. Albany: University of the State of New York, 1933. Facsimile Reprint. Charlestown, Massachusetts: Emporium Publications, 1971.

———. *The People Called Shakers*. 1953. Reprint. New York: Dover Publications, 1963.

Barbour, John D. *Versions of Deconversion: Autobiography and the Loss of Faith.* Charlottesville: University Press of Virginia, 1994.

Basch, Norma. "Invisible Women: The Legal Fiction of Marital Unity in Nineteenth-Century America." *Feminist Studies* 5 (Summer 1979): 346-366.

————. *In the Eyes of the Law: Women, Marriage, and Property in Nineteenth-Century New York.* Ithaca: Cornell University Press, 1982.

————. *Framing American Divorce.* Berkeley: University of California Press, 1999.

Bednarowski, Mary Farrell. "Outside the Mainstream: Women's Religion and Women Religious Leaders in Nineteenth-Century America." *Journal of the American Academy of Religion* 48 (June 1980): 207-231.

Bell, C. "The Noble Life and Sad Death of Brother Dyer." *New Hampshire Profiles* 13 (June 1964), 36-37.

Bellah, Robert and Frederick Greenspan, eds. *Uncivil Religion: Interreligious Hostility in America.* New York: The Crossroad Publishing, Co., 1987.

Blake, Nelson. "Eunice Against the Shakers." *New York History* 41 (October 1960): 359-378.

Bloch, Ruth. "American Feminine Ideals in Transition: The Rise of the Moral Mother, 1785-1815." *Feminist Studies* 4 (1978): 101-121.

Braude, Ann. *Radical Spirits: Spiritualism and Women's Rights in Nineteenth-Century America.* Boston: Beacon Press, 1989.

Brewer, Priscilla. *Shaker Communities, Shaker Lives.* Hanover, N. H..: University Press of New England, 1986.

Bromley, David G., ed. *Falling From the Faith: Causes and Consequences of Religious Apostasy.* Newbury Park, Calif.: Sage Publications, 1988.

————, ed. *The Politics of Religious Apostasy: The Role of Apostates in the Transformation of Religious Movements.* Westport, Conn.: Praeger, 1998.

Bromley, David G. and Anson D. Shupe. *Strange Gods: The Great American Cult Scare.* Boston: Beacon Press, 1981.

Bromley, David G., Anson D. Shupe and J. C. Ventimiglia. "Atrocity Tales, the Unification Church, and the Social Construction of Evil." *Journal of Communication* 29 (Summer 1979): 42-53.

Brown, Richard D. *Knowledge is Power: The Diffusion of Information in Early America, 1700–1865.* New York: Oxford University Press, 1989.

Burns, Deborah. *Cities of Peace, Love, and Union: A History of the Hancock Bishopric.* Hanover, N. H.: University Press of New England, 1993.

Carter, N. F. *The Native Ministry of New Hampshire.* Concord, N. H.: n.p., 1906.

Clark, Charles E. *The Eastern Frontier: The Settlement of Northern New England, 1610–1763.* Hanover, N. H.: University Press of New England, 1970. Reprint. New York: Alfred Knopf, 1983.

Clark, Elizabeth B. "'The Sacred Rights of the Weak:' Pain, Sympathy, and the Culture of Individual Rights in Antebellum America." *The Journal of American History* 82 (September 1995), 463-493.

Cott, Nancy F. *The Bonds of Womanhood.* New Haven: Yale University Press, 1977.

————. *Public Vows: A History of Marriage and the Nation.* Cambridge: Harvard University Press, 2000.

Coultrap-McQuin, Susan. *Doing Literary Business: American Women Writers in the Nineteenth Century.* Chapel Hill: The University of North Carolina Press, 1990.

Cross, Whitney. *The Burned Over District: The Social and Intellectual History of Enthusiastic Religion in Western New York, 1800–1850.* Ithaca: Cornell University Press, 1950.

Curry, Richard O. and Thomas More Brown, eds. *Conspiracy: The Fear of Subversion in American History.* New York: Holt, Rinehart, and Winston, Inc. 1972.

Davidson, Cathy, ed. *Reading in America: Literature & Social History.* Baltimore: The Johns Hopkins University Press, 1989.

———. *Revolution and the Word: The Rise of the Novel in America.* New York: Oxford University Press, 1986.

Davis, David B. "Themes of Counter-Subversion: An Analysis of Anti-Masonic, Anti-Catholic, and Anti-Mormon Literature." *The Mississippi Valley Historical Review* 47 (1960):205-224.

De Wolfe, Elizabeth A. "'So Much They Have Got for Their Folly:' Shaker Apostates and the Tale of Woe." *Communal Societies* 18 (1998): 21-35.

———. "Mary Marshall Dyer, Gender, and *A Portraiture of Shakerism.*" *Religion and American Culture* 8 (Summer 1998): 237-264.

———. "The Mob at Enfield: Community, Gender, and Violence Against the Shakers." In *Intentional Community: An Anthropological Perspective,* edited by Susan Love Brown. Albany: State University of New York Press, 2002.

Emlen, Robert P. "The Hard Choices of Brother John Cummings." *Historical New Hampshire* 34 (Spring 1979): 54-65.

Fabian, Ann. *The Unvarnished Truth: Personal Narratives in Nineteenth-Century America.* Berkeley: University of California Press, 2000.

Foster, Lawrence. *Religion and Sexuality: The Shakers, the Mormons, and the Oneida Community.* New York: Oxford University Press, 1981; Urbana: University of Illinois Press, 1984.

———. *Women, Family, and Utopia.* Syracuse, N. Y.: Syracuse University Press, 1991.

Garrett, Clarke. *Spirit Possession and Popular Religion: From the Camisards to the Shakers.* Baltimore: The Johns Hopkins University Press, 1987.

Gilje, Paul A. *The Road to Mobocracy: Popular Disorder in New York City, 1763–1834.* Chapel Hill: University of North Carolina Press for the Institute of Early American Culture, 1987.

Gilmore, William J. *Reading Becomes a Necessity of Life: Material and Cultural Life in Rural New England, 1780–1835.* Knoxville: University of Tennessee Press, 1989.

Givens, Terryl L. *The Viper on the Hearth: Mormons, Myths, and the Construction of Heresy.* New York: Oxford University Press, 1997.

Grant, Jerry. "The 'Secret Book of the Elders.'" *Shaker Historical and Bibliographical Register* 1 (Summer 1995):1-4.

Greven, Philip. *The Protestant Temperament: Patterns of Childrearing, Religious Experience, and the Self in Early America.* New York: Alfred A. Knopf, 1977.

Grossberg, Michael. *Governing the Hearth: Law and the Family in Nineteenth-Century America.* Chapel Hill: The University of North Carolina Press, 1985.

Ham, F. Gerald. "Shakerism in the Old West." Ph.D. diss., University of Kentucky, 1962.

Hartog, Hendrik. "Marital Exits and Marital Expectations in Nineteenth-Century America." *The Georgetown Law Journal* 80 (October 1991): 95-129.

———. *Man and Wife in America: A History.* Cambridge: Harvard University Press, 2000.

Hess, Wendell. *The Enfield (N. H.) Shakers: A Brief History.* [Enfield, New Hampshire]: 1993.

History of Coös County. Syracuse: W. A. Ferguson Co., 1888. Reprint. Somersworth, N. H.: New Hampshire Publishing Co., 1972

Humez, Jean M. "'Weary of Petticoat Government'" The Specter of Female Rule in Early Nineteenth-Century Shaker Politics." *Communal Societies* 11 (1991), 1-17.

———, ed. *Mother's First-Born Daughters: Early Shaker Writings on Women and Religion.* Bloomington: Indiana University Press, 1993.

————. "'A Woman Mighty to Pull You Down': Married Women's Rights and Female Anger in the Anti-Shaker Narratives of Eunice Chapman and Mary Marshall Dyer." *Journal of Women's History* 6 (Summer 1994): 90-110.

Johnson, Theodore E. "The 'Millennial Laws' of 1821." *Shaker Quarterly* 7 (Summer 1967), 35-58.

————. *Life in the Christ Spirit*. Sabbathday Lake, Maine: United Society of Shakers, 1969.

Kern, Louis. *An Ordered Love*. Chapel Hill: University of North Carolina Press, 1981.

Laws of New Hampshire, Vol.5, First Constitutional Period, 1784–1792. Concord, N. H.: Evans Printing Co., 1921.

Laws of New Hampshire, Vol. 9, Second Constitutional Period,1821–1828. Concord, N. H.: Evans Printing Co., 1921.

Lehuu, Isabelle. *Carnival on the Page: Popular Print Media in Antebellum America*. Chapel Hill: The University of North Carolina Press, 2000.

Lewis, Jan. "The Republican Wife: Virtue and Seduction in the Early Republic." *William and Mary Quarterly*, 3rd. ser., 44 (October 1987): 689-721.

Lilly, Paige. "The Shakers and the Media: An Examination of the Shaker Library." *Shaker Quarterly*, 17 (Fall 1989): 101-112.

Lyford, James O., ed. *History of Concord, New Hampshire*. 2 vols., Concord, N. H.: The Rumford Press, 1903.

Madden, Etta M. *Bodies of Life: Shaker Literature and Literacies*. Westport, Conn.: Greenwood Press, 1998.

Marini, Stephen. *Radical Sects in Revolutionary New England*. Cambridge: Harvard University Press, 1982.

McAdams, Ruth. "The Shakers in American Fiction." Ph.D. diss., Texas Christian University, 1985.

Moore, R. Laurence. *Selling God: American Religion in the Marketplace of Culture*. New York: Oxford University Press, 1994.

Morgan, David and Sally M. Promey, eds. *The Visual Culture of American Religions*. Berkeley: University of California Press, 2001.

Morse, Flo. *The Shakers and the World's People*. New York: Dodd, Mead & Company, 1980.

Murray, John E. "Communal Living Standards and Membership Incentives: The Shakers 1780–1880." Ph.D. diss., Ohio State University, 1992.

————. "The White Plague in Utopia: Tuberculosis in Nineteenth-Century Shaker Communes." *Bulletin of the History of Medicine* 68 (1994), 278-306.

Namias, June K. *White Captives: Gender and Ethnicity on the American Frontier*. Chapel Hill: University of North Carolina Press, 1993.

New Hampshire Revised Statutes Annotated. Orford, N. H.: Butterworth Legal Publishers, 1992.

Phillips, Roderick. *Putting Asunder: A History of Divorce in Western Society*. New York: Cambridge University Press, 1988.

————. *Untying the Knot: A Short History of Divorce*. New York: Cambridge University Press, 1991.

Prescott, L. W. "History of Stratford." Photocopied articles from *The Berlin Independent*, [Berlin, N. H., 1897], New Hampshire Historical Society.

Procter-Smith, Marjorie. *Women in Shaker Community and Worship*. Lewiston, N. Y.: Edwin Mellen Press, 1985.

Promey, Sally. *Spiritual Spectacles: Vision and Image in Mid-Nineteenth Century Shakerism*. Bloomington: University of Indiana Press, 1993.

Pugh, Michael. "A Thorn in the Text: Shakerism and the Marriage Narrative." Ph.D. diss., University of New Hampshire, 1994.

Rice, Franklin P. "Shaker Records of Enfield, New Hampshire." *New England Historical Genealogical Register* (April 1908): 119-128.

Richmond, Mary. *Shaker Literature*. 2 vols. Hancock. Mass.: Shaker Community, Inc., 1977.

Rothbaum, Susan. "Between Two Worlds: Issues of Separation and Identity After Leaving A Religious Community." In *Falling From the Faith: Consequences of Religious Apostasy.* edited by David G. Bromley. Newbury Park, Calif.: Sage Publications, 1988.

Sasson, Diane. *The Shaker Spiritual Narrative.* Knoxville: University of Tennessee Press, 1983.

Schneider, Barbara Taback. "Prayers for Our Protection and Prosperity at Court: Shakers, Children, and the Law." *Yale Journal of Law & The Humanities* 4 (1992): 33-78.

Schultz, Nancy Lusignan. *Veil of Fear: Nineteenth-Century Convent Tales, Rebecca Reed and Maria Monk.* West Lafayette, Indiana: NotaBell Books, 1999.

————. *Fire & Roses: The Burning of the Charlestown Convent, 1834.* New York: The Free Press, 2000.

Skees, Suzanne. *God Among the Shakers: A Search for Stillness and Faith at Sabbathday Lake.* New York: Hyperion, 1998.

Stein, Stephen. *The Shaker Experience in America.* New Haven: Yale University Press, 1992.

————. "Inspiration, Revelation, and Scripture: The Story of A Shaker Bible." *Proceedings of the American Antiquarian Society* vol. 105, part 2 (1996): 347-376.

————. "The 'Not-So-Faithful' Believers: Conversion, Deconversion, and Reconversion Among the Shakers." *American Studies* 38:3 (Fall 1997): 5-20.

Taves, Ann, ed. *Religion and Domestic Violence in Early New England: The Memoirs of Abigail Abbot Bailey.* Bloomington: Indiana University Press, 1989.

Thompson, Jeanette. *History of the Town of Stratford, N. H., 1773-1925.* Concord, N. H.: The Rumford Press, 1925.

Thurman, Suzanne. "Shaker Women and Sexual Power: Heresy and Orthodoxy in the Shaker Village of Harvard, Massachusetts." *Journal of Women's History* 10 (Spring 1998): 70-87.

————. *"O Sisters Ain't You Happy?": Gender, Family, and Community Among the Harvard and Shirley Shakers.* Syracuse, N. Y.: Syracuse University Press, 2002.

Tompkins, Jane. *Sensational Designs: The Cultural Work of American Fiction, 1790–1860.* New York: Oxford University Press, 1985.

Upton, Richard. "Franklin Pierce and the Shakers: A Subchapter in the Struggle for Religious Liberty." *Historical New Hampshire* 23 (Summer 1968): 3-18.

Weinbaum, Paul O. *Mobs and Demagogues: The New York Response to Collective Violence in the Early Nineteenth Century.* n.p.: UMI Research Press, 1979.

Weisbrod, Carol. *The Boundaries of Utopia.* New York: Pantheon Books, 1980.

Welter, Barbara. "The Cult of True Womanhood, 1820–1860." *American Quarterly* 18 (Summer 1966): 131-175.

Wessinger, Catherine, ed. *Women's Leadership in Marginal Religions: Explorations Outside the Mainstream.* Urbana: University of Illinois Press, 1993.

Wright, Stuart A. *Leaving Cults: The Dynamics of Defection.* Washington, D. C.: The Center for the Scientific Study of Religion, 1987.

Zboray, Ronald J. *A Fictive People: Antebellum Economic Development and the American Reading Public.* New York: Oxford University Press, 1993.

Index